Tertullian's *Aduersus Iudaeos*

North American Patristics Society
Patristic Monograph Series
Volume 19

Tertullian's *Aduersus Iudaeos*

A Rhetorical Analysis

Geoffrey D. Dunn

The Catholic University of America Press

Washington, D.C.

LIBRARY OF CONGRESS CATALOGING-IN-PUBLICATION DATA

Dunn, Geoffrey D., 1962–

Tertullian's Aduersus Iudaeos : a rhetorical analysis / Geoffrey D. Dunn.

p. cm.—(North American Patristic Society patristic monograph series ; v. 19)

Includes bibliographical references and index.

ISBN 978-0-8132-1526-6 (cloth : alk. paper)   1. Tertullian, ca. 160–ca. 230.

Adversus Judaeos.   2. Apologetics—History—Early church, ca. 30–600.

3. Judaism—Controversial literature—History and criticism.

4. Rhetoric, Ancient.   I. Title.   II. Series.

BR65.T3363D86 2008

239'.2—dc22   2007047672

Contents

Preface   vii

Abbreviations   xi

Introduction   I

1. Controversy Surrounding the
   Text and the Genre   5

   Those Who Doubt the Work's Integrity
       and Authenticity   6
   Those Who Accept the Work's Integrity
       and Authenticity   8
   Judaism and Christianity in Contact?   15
   A Rhetorical Reading   27

2. Readership   31

   Declamation and Eulogy   32
   Aduersus Iudaeos as *Controuersia*   36
   Second-Century Christian Rhetoric   38
   Real, Imagined, and Intended Readers   40
   Imagined Readers of *Aduersus Iudaeos*   43
   Intended Readers of *Aduersus Iudaeos*   50
   Conclusion   56

3. Structure   58

   Sider's Observations of General Structural
       Patterns in Tertullian   60
   Exordium   61
   Narratio   65
   Partitio   66
   Refutatio   72
   Confirmatio   75
   Peroratio   84
   Summary of Rhetorical Structure   86
   Comparison with Other Structural
       Arrangements of *Aduersus Iudaeos*   87
   Conclusion   95

Contents

4. Argumentation 97

    Classical Rhetoric on Argumentation 98

    Sider's Observations on
        Tertullian's Arguments 103

    Argumentation in *Aduersus Iudaeos* 105

    Conclusion 139

5. Style 142

    Classical Rhetoric on Style 143

    Style in Tertullian 146

    Style in *Aduersus Iudaeos* 148

    Conclusion 169

Conclusion 173

Bibliography . 183

General Index 197

Index of Citations to Tertullian 205

Index of Citations to Scripture 209

Preface

Within the field of Tertullian studies, *Aduersus Iudaeos* is a much neglected text. In his book *Ancient Rhetoric and the Art of Tertullian*, Robert Sider omitted any analysis of it because, as he stated elsewhere, the latter part of that work was an addition probably by someone other than Tertullian and taken from the third book of *Aduersus Marcionem*. Others have challenged that view of the work, but none has supported their arguments with detailed reference to the classical theory of rhetoric. The very method of investigation Sider himself used could fruitfully be employed in an examination of *Aduersus Iudaeos* in order to make a contribution to the question of the text's integrity and authenticity. This is what I have done by providing an analysis of *Aduersus Iudaeos* according to the rules of classical rhetoric with regard to its structure, its arguments, and its style.

A reading of my bibliography reveals works from across the disciplines of classical rhetoric, patristics, and Jewish-Christian relations. The methodology of classical rhetoric is applied to a piece of early Christian literature in order to determine its relevance to questions about the ongoing contact between two monotheistic faiths in late antiquity. Such a breadth of research should widen the appeal of what is a specialized study of a single piece of literature.

The results of this analysis indicate that whoever wrote the first part of the pamphlet (chapters 1 to 8) made sufficient comment about its structure to demonstrate that they planned to write on the topics that are found in the second part (chapters 9 to 14). This suggests that the work was the responsibility of one author. The position advanced by Säflund and Tränkle that *Aduersus Iudaeos* was written prior and not subsequent to *Aduersus Marcionem* is supported here. Repetition of material from one work to another does not imply the activity of some unidentified copyist any more than it does the idea that Tertullian himself found it convenient to re-use material from one to the other.

However, this does not mean that *Aduersus Iudaeos* is an outstanding piece of writing. There are several signs, especially in the second half, that what has survived is only an early draft of what is probably an unrevised essay. Some material is long-winded, out of place, peripheral to the main argument, or even repeated. Even though the work is incomplete, one can see where Tertullian was heading and how classical rhetoric was crucial to his thinking.

With the controversy about its authorship, this work has not played its proper part in the scholarly debate about the relationship between Judaism and Christianity in the centuries following Titus's capture of Jerusalem. Although those who have taken some interest in this work would conclude that it provides no information about interaction between Jews and Christians in Carthage at the end of the second century, the position I advance is that how and what one interpreted in the Hebrew Scriptures was the ongoing issue between them, just as it had been for the first followers of Jesus. The attempt by scholars to say that an anti-Judaic pamphlet was either for Jews to read and a sign of real contact, or for Christians to read and a sign of no contact is too limiting. A rhetorical interpretation supports the notion, I believe, that an author could have several objectives and readers in mind simultaneously.

My research on this pamphlet has been conducted in a series of published articles, in my doctoral dissertation, which was submitted at Australian Catholic University in 1999, and in the only English translation of the pamphlet to appear since the middle of the nineteenth century. The present volume is a revision of the doctoral dissertation. Further reflection upon Tertullian's text over the past five years, particularly in the light of the translation work, has enabled me to revise some of the points in the dissertation and to refine my presentation. The German translation by Regina Hauses in Fontes Christiani appeared too late for me to use in this volume.

I am grateful to my supervisor, Professor Pauline Allen, FAHA, director of the Centre for Early Christian Studies, Australian Catholic University, and to my associate supervisor, Rev. Dr. David Rankin, from Trinity Theological College, Brisbane. They offered me support and encouragement, judicious advice, a critical eye, and an unfailing commitment to scholarship of the highest level during the writing of the dissertation. My gratitude extends to my examiners—Professor Graeme Clarke of Australian National University; Dr. James Carleton Paget, Peterhouse, Cambridge; and Professor Robert Sider—and indeed to the editors and anonymous readers of the various journals in which my articles have appeared, for their valuable insights and suggestions for improvement. I am also grateful to those who read the various versions of this volume. Their comments were always insightful and often challenging. Even where I thought they missed my point, they helped me realize that I had not expressed my point clearly enough in the first place. Of course, whatever remains unclear is entirely my own fault. Professor Philip Rousseau, the director of the Center for the Study of Early Christianity at the Catholic University of America and the series editor, has been an encouraging friend and helpful advisor. My thanks go also to those at the Catholic University of America Press who have assisted in turning this typescript into a published reality. Finally, I wish to thank all my colleagues at the Centre for Early Christian Studies, Australian Catholic University, who have provided the stimulating and collaborative environment in which my research takes place.

Abbreviations

AJPh	*American Journal of Philology*
AntAfr	*Antiquités Africaines*
Arist.	Aristotle
Rh.	*Rhetorica*
Aristid.	Aristides
Or.	*Orationes*
BAGB	*Bulletin de l'Association Guillaume Budé*
Barn.	*Epistle of Barnabas*
CCSL	Corpus Christianorum, series Latina
CH	*Church History*
Cic.	Cicero
Brut.	*Brutus*
Opt. gen.	*De optimo genere oratorum*
De or.	*De oratore*
Inu. rhet.	*De inuentione*
Orat.	*Orator*
Part. or.	*De partitione oratoria*
CJ	*Classical Journal*
CPh	*Classical Philology*
CQ	*Classical Quarterly*
CSEL	Corpus Scriptorum Ecclesiasticorum Latinorum
F	*Codex Florentinus Magliabechianus,* Conv. Sopr. I, VI, 10, saec. XV
FC	Fontes Christiani
Front.	Fronto
Ad M. Caes.	*Ad M. Caesarem*
De eloq.	*De eloquentia*

Laud. fum. *et pul.*	*Laudes fumi et pulueris*
G&R	*Greece and Rome*
Gell. *N.A.*	Aulus Gellius *Noctes Atticae*
GRBS	*Greek, Roman, and Byzantine Studies*
HSCPh	*Harvard Studies in Classical Philology*
HTR	*Harvard Theological Review*
Ign. *Eph.*	Ignatius *Ephesians*
Iren. *Adu. haer.* *Dem.*	Irenaeus *Aduersus haereses* *Demonstratio Apostolicae Praedicationis*
JBL	*Journal of Biblical Literature*
JECS	*Journal of Early Christian Studies*
JEH	*Journal of Ecclesiastical History*
Jerm. *In Dan.*	Jerome *Commentarii in Danielem*
JJS	*Journal of Jewish Studies*
JQR	*Jewish Quarterly Review*
JRA	*Journal of Roman Archaeology*
JTS	*Journal of Theological Studies*
Jus. *1 Apol.* *Dial.*	Justin *1 Apologia* *Dialogus cum Tryphone*
Juv. *Sat.*	Juvenal *Satirae*
LCL	Loeb Classical Library
MEFRA	*Melanges de l'Ecole Française de Rome: Antiquite*
N	*Codex Florentinus Magliabechianus,* Conv. Soppr. I, VI, 9, saec. XV
NTS	*New Testament Studies*
P	*Codex Scelestadtensis* 439, saec. XI (Paterniacensis)

Philostr.	Philostratus
V.S.	*Vitae sophistarum*
Ph&Rh	*Philosophy and Rhetoric*
PhQ	*Philological Quarterly*
Plin.	Pliny the younger
Ep.	*Epistulae*
ps.-Aug.	pseudo-Augustine
Quaest. uet. et nou. test.	*Quaestionum ueteris et noui testamenti*
PTS	Patristische Texte und Studien
Q (Φ)	*Codex Fuldensis* amissus, cuius variae lectiones ex collatione Francisci Modii Aldenburgensis congestae sunt in adpendice editionis Uunianae, Franekerae, 1597
QJS	*Quarterly Journal of Speech*
Quint.	Quintilian
Inst.	*Institutio oratoria*
R	Consensus harum editorum, Beati Rhenani, 1521–1539
Rhet. Her.	*Rhetorica ad Herennium*
RSLR	*Rivista di Storia e Letteratura Religiosa*
SC	Sources Chrétiennes
Sen.	Seneca the elder
Controu.	*Controuersiae*
SJT	*Scottish Journal of Theology*
STh	*Studia Theologica*
Suet.	Suetonius
Rhet.	*De rhetoribus*
T	*Codex Trecensis 523, saec. XII*
Tac.	Tacitus
Dial.	*Dialogues de oratoribus*
Tert.	Tertullian
Ad mart.	*Ad martyras*
Ad nat.	*Ad nationes*
Ad Scap.	*Ad Scapulam*
Adu. Herm.	*Aduersus Hermogenem*
Adu. Iud.	*Aduersus Iudaeos*

Adu. Marc.	*Aduersus Marcionem*
Adu. Prax.	*Aduersus Praxean*
Adu. Val.	*Aduersus Valentinianos*
Apol.	*Apologeticum*
De an.	*De anima*
De carn.	*De carne Christi*
De cast.	*De exhortatione castitatis*
De cor.	*De corona*
De fug.	*De fuga in persecutione*
De idol.	*De idololatria*
De iei.	*De ieiunio*
De mon.	*De monogamia*
De pat.	*De patientia*
De praescr.	*De praescriptione haereticorum*
De pud.	*De pudicitia*
De res.	*De resurrectione mortuorum*
De spec.	*De spectaculis*
De test. anim.	*De testimonio animae*
De uirg.	*De uirginibus uelandis*
VChr	*Vigiliae Christianae*
YCS	*Yale Classical Studies*
ZAC	*Zeitscrift für Antikes Christentum*

Introduction

In the index of his 1971 monograph on the influence of classical rhetoric on Tertullian's writings, Robert Sider lists all of Tertullian's thirty-one works, with two exceptions: *Aduersus Iudaeos* and *Ad Scapulam*.[1] Although Tränkle's commentary on *Aduersus Iudaeos* is contained within Sider's bibliography, there is no reference to the treatise in his text, not even where one might expect it, viz., in conjunction with the third book of *Aduersus Marcionem*.[2]

Without any statement from Sider himself one is left to hypothesize. Could it be that *Aduersus Iudaeos* (and *Ad Scapulam* for that matter)[3] displays no classical rhetorical influence and thus was not suitable for inclusion in his volume? A more plausible reason is found in the controversy that has surrounded the work's authenticity and integrity. Sider suggests elsewhere that this is the case, when he writes concerning *Aduersus Iudaeos*:

Unfortunately, we do not know how much of the debate is represented in this treatise since the latter part (chapters 9–14) is an addition, probably by another hand, with material gathered from Book III of Tertullian's treatise *adversus Marcionem*.[4]

1. Robert Dick Sider, *Ancient Rhetoric and the Art of Tertullian* (Oxford: Oxford University Press, 1971), 141–42. The commentary of A. Quacquarelli, ed., *Q. S. F. Tertulliani: "Ad Scapulam." Prolegomeni, testo critico, traduzione e commento*, "Opuscula patrum 1" (Rome: Desclée, 1957), is listed in Sider's bibliography, though I can discover no discussion of the treatise in the work itself. Even though I am unable to find any reference to these two works in Sider, Ernest Evans, ed. and trans., *Tertullian: "Adversus Marcionem,"* vol. 1: *Books 1 to 3*, Oxford Early Christian Texts (Oxford: Clarendon Press, 1972), xxiii, states that "every one of Tertullian's works is meticulously examined" in Sider.

2. Sider, *Ancient Rhetoric*, 139, 54–55.

3. See Geoffrey D. Dunn, "Rhetorical Structure in Tertullian's *Ad Scapulam*," *VChr* 56 (2002): 47–55, for an examination of the rhetorical influence in the structure of Tert., *Ad Scap*. There is no debate about the authorship of *Ad Scap.*, so its omission from consideration is puzzling. Perhaps it was mere oversight.

4. Robert Dick Sider, *The Gospel and its Proclamation*, Message of the Fathers of the Church 10 (Wilmington, Del.: Michael Glazier, 1983), 45.

In stating this Sider merely accepts and repeats the opinion of a number of scholars from the last few centuries about this treatise. I believe that had Sider considered the rhetorical influences present in *Aduersus Iudaeos,* as he had with twenty-nine of the other treatises of Tertullian, he could have made a valuable contribution to the question about the integrity of the treatise and its authorship.

My intention is to examine *Aduersus Iudaeos* from the perspective of classical rhetoric. Although many scholars have offered their opinions about whether one author wrote the whole work and whether that author was Tertullian, none has made extensive use of classical rhetoric in conducting the research. This will be the first time that a rhetorical analysis of *Aduersus Iudaeos* has ever been undertaken.

This is a work that concerns the relationship between Jews and Christians. The question of the contact between these two groups in the years after Titus captured Jerusalem is one that has been hotly contested in scholarship in recent years. There are those who believe that the two went their separate ways and that the anti-Judaic literature produced by early Christians was written for internal consumption, to assist with issues of self-definition; and there are those who believe that the two groups remained in contact much longer than was once thought and that we ought to take these pieces of early Christian literature at face value, as reflecting ongoing contact. In this debate Tertullian's *Aduersus Iudaeos* is most often pushed to one side because of the controversy that surrounds it.

In the opening chapter of this volume I wish to outline the nature of those two controversies: the integrity and authenticity of *Aduersus Iudaeos,* and the reality of Jewish-Christian engagement in late antiquity.

My argument is that when we examine the rhetorical structure of the work (chapter 3), when we examine the arguments that are presented (chapter 4), and when we consider the style of writing (chapter 5), what we discover is that the work was written by one author, that its quality as a piece of writing deteriorates the further one reads it because it is an unrevised work, that there is one example of interpolation at the very end of the text, that it was written prior to *Aduersus Marcionem,* and that its verbosity and rambling nature are indicative of Tertullian's early style. All of this suggests to me that one should take the claim at the beginning of *Aduersus Iudaeos* that it was written in response to an earlier debate between a Christian and a proselyte Jew as evidence that there was some ongoing contact between Christians and

Jews at least in Carthage in the Severan age. A consideration of what the text tells us about questions of readership (chapter 2) suggests that although the work might not have been addressed specifically to Jews, it was written almost as a template by Tertullian for other Christians to use in their own encounters with Jews. It must be pointed out that Tertullian's *Aduersus Iudaeos* is not the record of a particular encounter but an idealized version of the Christian side that could be used in future debates.

In the pamphlet, Tertullian argued for supersession: the Christians had replaced the Jews as God's people. The work was meant to be the definitive case to refute those who believed that the Jews were still the only people of God. It has all the hallmarks of forensic rhetoric. The point of difference was over the interpretation of the Hebrew Scriptures. Tertullian highlighted how Christians accepted that, through the life and death of Jesus, the scriptural passages that referred to the one who was to come had been fulfilled. Against those modern scholars who argue that because Christian anti-Judaic literature did not address current events it must be taken as proof that there was no contact between the two groups, I want to advocate strongly that Christians and Jews continued to engage each other in debate, not on current events but on the one topic that meant something to them both, viz., the true meaning of Scripture. It was Scripture that would give legitimacy to one or the other group's claim to be the authentic people of God, and it is my position that Christians and Jews never tired of arguing with one another on this very point time and again in late antiquity. At the same time a work like Tertullian's *Aduersus Iudaeos* was designed also for purposes of reinforcing a Christian self-understanding. One need not succumb to the tendency to choose between engaging the other in debate or writing for an internal audience. A classical rhetorical perspective helps us appreciate that both aims could be met in the one piece of literature.

CHAPTER ONE

Controversy Surrounding the Text and the Genre

By way of background, in this opening chapter I wish to survey the debate that has engaged scholars over the past couple of centuries about the integrity and authenticity of *Aduersus Iudaeos,* before engaging with the text itself and making my own contribution to that debate in the remainder of this volume, where I shall apply Sider's rhetorical methodology. It is not my intention in this preliminary chapter to critique the assessments offered by other scholars as much as it is simply to highlight the controversy that has surrounded this work in order to suggest that the disagreement among scholars about its integrity (whether or not the work is a complete piece written by one person) and authenticity (whether or not the work was written by Tertullian) explains why many other scholars interested in early Christianity's relationship with Judaism have neglected it (a fact that can be demonstrated by a survey of such scholarship). No one has yet approached *Aduersus Iudaeos* from the perspective of classical rhetoric in order to address the issues of its integrity and authenticity. While many of the points I shall make in the later chapters have been made before, the fact that I shall make them employing a different methodology should help tip the balance in favor of those who argue in support of the integrity of *Aduersus Iudaeos* and of Tertullian as its author. Furthermore, I believe that *Aduersus Iudaeos* has valuable information to contribute to the debate about the reality of ongoing contact between Jews and Christians, once the controversy that surrounds the work itself has been resolved.

Those Who Doubt the Work's
Integrity and Authenticity

Kroymann, whose 1942 CSEL edition,[1] with only a few emendations from Borleffs, is utilized in CCSL as the standard edition of Tertullian's *Aduersus Iudaeos*,[2] accepted only the first eight chapters as Tertullian's own work.[3] His position was endorsed by the series general editor.[4] However, the assertion of non-Tertullianic authorship for the second half of the treatise is qualified immediately: "attamen nonnullas sententias haurire uidetur ex schedis plagulisque imperfectis ipsius Tertulliani."[5]

Aulisa points out that doubts about Tertullian's having written a treatise against the Jews did not exist in late antiquity.[6] They first appeared in the eighteenth century with Johann Semler.[7] This leading German Enlightenment scholar, who pioneered biblical higher criticism, not only had strong suspicions about the entire work, but believed that *Aduersus Marcionem* was not by Tertullian either, and that they were both by some forger. While his radical notions about the latter work did not find favor, the nineteenth-century English scholar Burkitt also rejected Tertullian as the author of *Aduersus Iudaeos*, arguing that the scriptural citations that appear in the second half of the work were taken from *Aduersus Marcionem*, and that those in the first half of the work have more in common with Cyprian's *Testimonia* than with Tertullian's normal method of citing Scripture. In particular, he noted that Tertullian normally cited Daniel from the Septuagint, whereas in *Aduersus Iudaeos* 8.4–6 Theodotion was used.[8]

---

1. Emil Kroymann, ed., *Tertulliani Opera*, II, 2. CSEL 70 (Vienna: Verlag der Österreichischen, Akademie der Wissenschaften, 1942), 251–331.

2. Emil Kroymann, ed., "[Q. S. F. Tertulliani]: *Aduersus Iudaeos*," in *Tertulliani Opera*, part 2: *Opera Montanistica*, ed. Eligius Dekkers et al., CCSL 2 (Turnhout: Brepols, 1954), 1338.

3. Ibid., 1364.

4. Ibid., 1338.

5. Ibid. See also Eligius Dekkers, ed., *Clavis Patrum Latinorum*, 3rd ed., CCSL (Turnhout: Brepols, 1995), 9.

6. Immacolata Aulisa, ed., *Tertulliano. Polemica con i Giudei,* Testi Patristici 140 (Rome: Città Nuova, 1998), 43. She refers to ps.-Aug., *Quaest. uet. et nou. test.* 44.14 (CSEL 50.79–80), and Jerm., *In Dan.* 9.24 (CCSL 75A.880–81). On Ambrosiaster as the author of *Quaest. uet. et nou. test.* see Alexander Souter, *A Study of Ambrosiaster,* Texts and Studies 7 (Cambridge: Cambridge University Press, 1905).

7. Johann Salomo Semler, ed., *Q. S. Fl. Tertullianus, Opera recensuit,* 6 vols. (Halle: Hendel, 1770–1776), 5:221–45.

8. F. C. Burkitt, *The Old Latin and the Itala* (Cambridge: Cambridge University Press, 1896), 7, 29.

In the 1940s Quispel suggested that *Aduersus Iudaeos* was connected with the apostate brother who stole and published what amounted to the second edition of *Aduersus Marcionem*.[9] He believed that the apostate wrote chapters 9–14 of *Aduersus Iudaeos* from the now lost second edition of *Aduersus Marcionem*. There seems to be evidence, he claimed, that the apostate did not understand what was in the work he stole and that this ignorance is obvious in *Aduersus Iudaeos*. According to Quispel, what we find in the first eight chapters has been reworked so much by the apostate that it cannot be called Tertullian's at all. Johannes Quasten agreed with Quispel, but made no comment about the authenticity of the first eight chapters.[10]

Other scholars, while sharing in the belief that the second half of the work was not by Tertullian, take a more positive approach to the question of his authorship of the first eight chapters. Augustus Neander claimed that, because the passages in *Aduersus Marcionem* were necessary for the integrity of the argument while those same passages in *Aduersus Iudaeos* were not, the second half of *Aduersus Iudaeos* derived from *Aduersus Marcionem*, and was not by Tertullian himself but by a foreign hand.[11] He was unsure when in Tertullian's career (before or after *Aduersus Marcionem*, before or during his Montanist phase) the first eight chapters had been written.[12] In a brief appendix he offered his proof.[13] Objections that one could imagine Marcion making to the interpretation of some passages from the Hebrew Scriptures do not sound nearly as authentic when placed on the lips of the Jewish opponent in *Aduersus Iudaeos*. Further, there are grammatical infelicities that occurred when the compiler attempted to alter clauses and sentences that referred to Marcion.

Åkerman believed that the later chapters were a mere forgery and a "ziemlich miserable Interpolation."[14] De Labriolle repeated the same general opinion, that, because of an uncharacteristic clumsiness in the last six chapters, they must have been borrowed from the *Aduersus Marcionem* by someone

9. Gilles Quispel, *De bronnen van Tertullianus' Adversus Marcionem* (Utrecht: Burgersdijk en Niemans, 1943), 61–79.

10. Johannes Quasten, *Patrology*, vol. 2: *The Ante-Nicene Literature after Irenaeus* (Utrecht: Spectrum, 1953), 269.

11. Augustus Neander, *History of the Planting and Training of the Christian Church by the Apostles*, vol. 2: *Antignostikus, or the Spirit of Tertullian*, trans. J. E. Ryland (London: Henry G. Bohn, 1851), 530.

12. Ibid., 530–33.   13. Ibid., 534–36.

14. Malte Åkerman, *Über die Echtheit der letzteren Hälfte von Tertullians Adversus Iudaeos* (Lund: Lindstroem, 1918), 11.

other than Tertullian.[15] Efroymson accepts this as the majority view among
scholars today and, for this reason, ignores *Aduersus Iudaeos* when commenting on Tertullian's attitudes toward Judaism.[16]

Variations on these positions also have been put forward by several scholars. Corssen agreed with Neander that the second half of the treatise was
noticeably different from the first. Yet, he argued that the second half contained not only material that came from *Aduersus Marcionem* and other material that was written by the forger himself, but also some material that was
Tertullian's own.[17] These passages (particularly 13.1–23) would have followed
on originally from chapter 8 but the forger has inserted his own material and
the extracts from book 3 of *Aduersus Marcionem,* thereby separating them. Evans suggests, on the other hand, in a rather ambiguous clause, that the early
chapters are the ones of the most doubtful validity because they lack Tertullian's usual vigor and that the second half was either copied from Tertullian
or was his own draft.[18]

Those Who Accept the Work's Integrity and Authenticity

The popularity of Quasten's multivolume introduction to early Christian
literature has ensured that the negative assessment of Tertullian's involve-
ment in at least the second half of *Aduersus Iudaeos* is the most readily accessible and most often repeated, despite the fact that a number of scholars have
tried to repudiate it.

In the nineteenth century Noeldechen argued that Tertullian used his
own *Aduersus Iudaeos* as a draft for the third book of *Aduersus Marcionem,* the
first eight chapters of the former being the more finished part of the draft.
His criticism of Semler was that he was unable to appreciate early Christian
literature in its own context.[19] He believed that the differences between the
two halves of the treatise seduced Neander ("verführte ihn") into believing

15. Pierre de Labriolle, *Histoire de la Littérature latine chrétienne,* 3rd ed., Collection d'Études
Anciennes (Paris: G. Bardy, 1947), 121.

16. David Efroymson, "The Patristic Connection," in *Anti-Semitism and the Foundation of
Christianity,* ed. Alan T. Davies (New York: Paulist, 1979), 116, n. 6.

17. P. Corssen, *Die Altercatio Simonis Judaei et Theophili Christiani auf ihre Quellen geprüft* (Berlin: Weidmann, 1890), 2–10.

18. Evans, *Tertullian: "Adversus Marcionem,"* xx.

19. Ernst Noeldechen, *Tertullian's Gegen die Juden auf Einheit, Echtheit, Entstehung,* Texte und
Untersuchung zur Geschichte der altchristlichen Literatur 12.2 (Leipzig: J. C. Hinrichs, 1894), 15.

that the second half was the work of someone incompetent.[20] Those who followed Neander were accused of merely repeating his opinion without investigating it for themselves.[21] Noeldechen's criticism of Corssen was that the latter had not investigated his claim sufficiently and that by creating four sources for the treatise (genuine Tertullian in the first eight chapters, material from *Aduersus Marcionem* 3, the forger's own material, and genuine Tertullian in the second half), it became too convenient to label any difficult passage as non-genuine, thereby not engaging the text as we have it.[22]

Noeldechen could point approvingly to the earlier work of the German scholar Grotemeyer, who had argued that the themes found in the second half of *Aduersus Iudaeos* were announced in chapter 6, thus indicating a "Gedankenordnung."[23] Grotemeyer had accepted the untidiness of the second half compared with the first, and so did Noeldechen. Throughout his treatment of the relationship between *Aduersus Iudaeos* and book 3 of *Aduersus Marcionem*, Noeldechen argued that the latter was derived from the former, and that this could be explained simply as the same author himself reusing older material in a new context.[24] Even though *Aduersus Iudaeos* does not have a clear rhetorical conclusion, what there is still relates back to the rest of the treatise and is consistent with how Tertullian ended a number of works.[25]

A few years earlier Noeldechen had made some general comments about *Aduersus Iudaeos*. He indicated that he believed it was a genuine response to a genuine debate, because the opponent in the debate was presented not simply as a Jew but as a proselyte. In many regards it lacks the falsity one associates with feigned debates and the overall tone is mild rather than harsh.[26] He dated the work to early 196 because of the statements in 9.12 about Roman provincial matters with regard to the division of Syria, and in 7.4, 7–8 about Roman interaction with the Parthians and Gaetulians.[27] It is to be noted that Tertullian's comments about Syria match those in Justin's *Dialogus* 78.10, written well before the actual division in 194, which suggests that this is a gloss in Justin.

20. Ibid.   21. Ibid., 16.

22. Ibid., 19–20.

23. Ibid., 17–18. See Hermann Grotemeyer, "Excurs über die Echtheir der Schr. adv. Jud. und die Zeit ihrer Abfassung," *Jahresbericht des Gymnasium Thomaeum zu Kempen* (1865): 16–26.

24. Noeldechen, *Tertullian's Gegen die Juden*, 46–74.

25. Ibid., 91.

26. Ernst Noeldechen, *Tertullian* (Gotha: Friedrich Undreas Berthes, 1890), 72–76.

27. Ernst Noeldechen, *Die Abfassungszeit der Schriften Tertullians*, Texte und Untersuchung zur Geschichte der altchristlichen Literatur 5 (Leipzig: J. C. Hinrichs, 1888), 48–49.

Although he accepted the genuineness of the entire work, Adolf Harnack argued that the first eight chapters were written after the first edition of *Aduersus Marcionem* and that the last chapters were taken from *Aduersus Marcionem*.[28]

In 1935 Lukyn Williams accepted that the entire piece was by Tertullian, that it depended upon *testimonia,* and that, when Tertullian later wrote *Aduersus Marcionem,* he relied again upon *testimonia,* or on the extracts he had combined already in *Aduersus Iudaeos,* which were then interpreted to suit a new purpose or context.[29] He rejected any notion that the later chapters did not belong: "[t]hey do in fact continue the argument, though as it seems, in a rougher, more detailed, and less polished form."[30]

Gösta Säflund dates the work early in Tertullian's career and follows Noeldechen in believing, on stylistic and philological grounds, that it was employed later in the composition of the third book of *Aduersus Marcionem.*[31] After a thorough examination of Tertullian's use of scriptural texts, Säflund comes to the conclusion that our treatise is a single work. He explains the problems concerning the two halves of the treatise, particularly the repetitions, as being the result of the author's change of mind during composition, writing more than had been intended initially.[32] In particular, he takes exception to the arguments of Åkerman. Säflund seems to accept that, even though Tertullian had begun work on chapters 9 to 14, someone else, not up to the task, put the material together and attached it to the earlier chapters.[33] A number of "problems" in the second half of the treatise, from which Åkerman reached his conclusion that this half was a forgery, are found by Säflund to occur in the earlier parts of the treatise and in some other treatises of Tertullian as well. He considers passages in the second half of the treatise that are without parallel in *Aduersus Marcionem,* viz., 11.1–10 and 13.1–23, as displaying characteristics of Tertullian's writing.[34] Regarding those passages in the second half that do have a parallel to passages in *Aduersus Marcionem,* Säflund

---

28. Adolf Harnack, *Geschichte der altchristlichen Literatur bis Eusebius,* part II: *Die Chronologie,* vol. 2: *Die Chronologie der Literatur von Irenaeus bis Eusebius* (Leipzig: J. C. Hinrichs, 1904), 288–92.

29. A. Lukyn Williams, *"Adversus Judaeos": A Bird's-Eye View of Christian "Apologiae" until the Renaissance* (Cambridge: Cambridge University Press, 1935), 45.

30. Ibid., 48.

31. Gösta Säflund, *De pallio und die stilistische Entwicklung Tertullians,* Skrifter utgivna av Svenska Institutet I Rom, 8, VIII (Lund: C. W. K. Gleerup, 1955), 128–208.

32. Ibid., 206.   33. Ibid., 207.

34. Ibid., 161–66.

concludes that it makes more sense to see parts of *Aduersus Iudaeos* as having been deleted or made more concise for inclusion in the later *Aduersus Marcionem*.[35]

The most thorough investigation of *Aduersus Iudaeos* has been conducted by Hermann Tränkle. His 1964 critical edition and German commentary is also the most recent we have. He rejects the position of scholars like Neander, Burkitt, Corssen, and Quispel quite explicitly, stating that the evidence Quispel offered was only "spärliche Material," insufficient to prove his point. He argues that Burkitt's claim about Tertullian's exclusive use of Theodotion in *Aduersus Iudaeos* and the Septuagint in the rest of his works is exaggerated.[36] As a result Tränkle believes "sondern erklärt auch keine der bei den früheren Verfechtern der Unechtheit der zweiten Hälfte offen gebliebenen Fragen."[37] He agrees with Noeldechen about the genuineness of the work and argues that the second half of the treatise displays lecture-like characteristics no less than the first, indicating that the second half has the same form.[38] In fact, Tränkle distinguishes between the work's unity and its authenticity, a point he borrows from C. Becker.[39] Even though he has some questions about the first in a few places, he has none about the second.[40] For Tränkle, the style of the first eight chapters matches that of the second half and that of *Aduersus Marcionem* 3. All he concedes is that if the second half was not by Tertullian it was by someone who could imitate him particularly well.[41]

Tränkle accepts the priority of *Aduersus Iudaeos* over *Aduersus Marcionem*, arguing, through a detailed contrast of a number of extracts, "daß die Formulierungen in Marc. III viel knapper und straffer, in Iud. dagegen schlaffer und umständlicher sind."[42] Not only is the wording tighter and more concise in *Aduersus Marcionem*, but sentence structure too reveals that what takes

---

35. Ibid., 166–89.

36. Hermann Tränkle, *Q. S. F. Tertullian, "Adversus Iudaeos." Mit Einleitung und kritischem Kommentar* (Wiesbaden: Franz Steiner Verlag, 1964), xii–xiv.

37. Ibid., xxi.   38. Ibid., xvii.

39. Ibid., xxii.

40. Ibid., xvi. Even though he agrees with Corssen that ch. 13 seems to follow ch. 8, stating how "wertvoll und, wie mir scheint, richtig diese Behauptung ist," he criticized him for not having then addressed the questions this would raise about why they were separated in the first place, and about why 11.1–9 was added where it was, rather than with ch. 13. On p. xxii Tränkle indicates that he disagrees with Säflund on the question of the work's unity because of the repetitions and disjointed structure in several places.

41. Ibid., lix.

42. Ibid., liii.

several sentences in *Aduersus Iudaeos* and involves much that is long-winded, is abbreviated in *Aduersus Marcionem.*[43] In contrast with it, the second half of *Aduersus Iudaeos* is less organized and less structurally coherent, such that it lacked "Lebendigkeit und Schlagkraft."[44] For Tränkle questions about the date of composition of *Aduersus Iudaeos* must remain unanswered because, given the sketch-like quality of the treatise ("nur als Entwurf erhalten ist"), points like the omission of the Parthians could be explained by any number of factors. At the same time he does support a date early in Tertullian's literary career,[45] before *Apologeticum.*[46]

Further, the work, having so much in common with other, earlier examples of the anti-Judaic genre of Christian literature, does not reflect for him contact with contemporary Judaism but simply repeats older arguments.[47] Further still, Tränkle believes that, like Justin's *Dialogus cum Tryphone,* Tertullian's treatise was not directed to Jews but to pagans, and hence each of these works was "Scheinpolemik."[48] He thinks that Tertullian abandoned this treatise when he could engage in real polemic against the popularity of Marcionism.[49] Although he offers an extended commentary on the structure of the work, Tränkle indicates rhetorical elements only briefly.[50]

Jean-Claude Fredouille reviewed the state of this question in 1972. Two issues were of paramount interest to him: whether *Aduersus Iudaeos* was by Tertullian and whether it showed that its author had contact with a contemporary Jewish community. He took a positive stance on both issues.[51] Fredouille lists commentators under several headings:[52] those, like himself, who believed that the work was authentically Tertullian's and that it reflected a real controversy (Monceaux, Säflund, Braun);[53] those who believed that the

43. Ibid., lvi.
44. Ibid., lix.
45. Ibid., lx–lxi.
46. Ibid., lxvii.
47. Ibid., lxviii–lxxxviii.
48. Ibid., lxxii.
49. Ibid., lxxiv.

50. Ibid., xxiii–liii. On p. xxiv he speaks of "[d]ie eigentliche Steitfrage" about the validity of the Jewish law appearing at the beginning of ch. 2. On p. xxx he indicates that Tertullian began "der Nachweis" at the start of ch. 6.

51. Jean-Claude Fredouille, *Tertullien et la conversion de la culture antique,* Collection des Études Augustiniennes Série Antiquité 47 (Paris: Études Augustiniennes, 1972), 254–55.

52. Ibid., 92.

53. Paul Monceaux, *Histoire littéraire de l'Afrique chrétienne,* vol. 1: *Tertullien et les origines* (Paris: Ernest Leroux, 1901), 293–94, believed *Adu. Iud.* to be prior to *Adu. Marc.* and that it was Tertullian who revised his own earlier work in the later. For Säflund see n. 31; René Braun, "Aux origines de le chrétienté d'Afrique: un homme de combat, Tertullien," *BAGB* 4th series (1965): 196.

work, at least the last chapters, was not by Tertullian, although it reflected a real controversy (de Labriolle, Quispel, Quasten, Altaner);[54] and those who believed that the work was authentically Tertullian's, although it did not reflect any real contact with contemporary Judaism (Harnack, Tränkle).[55] His fourth category was for those who accepted the reality of this work as coming from contact with contemporary Judaism but who were not interested in questions of the work's integrity (Williams, Simon, Judant).[56] Fredouille argues that Tertullian was dependent upon Justin and Irenaeus and that his urgent concern was to demonstrate the novelty of Christ's new law, which was more important than a coherent treatise about salvation history.[57]

Another French scholar, Claude Aziza, raises a number of questions, although a number of his conclusions have been labeled as "unbridled speculation,"[58] and he is criticized because he seems "to have underplayed Tertullian's antagonism toward Judaism and seriously overstated his knowledge of Judaism."[59] Aziza rejects the view that *Aduersus Iudaeos* was written after, and partly from, *Aduersus Marcionem*.[60] He reaches this position because he believes that the entire work displays a coherence and integrity in the development of themes that necessitate chapters 9–14 being part of the intended structure of the work, such that the treatise had to be written prior to 207–208, the date accepted for *Aduersus Marcionem*.[61] Even though the last chapters may lack vigor, Aziza does not believe that they were taken from *Aduersus Marcionem*.[62] The seemingly ill-fitting nature of the work was part of the deliberate intention of the author. The two themes of the coming of the Christ and the rejection of the Jews are intermingled throughout the work,

54. For de Labriolle see n. 15; for Quispel see n. 9; for Quasten see n. 10; B. Altaner, *Patrologie. Leben Schriften und Lehre der Kirchenväter*, 8th ed., rev. Alfred Stuiber (Freiburg: Herder, 1978), 153, in the most recent edition of his work, modifies his position somewhat: "Auch der 2. Teil (9/14) ist echt und wurde später im 3. Buch *Adversus Marcionem* verwertet."

55. For Harnack see n. 28; for Tränkle see n. 36.

56. For Williams see n. 29; Marcel Simon, *"Verus Israel": A Study of the Relations between Christians and Jews in the Roman Empire (AD 135–425)*, 2nd Eng. ed., trans. H. McKeating, The Littman Library of Jewish Civilization (London: Vallentine Mitchell, 1996), 139; D. Judant, *Judaïsme et christianisme. Dossier patristique* (Paris: Les Editions du Cèdre, 1969), 98, 111.

57. Fredouille, *Tertullien et la conversion*, 256.

58. John G. Gager, *The Origins of Anti-Semitism: Attitudes Toward Judaism in Pagan and Christian Antiquity* (Oxford: Oxford University Press, 1983), 296, n. 14.

59. David Efroymson, "Tertullian's Anti-Jewish Rhetoric: Guilt by Association," *Union Seminary Quarterly Review* 36 (1980): 37, n. 8.

60. Claude Aziza, *Tertullien et le judaïsme*, Publications de le Faculté des Lettres et des Sciences Humaines de Nice 16 (Nice: Les Belles Lettres, 1977), 104.

61. Ibid., 107.   62. Ibid., 105.

sometimes one more to the fore than the other.[63] He argues further for real contact between Tertullian and Jews in Carthage, suggesting that Tertullian would have been unlikely to invent the proselyte, whom he mentioned in the opening lines of the treatise, if there had not been one, as his readers would have known this.[64]

In the introduction to his Italian translation of a number of Tertullian's works, Moreschini adopts Tränkle's findings that the work predates *Aduersus Marcionem,* that it was all by Tertullian, that the first eight chapters and chapters 9–12 were "un abbozzo incompiuto," where sections repeat themselves, and that the work was probably published after Tertullian's death with some additions in the latter half.[65] For these reasons he describes *Aduersus Iudaeos* as "una delle più singolari opere di Tertulliano."[66]

This is also the view of Schreckenberg: that the work is early (prior to *Aduersus Marcionem*), only written in draft form, and never intended by Tertullian to be published in the state we have it now.[67] That material is common to both should not lead one to the conclusion that the second half of *Aduersus Iudaeos* is spurious or that it was written after, and from, *Aduersus Marcionem.*[68] He describes *Aduersus Iudaeos* as possessing "die skizzenhafte Unfertigkeit des Frühwerkes" when compared with *Aduersus Marcionem,* and being "theologisch aber nicht so durchdacht und folgerichtig angelegt . . . wie andere seiner Werke."[69] Further, in contrast with the position taken by Aziza on the reality of Tertullian's contact with the Jews, he believes the work to be "eine literarische Fiktion" and "deren Rahmenhandlung keineswegs ein reales Geschehen widerspiegeln muß."[70]

Timothy Barnes is one of the few English-speaking scholars to have commented on *Aduersus Iudaeos* in the twentieth century. Relying on both Säflund and Tränkle, he also accepts this to be an early, genuine, though unrevised and later self-plundered work of Tertullian.[71] In the second edition

63. Ibid., 106–107.   64. Ibid., 108.

65. Claudio Moreschini, trans., *Opere scelte di Quinto Settimio Florente Tertulliano,* Classici delle Religioni, sezione Quarta: La religione cattolica (Turin: Unione Tipografico-Editrice Torinese, 1974), 48–49.

66. Ibid., 48.

67. Heinz Schreckenberg, *Die christlichen Adversus-Judaeos-Texte und ihr literarisches und historisches Umfeld (1.–11.Jh.)* (Frankfurt am Main: Peter Lang, 1982), 217.

68. Ibid.   69. Ibid.

70. Ibid.

71. Timothy D. Barnes, *Tertullian: A Historical and Literary Study,* 2nd ed. (Oxford: Clarendon Press, 1985), 53.

of his biography of Tertullian, he withdrew his earlier bald statement that Tertullian's knowledge of Judaism was derived not from contemporary experience but only from reading the pages of the Hebrew Scriptures, such that "[f]or Tertullian . . . Judaism was an unchanging, fossilized faith, not to be taken seriously."[72] What he has replaced it with is a sense that Tertullian had a detached awareness of contemporary Jews in Carthage.[73]

To this list of names we could add the research of Otranto. He dates *Aduersus Iudaeos* to before the third edition of *Aduersus Marcionem,* around the same time as the first drafts of the latter. Otranto wants to date the work to 202 because the edict of Septimius Severus against proselytizing in that year would have rendered useless the need for Tertullian to complete his work against the Jews.[74]

Judaism and Christianity in Contact?

This then is the state of the question with regard to the integrity and authenticity of *Aduersus Iudaeos*. Although my comments have been largely summary in nature, it is important, I believe, to have a thorough and accurate picture of the nature of the controversy that has surrounded this text in order that the results of my rhetorical analysis of its authenticity and integrity in the following chapters be appreciated fully. There remains much division in the scholarly community about this work, and by highlighting the nature of the disagreement I believe that I have pointed to precisely those kinds of concerns that can be addressed by offering the first-ever rhetorical analysis of this piece of literature. That my rhetorically derived conclusions will endorse many of the points made already by those who support the work's authenticity and integrity should help resolve this controversy. In addition, as we have seen, some of those who have considered this work have also made comment about the reality of the occasion that prompted its writing and the reality of Tertullian's contact with Jews in early third-century Carthage. The broader issue of the contact between Christians and Jews in late antiquity has been of growing importance to scholarship on both early Christianity and early rabbinic Judaism in recent decades. In this debate this work ascribed

72. Ibid., 92.
73. Ibid., 330.
74. G. Otranto, *Giudei e cristiani a Cartagine tra II e III secolo. L'Adversus Iudaeos* (Bari: Adriatica, 1975), 161–62.

to Tertullian is often neglected because of the controversy that surrounds it. It is appropriate in this chapter to outline the debate concerning Christians' contact with Jews as well, in particular because I intend to demonstrate that many other brief summaries of that question contain inaccurate presentations of what other scholars have said about the topic. In the conclusion to this volume I shall return to this more specific question of Tertullian's contact with Carthaginian Jews to offer my own contribution.

We may begin with Williams, who commented on the purpose of Tertullian's treatise. He wrote, "There was therefore sufficient reason for the *Adversus Judaeos* to be composed, both as a protection to Christians and as a means of winning Jews."[75] Many of those who argue that the work (and others like it) was intended for Jews do so because they accept that Judaism and Christianity were engaged in a lively interaction during these centuries, while those who argue that such works were intended for Christians, not Jews, do so because they believe that the two had gone their separate ways by this time. This point has been well made by several scholars in recent years. Guy Stroumsa states that those who support the first position argue for social interaction and those who argue for the second focus on Christian self-definition.[76] James Carleton Paget expresses the question in similar fashion:

Did the Christian *Adversus Judaeos* tradition, and indeed Christian anti-Judaism in general, reflect genuine disputes between Christians and Jews, so that it could be understood either as a response to a threat posed by the Jewish community to the nascent church, or as an attempt to convert Jews to Christianity? Or, contrary to this thesis, was it literature which should be understood without any reference to an outside Jewish reality, and seen rather as the result of internal tendencies within Christian theology and parenesis?[77]

The notion that Jews and Christians had gone their separate ways has been the subject of increasing interest in academic circles.[78] As the papers at the Oxford-Princeton Research Partnership "Culture and Religion of the Eastern

---

75. Williams, *"Adversus Judaeos,"* 43. On p. 52, however, he stated that Tertullian's personal knowledge of contemporary Jews was inferior to Justin's.

76. Guy G. Stroumsa, "From Anti-Judaism to Antisemitism in Early Christianity?" in *Contra Iudaeos: Ancient and Medieval Polemics Between Christians and Jews,* ed. Ora Limor and Guy G. Stroumsa, Texts and Studies in Medieval and Early Modern Judaism 10 (Tübingen: J. C. B. Mohr [Paul Siebeck], 1996), 3.

77. James Carleton Paget, "Anti-Judaism and Early Christian Identity," *ZAC* 1 (1997): 195.

78. James D. G. Dunn, *The Parting of the Ways between Christianity and Judaism and their Significance for the Character of Christianity* (Philadelphia: Trinity Press International, 1991); R. Bauckham, "The Parting of the Ways: What Happened and Why," *STh* 47 (1993): 135–51; James

Mediterranean" Project early in 2002 at Princeton University demonstrate, more scholars are finding evidence of contact between Jews and Christians extending much later than previously imagined. However, Tertullian's *Aduersus Iudaeos* is not mentioned explicitly in any of the papers presented at that conference.

Stroumsa and Carleton Paget have divided a number of their colleagues into two camps, each representing one of the two approaches. Juster, Simon, Krauss, Williams, Parkes, Blumenkranz, Wilken, Blanchetière, Horbury, de Lange, Wilson, and MacLennan are allocated to the first group, who support the notion of ongoing contact between Christians and Jews.[79]

Samuel Krauss, for example, considered the Jews to have continued to be a significant group in certain parts of the Mediterranean world until well into the fourth century and to have remained in competition with the Christians.[80] In addition, Krauss noted that the disagreement between Jews and Christians centered on the exegesis of Scripture.[81] Interestingly enough, he made no mention of Tertullian's treatise.

We may take Marcel Simon, whose work first appeared in French in 1948, as the primary exponent of this view, and hence I should like to devote a little more attention to his arguments.[82] Writing in the aftermath of the Second World War, Simon was concerned with distinguishing historic Christian anti-Judaism from contemporary Nazi anti-Semitism.[83] For him, the anti-Judaic literature[84] only made sense as part of a significant and ongoing in-

---

D. G. Dunn, *Jews and Christians: The Parting of the Ways, A.D. 70–135,* rev. Eng. ed., The Second Durham-Tübingen Research Symposium on Earliest Christianity and Judaism, Durham 1989 (Grand Rapids, Mich.: Eerdmans, 1999); Adam Becker and Annette Yoshiko Reed, eds., *The Ways That Never Parted: Jews and Christians in Late Antiquity and the Early Middle Ages,* Texts and Studies in Ancient Judaism 95 (Tübingen: Paul Siebeck, 2003); and Daniel Boyarin, *Border Lines: The Partition of Judaeo-Christianity,* Divinations: Rereading Late Ancient Religion (Philadelphia: University of Pennsylvania Press, 2004).

79. Stroumsa, "From Anti-Judaism to Antisemitism," 10–16; Carleton Paget, "Anti-Judaism and Early Christian Identity," 196–97.

80. Samuel Krauss, "The Jews in the Works of the Church Fathers, part 2," *JQR* 6 (1894): 89.

81. Ibid., 129.

82. Cf. Efroymson, "Tertullian's Anti-Jewish Rhetoric," 25, who puts Simon and Ruether together as representative of the view that the anti-Judaic literature was about Christian self-definition. See G. N. Stanton, "Aspects of Early Christian-Jewish Polemic and Apologetic," *NTS* 31 (1985): 377.

83. Simon, *"Verus Israel,"* 397–98; Albert I. Baumgarten, "Marcel Simon's *Verus Israel* as a Contribution to Jewish History," *HTR* 92 (1999): 465–66; and Michele Murray, *Playing a Jewish Game: Gentile Christian Judaizing in the First and Second Centuries CE,* Études sur le christianisme et le judaïsme 13 (Waterloo, Ontario: Wilfrid Laurier University Press, 2004), 137–41.

84. Like many scholars I see a difference between the terms "anti-Judaism" and "anti-

teraction between Christians and Jews. He wanted to answer the question about the purpose of anti-Judaic literature and to do so neither asserting unquestioningly, as he believed Williams had done, that such literature reflected real controversies, nor asserting the opposite, as he believed Harnack had done, that the writings "do not contain any real answer to objections actually raised by Jews."[85] He raised a number of pertinent questions about why one would write treatises against Jews unless there was contact and why one would write indirectly if they were intended for pagans.[86]

Simon drew attention to the fact that the arguments in this literary genre derived from Scripture, that it should not be surprising that the same passages and interpretations could be used against Jews, pagans, and heretics alike, and could be used repeatedly,[87] and that, with regard to our work, just because parts of it were reused without much modification in *Aduersus Marcionem* one should not reach the conclusion that the opponent in *Aduersus Iudaeos* was really pagan. Given the greater use of Scripture in treatises designed ostensibly for Jews than in those explicitly directed to pagans, perhaps one should accept that the Jews were the intended recipients.[88]

Simon responded also to one of Harnack's points, that in the dialogues the Jewish participant seems to be a conventional and literary character rather than a real person, by noting that dialogues only represent a small part of this anti-Judaic genre, and that, even if the character was the construct of the author to some degree, real encounters might still underlie the literary trap-

---

Semitism," reserving the former for theological and religious disputes and the latter for racial and ethnic ones. See Craig A. Evans, "Faith and Polemic: The New Testament and First-century Judaism," in *Anti-Semitism and Early Christianity: Issues of Polemic and Faith,* ed. Craig A. Evans and Donald A. Hagner (Minneapolis: Fortress Press, 1993), 1; and Stroumsa, "From Anti-Judaism to Antisemitism," 2. Gager, *The Origins of Anti-Semitism,* 8–10, accepts the distinction between these terms but argues that there are instances where neither one applies. Cf. Rosemary Radford Ruether, *Faith and Fratricide: The Theological Roots of Anti-Semitism* (New York: Seabury Press, 1974), 3, and Gavin Langmuir, "Anti-Judaism as the Necessary Preparation for Anti-Semitism," *Viator* 2 (1971): 383–89, who argue that anti-Judaism always finds social expression in anti-Semitism. For an even more extreme view, that theological differences are the first step in racial anti-Semitism, see Fred Gladstone Bratton, *The Crime of Christendom: The Theological Sources of Christian Anti-Semitism* (Santa Barbara, Calif.: Fithian Press, 1969), x–xi. For a response to Langmuir see Peter Schäfer, *Judeophobia: Attitudes toward the Jews in the Ancient World* (Cambridge, Mass., and London: Harvard University Press, 1997), 197–211. Of course, no matter what the definitions, the question to ask is whether we can distinguish in practice (and for my purposes I am interested only with regard to Tertullian) between a negative attitude toward Jewish religious thinking and toward Jews as people.

85. Simon, *"Verus Israel,"* 137.   86. Ibid., 138.
87. Ibid., 145.   88. Ibid., 139.

pings. It made no sense to Simon for Christians to continue employing this genre long after its original use supposedly disappeared.[89]

If that says something about Simon's position with regard to the reality of the interaction that lay behind the texts, one has to ask about the purpose of this literature. He noted that Hulen's assessment that this genre could be classified according to the purpose a work fulfilled (expository, argumentative, or denunciatory)[90] seemed too rigid and artificial. Simon offered a modification of Hulen's position, particularly with regard to works where the emphasis appeared primarily to be one of refuting, such that a work that refuted Jewish beliefs rather than just responded to Jewish criticisms of Christianity could be taken as genuinely directed against Jews.[91] When the emphasis appeared apologetic, Simon agreed with Harnack that such works might not have been polemical at all but addressed to an internal Christian audience. Simon's position, though, is more nuanced than Harnack's, arguing that a work could have been written with several objectives simultaneously in mind.[92] He mentioned Tertullian's treatise as demonstrating this double purpose with a first part (chapters 1–5) and a second part (chapters 6–14).[93]

The main point in Simon's groundbreaking work was delivered when he reminded his own readers that the discussion about whether real encounters lay behind each piece of writing or whether these works actually were addressed to Jews was secondary to the issue of whether Judaism posed a real threat to Christianity. Christian Judaizing tendencies arose because of an outside stimulus.[94] Simon believed that Judaism remained a vital force in antiquity for longer than had been accepted previously.[95]

I have spent considerable time presenting Simon's position in some detail because I believe that some of the efforts of more recent scholars who survey this field are too simplistic in their summation of Simon's position. Stroumsa rightly highlights the fact that Simon pointed to social factors as being important because he believed that Judaism remained a dynamic force far lon-

---

89. Ibid., 140.

90. B. Hulen, "The Dialogues with the Jews as Sources for the Early Jewish Argument Against Christianity," *JBL* 51 (1932): 58–70. On pp. 143–44, Simon noted that, in broad outline, he agreed with Hulen that these three categories have some chronological pattern.

91. Simon, *"Verus Israel,"* 143.

92. Ibid. On p. 156 Simon restated his position with regard to the purpose of this genre: "The anti-Jewish writers pursue a double aim, to demonstrate from scripture the truth of Christianity, and by the same means to refute the claims of Judaism."

93. Ibid., 156.   94. Ibid., 145.

95. Ibid., xi.

ger than credited previously,[96] but Stroumsa does not make any comment about the purpose of anti-Judaic writings, especially about Simon's carefully stated position that some of this literature was written for an internal reason as well as for external ones. It is important to look carefully at Simon, because his argument was more nuanced than many acknowledge. Stroumsa has been influenced greatly by Miriam Taylor, in a work in which she acknowledges that she is creating typologies and categories.[97] The trouble with such things is that they are generalizations that tend to obliterate important evidence that does not fit within the category.

With reference to Tertullian in particular, it has been noted already that Fredouille, Monceaux, Säflund, and Braun believe he had contact with Jews and, on this basis, conclude that he intended his work for Jews.[98] William Frend, surveying Tertullian's corpus of writing and Carthaginian archaeology, accepts that Tertullian was in touch with contemporary Jews.[99] Aziza goes one step further and suggests that Tertullian's legalism and agitated personality might have stemmed from the fact that before he became a Christian he could once have had leanings toward Judaism.[100] Scholer accepts the opinion of scholars like Aziza, Frend, and Horbury that Tertullian did have knowledge of contemporary Judaism in Carthage, but he rejects the view of Frend that Tertullian provides us with evidence of a Jewish persecution of Christians.[101]

Between them Stroumsa and Carleton Paget have allocated scholars like Harnack, Barnes, Rokeah, Schreckenberg, Ruether, Taylor, Johnson, Gaston,

96. Stroumsa, "From Anti-Judaism to Antisemitism," 11.

97. Miriam Taylor, *Anti-Judaism and Early Christian Identity: A Critique of the Scholarly Consensus,* Studia Post-Biblica 46 (Leiden: E. J. Brill, 1995), 3.

98. Fredouille, *Tertullien et la conversion,* 269–71.

99. W. H. C. Frend, "The Persecutions: Some Links between Judaism and the Early Church," *JEH* 9 (1958): 156–57; Frend, "The *Seniores laici* and the Origins of the Church in North Africa," *JTS* n.s. 12 (1961): 280–84; Frend, "Tertulliano e gli Ebrei," *RSLR* 4 (1968): 3–10; Frend, "A Note on Tertullian and the Jews," in *Studia Patristica* 10, part 1, ed. F. L. Cross, papers presented to the fifth International Conference on Patristic Studies, Oxford 1967 (Berlin: Akademie-Verlag, 1970), 293–96; Frend, "A Note on Jews and Christians in Third-Century North Africa," *JTS* n.s. 21 (1970): 92–96; and Frend, "Jews and Christians in Third-Century Carthage," in *Paganisme, Judaïsme, Christianisme. Influences et affrontements dans le monde antique,* ed. A. Benoit (Paris: de Boccard, 1978), 191–93.

100. Aziza, *Tertullien et le judaïsme,* 221.

101. D. M. Scholer, "Tertullian on Jewish Persecution of Christians," in *Studia Patristica* 17, part 2, ed. Elizabeth A. Livingstone, papers presented to the eighth International Conference on Patristic Studies, Oxford 1979 (Oxford: Pergamon, 1982), 821–28. See William Horbury, "Tertullian on the Jews in the Light of *De Spectaculis* XXX.5–6," *JTS* n.s. 23 (1972): 455–59.

and Efroymson into the second camp of those who assert that the anti-Judaic literature was written for a Christian readership to help with questions of self-identity.[102] Harnack argued that Christianity sought to see itself as the fulfillment of Old Testament prophecy and as such was not engaged in ongoing opposition to Jews but to some stereotypical straw figure in order to address pagan challenges.[103] As the Christian anti-Judaic literature was designed for an internal readership Harnack described it as apologetic rather than polemical.[104] More recently, Taylor describes the position of Simon and others as the "conflict theory" of Jewish-Christian relations.[105] She offers a critique of this now dominant approach, which she divides into two: "competitive anti-Judaism" and "conflictual anti-Judaism." The first assumes that Christianity and Judaism were equal religions locked in a struggle for converts. It is divided into three kinds: "polemical and apologetic" anti-Judaism, which grew out of the literary controversies between Christians and Jews about the messiah and who was now God's people; "defensive" anti-Judaism, a reaction to the Judaizing tendencies among some Christians; and "embittered or disillusioned" anti-Judaism, which is grounded in the Christian failure to convert many from Judaism.[106]

Several criticisms of the polemical and apologetic model are offered by Taylor. First, it presumes that Jews would have been interested in debating these particular issues with Christians. Second, the themes remained repetitive over centuries, which Taylor takes as indicating that the debates were not genuine, for real ones would be attentive to changing circumstances. Third, the Jewish opponent lacks substance and independence, suggesting that such a figure is more likely to have been a literary construct. Fourth, this model is based upon presumptions of rivalry and evidence is made to fit it.[107] Last,

---

102. Stroumsa, "From Anti-Judaism to Antisemitism," 10–16; Carleton Paget, "Anti-Judaism and Early Christian Identity," 196–97.

103. Adolf Harnack, *Die Altercatio Simonis Iudaei et Theophili Christiani nebst Untersuchungen über die antijüdische Polemik in der alten Kirche,* Texte und Untersuchung zur Geschichte der altchristlichen Literatur 1/3 (Leipzig: J. C. Hinrichs, 1883), 56–57, 63–64.

104. Ibid., 64. See Murray, *Playing a Jewish Game,* 129–33.

105. Taylor, *Anti-Judaism and Early Christian Identity,* 2. See Murray, *Playing a Jewish Game,* 149–51.

106. Taylor, *Anti-Judaism and Early Christian Identity,* 7–45. On p. 21, however, where she sets out her plan for the section on competitive anti-Judaism, Taylor makes no mention of the third type, which appears without warning on p. 41.

107. See Baumgarten, "Marcel Simon's *Verus Israel,*" 475–77, for an assessment of Taylor's response to Simon on Jewish proselytizing.

any weaknesses in the model are explained as being due to the apologetic and polemical needs of the Christian authors.

The criticisms that Taylor offers of defensive anti-Judaism are that it presumes that Christian attraction to Jewish practices must be the result of a healthy Judaism and that scholars seem to find their evidence for this Judaizing from the fourth century and read it back into earlier ones. In response to those who put forward embittered anti-Judaism Taylor counters that it is dangerous to introduce psychology into history and that a reading of these texts reveals an abstract dislike for what the Jews represent rather than a dislike for contemporary Jews themselves.[108]

The second typology, conflictual anti-Judaism, recognizes not two equal groups but the inequality in the struggle between Christians and Jews and its political and social, as well as religious, dimensions.[109] Taylor divides this typology into three kinds: "reactive" anti-Judaism, which derived from a Christian inferiority complex at Judaism's social acceptability; "strategic" anti-Judaism, in which Christians positioned themselves to usurp the privileges of the Jews from their Roman overlords; and "recriminatory" anti-Judaism, which contained the Christian response to active Jewish antagonism against them. This typology too comes in for critical evaluation, almost exclusively through a reexamination of Melito of Sardis. There is no evidence, Taylor asserts, to conclude definitively that Jews in the second century were wealthy and secure, that Christians in the same period were poor and oppressed, and that this resulted necessarily in a particular attitude of Christians toward Jews. Strategic anti-Judaism is dismissed as being without any foundation with regard to Melito's currying Rome's favor at the expense of the synagogue. The idea of a Jewish persecution of Christians is likewise dismissed as speculative, because it is not found even in the Christian writers where many other modern scholars assert it is to be found.[110]

Yet more categories are offered: there is "inherited" anti-Judaism. That which was inherited from the pagan prejudices against Jews is labeled "en-

---

108. Taylor, *Anti-Judaism and Early Christian Identity,* 44.

109. Ibid., 47–114.

110. Steven T. Katz, "Issues in the Separation of Judaism and Christianity after 70 CE: A Reconsideration," *JBL* 103 (1984): 43–76, argues that much of what has been understood traditionally as being evidence of Jewish antagonism toward Christianity is really Jewish antagonism against all heretics not just Jewish Christians in particular and that, as a result, there is no evidence until at least the Bar Kochba revolt of a sharp separation between Jews and Christians. We will return later to discuss the term "Jewish Christians."

vironmental" anti-Judaism, and that inherited from what is found in the He-brew Scriptures themselves is called "traditional" anti-Judaism. More criti-cisms of these are offered.[111]

As an alternative, in the second half of her book, Taylor offers a "symbol-ic" anti-Judaism. In this typology she suggests that "the writings of the fathers make much more sense as expressions of an anti-Judaism rooted in theologi-cal ideas than as responses to contemporary Jews in the context of an on-going conflict."[112] For Taylor, this theological need is centered on Christian self-definition, i.e., how both to preserve a continuity with their Jewish heri-tage and to maintain a distinction, even supersession. It is here that Taylor sees the use of Scripture as the basis of the first of her approved typologies: "theological" anti-Judaism. "It is grounded in a hermeneutic of the Holy Scriptures which condemns not the contemporary actions of Jews, but judges them rather in terms of historical crimes with a theological significance."[113]

According to Taylor, this need for theological self-definition cannot co-exist with Christian interaction with contemporary Jews, for the texts of anti-Judaism do not reveal, Taylor postulates as a hermeneutical principle, Christian identity in all its social dimensions, but only its theological ones.[114] She takes an "all or nothing" stance and therefore places Simon totally in the opposite camp, even though, as we have seen, he would not place him-self there.[115] Taylor finds in the comments and writings of Gaston, Efroym-son, and Ruether a refusal or an inability to rule out the "conflict theory," even though, like her, they all support the idea that the primary purpose of Christian anti-Judaic literature was for internal, theological needs of self-definition.[116] These writings provided the basis for the reaffirmation of the Christian argument against Marcion ("reaffirmative" anti-Judaism)[117] and provided a source of symbolism that Christians could use for a variety of

111. Taylor, *Anti-Judaism and Early Christian Identity*, 115–25.

112. Ibid., 127.   113. Ibid., 139.

114. Ibid., 140–41.

115. Cf. ibid., 128, where Taylor, quoting Gager, says that Simon declared that Christian anti-Judaism was tied up with questions of self-identity. However, he is in no way rehabilitated by this.

116. Ibid., 144–51.

117. Ibid., 170–77. As an example of the position Taylor criticizes one could refer to the opin-ions of J. Massingberd Ford, "Was Montanism a Jewish-Christian Heresy?" *JEH* 17 (1966): 154–58, where it is suggested that Tertullian's interest in Judaism might have come from contact with Jewish figures whose advice he sought in preparation of material to use against Marcion. A de-scription of the instances in Tertullian's writings that demonstrate his acquaintance with Jewish thought is provided as well.

other purposes, particularly as an exhortation to virtue and as a tool against other Christian opponents ("fortifying" anti-Judaism and "associative" anti-Judaism).[118] Tertullian's *Aduersus Iudaeos* receives several brief mentions, and Taylor sees it as an example of theological anti-Judaism that focuses on appropriating Scripture for solely Christian use and posits the abrogation of the old law by the new.[119]

I have provided an extensive summary of Taylor's work because hers is the most recent and her case is well made and forcefully argued. It cannot be dismissed lightly. Stroumsa has responded to her position by stating that if the "conflict theory" suffers from the weakness of only considering the social at the expense of the theological, Taylor's position suffers from the opposite weakness. He argues for a more dynamic critique, one that recognizes change over time and one that acknowledges a variety of discourses.[120] Carleton Paget offers just such a sustained critique of Taylor. He claims that she has not recognized or dealt with significant primary and secondary literature and that she presumes that all scholars who support the "conflict theory" agree that it is founded on the basis of proselytizing. He questions whether Judaism was as uninterested in proselytizing as Taylor claims and whether Judaizing among Christians did not have any connection with Judaism. He objects to Taylor's failure to acknowledge contact between Jews and Christians in terms of biblical exegesis.[121] Carleton Paget also raises the question of Jewish anti-Christianity as being insufficiently explored in Taylor's monograph. He also responds to Taylor's assertion that the arguments of this genre remained static. He notes that much of this literature is polemical, a style in which it was not important to represent an opponent's point of view accurately. Further, the form of the literature could vary, as could its tone.[122] He agrees with Taylor that in assessing the purpose of this writing we are often left only with the texts themselves and that oftentimes the interpretation of texts is based on certain assumptions. Unlike Taylor, Carleton Paget does not seem disturbed by this.[123] He concludes that we should not be limited to "either-or" choices.[124]

---

118. Taylor, *Anti-Judaism and Early Christian Identity,* 178–87. In the section on associative anti-Judaism Taylor relies upon Efroymson's analysis of the ways in which Tertullian linked his opponents to Jewish characteristics.

119. Ibid., 132–34.

120. Stroumsa, "From Anti-Judaism to Anti-Semitism," 17.

121. Carleton Paget, "Anti-Judaism and Early Christian Identity," 213.

122. Ibid., 218–19.   123. Ibid., 221.

124. Ibid., 224.

Stroumsa and Carleton Paget are not alone in rejecting this "either-or" approach to scholarship on the question of the relationship between Jews and Christians in late antiquity. Judith Lieu offers a dynamic approach in that she is aware that one cannot make too hasty a generalization about it. Some texts give evidence of contact and others do not. There is recognition of the rhetorical nature of the anti-Judaic literature in that Christian knowledge of Jews helped shape the image of them that the Christians presented, which, in turn, became a part of the reality for a new generation.[125] For her, Tertullian, although aware of the Jews in Carthage, had little to do with them.[126] As we shall discover next, these points are derived from Efroymson's work, and the problem with Efroymson is that he has accepted the view that Tertullian did not write *Aduersus Iudaeos,* at least not in its entirety. It seems to me that Lieu has overlooked the implication of what she starts to say in that last sentence. If Tertullian's comments are less strident in a work addressed to the Jews, does this not suggest that he intended for them actually to read it and that he therefore had more contact with them than she was prepared to accept? We shall see how Efroymson handles that problem, but Lieu simply passes over it, seemingly unaware of its challenge.

Part of the confusion that I believe exists in this field of study comes from the distribution of scholars into two neatly defined and mutually exclusive camps. Even though Stroumsa and Carleton Paget argue for an approach that allows for a multiplicity of purposes in anti-Judaic literature, they have not recognized that some earlier scholars have accepted this and therefore they cannot be divided too neatly into two separate camps. Here I have made some mention of how a close reading of Simon reveals that, although he favored one position more than the other, he was not limited to believing that actual interaction between Jews and Christians was the total picture. Taylor, for example, seems to think that every other scholar besides herself is tainted to some degree by holding a "conflict theory" position. Timothy Horner's summary of scholarship on the reality of Trypho in Justin's *Dialogus* reflects a more carefully delineated range of opinion, from that work's being a ver-

125. Judith Lieu, *Image and Reality: The Jews in the World of the Christians in the Second Century* (Edinburgh: T. & T. Clark, 1996), 12. On p. 105 she dates Tert., *Adu. Iud.* to early in the third century, which, besides the fact that it was not from Asia Minor, may explain why she did not deal with it.

126. Judith Lieu, "History and Theology in Christian Views of Judaism," in *The Jews Among Pagans and Christians in the Roman Empire,* rev. ed., ed. Judith Lieu, John North, and Tessa Rajak (London: Routledge, 1994), 86–87.

batim account of an actual encounter, to a work where Justin has recast an
actual encounter to suit his purposes better, to a work not based on a real encounter and not having anything to do with Judaism.[127]

In all of this discussion about Christian anti-Judaism Tertullian often receives little mention and his *Aduersus Iudaeos* even less.[128] Some of those
who have considered Tertullian in their overviews rely on Efroymson.[129] He
makes a rhetorical assessment of Tertullian's anti-Jewish references and concludes that they helped Tertullian define who was and was not a Christian.
For Tertullian, anything that he believed was opposed to Christianity he could
label as Jewish; whether it actually was or not was irrelevant.[130] Efroymson
illustrates this convincingly with reference to a number of Tertullian's treatises. Thus, even though throughout *Aduersus Marcionem* he sought to rescue
the Hebrew Scriptures from Marcion's excision of them from Christian use,
Tertullian could still identify him as adopting Jewish thinking in his attitudes
about the coming of the messiah for example.[131] Efroymson makes the point
that it is in *Aduersus Marcionem* that we find the largest block of Tertullian's
anti-Jewish material.[132]

This is true only because Efroymson does not investigate Tertullian's *Aduersus Iudaeos,* since he follows the majority of scholars in accepting only the
first eight chapters as authentically Tertullian's.[133] What scholars tend to
overlook is that Efroymson does not say that *Aduersus Marcionem* has more
anti-Judaic material than *Aduersus Iudaeos.* What he does is rule out *Aduersus
Iudaeos* from consideration as being by Tertullian.

I shall argue in the pages of this investigation as we begin to engage with
the text itself that a rhetorical reading of Tertullian's *Aduersus Iudaeos* allows
us to see how this work might well have been written to fulfill a variety of

127. Timothy J. Horner, *Listening to Trypho: Justin Martyr's Dialogue Reconsidered,* Contribu-
tions to Biblical Exegesis and Theology 28 (Leuven: Peeters, 2001), 16–31.

128. Stephen G. Wilson, *Related Strangers: Jews and Christians 70–170 C.E.* (Minneapolis: Fortress Press, 1995), xiv, notes that many investigations into the relationship between Jews and
Christians jumps from the New Testament to the third or fourth centuries, with John Chrysostom in particular. His book sought to redress that imbalance. However, even his work goes
only to 170. Tertullian remains in a black hole.

129. E.g., Lloyd Gaston, "Retrospect," in *Anti-Judaism in Early Christianity,* vol. 2: *Separation
and Polemic,* ed. Stephen G. Wilson, Études sur le christianisme et le judaïsme 2 (Waterloo, Ontario: Wilfrid Laurier Press, 1986), 163–64.

130. Efroymson, "Tertullian's Anti-Jewish Rhetoric," 25.

131. Ibid., 29–30.

132. Efroymson, "The Patristic Connection," 100.

133. Ibid., 116, n. 6.

purposes, not just one. I believe the multidimensional answer to be the most fruitful.[134] Claudia Setzer's statement that "there is no either-or view of biblical Jews or of contemporary Jews, but rather a tendency to project one on top of the other, or to understand one in the light of the other" makes perfect sense.[135] The historical and social realities of interaction between Christians and Jews were intertwined with Christian theological needs for self-definition. Thus, Tertullian could declare a parting of the ways between Christianity and Judaism on the theological level, yet still be engaged with Jews on a social basis.[136]

A Rhetorical Reading

The controversy about the integrity and authenticity of *Aduersus Iudaeos* has affected the degree to which it is used as evidence for scholarly assessment in questions of the relationship between Jews and Christians in late antiquity. Even though there is a growing chorus of scholars asserting Tertullian as author of the entire work, still more research is needed to tip the scales. While Williams's claim in the 1930s, that questions of the unity and authorship of *Aduersus Iudaeos* are of little more than academic interest,[137] may be acceptable for a sweeping review of the entire genre of anti-Judaic polemic, it will not suffice for the purposes of an analysis of the work itself. Nor will the mere repetition of views from one scholar to the next without reexamination.[138] Although Sider may have omitted this book because he accepted uncritically the opinion that the work lacked complete unity and in-

134. Geoffrey D. Dunn, *Tertullian*, The Early Church Fathers (London and New York: Routledge, 2004), 51.

135. Claudia Setzer, "Jews, Jewish Christians and Judaizers in North Africa," in *Putting Body and Soul Together: Essays in Honor of Robin Scroggs*, ed. Virginia Wiles, Alexandra Brown, and Graydon F. Snyder (Valley Forge, Pa.: Trinity Press International, 1997), 187.

136. A distinction I take from Robert A. Kraft, "The Weighing of the Parts: Pivots and Pitfalls in the Study of Early Judaisms and their Early Christian Offspring," in *The Ways That Never Parted: Jews and Christians in Late Antiquity and the Early Middle Ages*, ed. Adam Becker and Annette Yoshiko Reed, Texts and Studies in Ancient Judaism 95 (Tübingen: Paul Siebeck, 2003), 87. Whether or not modern scholars no longer see the relationship between Christians and Jews in late antiquity in terms of supersessionism (see Andrew S. Jacobs, "The Lion and the Lamb: Reconsidering Jewish-Christian Relations in Antiquity," in Becker and Reed, eds., *The Ways That Never Parted*, 97–105), Tertullian himself certainly did.

137. See n. 35.

138. Tränkle, *Tertullian*, *"Adversus Iudaeos,"* xiv, describes Neander's opinion about the second half of *Adu. Iud.*, an opinion that remained largely uncontested for so long, as "die gefährliche Unbestimmtheit."

tegrity, I believe that a rhetorical analysis, along the lines Sider himself followed with Tertullian's other works, is an appropriate exercise. My survey has needed to be as extensive as it is in order to demonstrate the variety and complexity of opinions, which sometimes rest upon an inaccurate generalization of other secondary literature. Classical rhetoric offers us, I believe, a way of analyzing style and structure that will give us fresh insight in terms of integrity, authorship, structure, argumentation, and purpose.

I am convinced, however, that such an analysis will yield other benefits. An appreciation of the extent to which this is a rhetorical work will provide a hermeneutical context for interpretation. That its author was engaged in debate, seeking to prove a point, to win an argument, and to be persuasive, will, to the extent they are aware of it, shape the way modern readers approach it. I would contend that it is probably inappropriate for us to describe much of early Christian literature, as we have done, as treatises. That term implies that a work is objective, comprehensive, and systematic. Tertullian (and he was not alone in this) did not engage in exposition but in advocacy; he did not report and investigate, he urged. Perhaps we would do better to describe his writings as pamphlets, in the sense that they are occasional essays dealing with one aspect of a topic and involving some form of recommendation. His works are like proposals or briefs; they had a position to adopt or a case to argue. Classical rhetoric was all about the art of argument. An appreciation of the rhetorical nature of much of early Christian literature will help us read it appropriately. In other words, one should not be surprised, as Taylor appears to be, that Christian writers cast their Jewish opponents as ineffectual debaters with weak arguments. This is not a sign that engagement did not take place. The authors of anti-Judaic literature were not trying to be fair and accurate; they were lobbyists trying to be persuasive and victorious before a particular audience. Recasting an opponent from a real debate as a straw figure was one way of winning, at least on paper. It is a question of determining the audience. However, as we shall soon see, Tertullian's *Aduersus Iudaeos* is not even cast in the form of a dialogue involving a Jewish opponent. An opponent from an earlier encounter is mentioned in the beginning of the work only in order to provide the occasion for Tertullian to write his theological monologue, if one may call it that, about the limitations of Judaism.

Tertullian and rhetoric is a topic that needs little justification.[139] Indeed,

139. Dunn, *Tertullian*, 25–29.

that was the whole point of Sider's presentation. Barnes too has commented on the importance of rhetoric for Tertullian.[140] Averil Cameron has no
doubts that Tertullian was "a writer deeply imbued with traditional rhetoric"
who "applied to Christian themes the skill of traditional rhetoric."[141] With
regard to *Aduersus Iudaeos* in particular, Robert MacLennan describes it as
"Christian rhetoric" but then provides only the most rudimentary comments
about the structure of the work or the impact of classical rhetoric.[142] It is
one of my primary intentions to use classical rhetoric to make a further contribution in support of Tertullian's authorship of *Aduersus Iudaeos.*

One of the benefits of highlighting the rhetorical influence on Tertullian
is that it complements the research carried out on the other influences that
are discernible in his writings. For instance, Eric Osborn has drawn attention to the importance of Stoicism in Tertullian, particularly the philosophy
of opposites.[143] While this philosophical influence is important, so too is the
educational influence: trained in oratory, Tertullian would naturally have developed the skills of contrasting opposites and of being argumentative.[144] A
sound grasp of oratory was something that anyone with a typical good Roman education would have had.[145]

Whether or not *Aduersus Iudaeos* was composed by Tertullian in whole or
in part is an issue of interest here, and comment will be made with regard

140. Timothy D. Barnes, "Tertullian the Antiquarian," in *Studia Patristica* 14, ed. Elizabeth A.
Livingstone, papers presented to the sixth International Conference on Patristic Studies, part 3,
Oxford 1971 (Berlin: Akademie-Verlag, 1976), 6.

141. Averil Cameron, *Christianity and the Rhetoric of Empire: The Development of Christian Discourse* (Berkeley: University of California Press, 1991), 85, 115.

142. Robert MacLennan, *Early Christian Texts on Jews and Judaism*, Brown Judaic Studies 194
(Atlanta: Scholars Press, 1990), 118.

143. Eric Osborn, "The Conflict of Opposition in the Theology of Tertullian," *Augustinianum* 35 (1995): 623–39.

144. See Stanley F. Bonner, *Education in Ancient Roman: From the elder Cato to the younger Pliny*
(Berkeley: University of California Press, 1977), 250–327. Earlier (*Roman Declamation in the Late
Republic and Early Empire* [Liverpool: University Press of Liverpool, 1949], vi), he had written:
"It is clear to any student of the Roman educational system that preparation for public speaking was the chief preoccupation of teachers, parents, and pupils alike, and that education was
accordingly mainly linguistic and literary in its earlier stages, and predominantly oratorical and
legal in its more advanced form."

145. Whether Tertullian ever utilized his oratorical training in the law courts or whether he
was a jurist (a teacher or commentator on the law) may be left to one side. See Gerald Bray,
"The Legal Concept of Ratio in Tertullian," *VChr* 31 (1977): 94–116; Barnes, *Tertullian*, 22–29; David I. Rankin, "Was Tertullian a Jurist?" in *Studia Patristica* 31, ed. Elizabeth A. Livingstone, papers presented to the twelfth Oxford Patristics Conference, Oxford 1995 (Leuven: Peeters, 1997),
335–42; and Dunn, *Tertullian*, 3–4.

to this issue in the course of my presentation, as the results of the rhetorical analysis are established. Yet this issue can be bracketed to some extent. For a significant part of the past eighteen hundred years *Aduersus Iudaeos* has existed in its present state. Whether by one author or several, whether conceived of as a single literary unit or not, whether a draft left unrevised or a treatise culled from earlier work, whether its final shape was deliberate or accidental, and whether it was meant to be read by Jews, Christians, or pagans, *Aduersus Iudaeos* has an existence today independent of its author's intentions. If not Tertullian himself, someone was responsible for the work existing as it does today and it is quite legitimate to analyze it rhetorically as it is: as a literary entity in its own right.[146]

Tertullian's *Aduersus Iudaeos* does have a valuable contribution to make to scholarship on the relationship between early Christians and Jews. I seek to reintroduce this pamphlet into the mainstream of that debate, which is an important one for many aspects of early Christian studies, as Shoemaker's article on the early traditions of the dormition of Mary as part of Jewish-Christian relations reveals.[147] My own work is also a piece of rhetoric. I am seeking to persuade my readers that my argument is correct. The *partitio,* the point at issue, is whether or not *Aduersus Iudaeos* was written by Tertullian as a complete work according to the rules of classical rhetoric, and my thesis is that it was. What will be argued in these pages is that *Aduersus Iudaeos* is an example of a *controuersia*—the juridical, declamatory exercise so common in Tertullian's time. In order that we may appreciate the rhetorical techniques employed in the composition of this pamphlet, attention in the next chapter will be given to questions of readership.

146. See Mark Allen Powell, *What Is Narrative Criticism?* (Minneapolis: Fortress Press, 1990), 7: "Literary criticism does not deny these observations regarding the development of the text, but it does ignore them. Ultimately, it makes no difference from a literary interpretation whether certain portions of the text once existed elsewhere in some other form. The goal of literary criticism is to interpret the current text, in its finished form."

147. Stephen J. Shoemaker, "'Let Us Go and Burn Her Body': The Image of the Jews in the Early Dormition Traditions," *CH* 68 (1999): 775–823.

CHAPTER TWO

ꙮ

Readership

In the first half of this chapter I shall anticipate some findings of the following chapters and argue that *Aduersus Iudaeos* is an example of *controuersia,* a forensic rhetorical exercise. Unlike his near contemporaries, including fellow Africans like Apuleius and Fronto, whose emphasis was on achieving a pleasing form, Tertullian, I believe, used this genre in a more traditional manner, in that he sought to persuade his readers about a relevant and pressing subject matter rather than delight them with his skill in presentation. I shall demonstrate this by locating Tertullian within the rhetorical and literary context of his age, which will reveal the extent to which he stood apart from the Second Sophistic norm. The explanation for this difference is due to the place Christianity occupied within its wider society.

I shall argue that this context suggests a solution to the questions about the readership and purpose of the pamphlet. Classical rhetoric acknowledged the importance of one's audience or readers as the judge of one's effectiveness. Knowing something about the readers to whom the author addressed *Aduersus Iudaeos* will help answer the historical questions of the relationship between Christians and Jews in the late second century. Utilizing modern literary criticism's distinction between imagined and intended readers, and based on a close statistical reading of the evidence in *Aduersus Iudaeos* itself, my conclusion is that Tertullian imagined that both Jews and Christians were the readers of his work, while it was intended for Christians. Its purpose, I would propose, should be seen both in terms of promoting Christian self-identity and legitimacy in the face of ongoing Jewish criticism, and of providing a template for Christians to use in future encounters with Jews in arguing about their religious truth claims.

Declamation and Eulogy

Like its near relation the *suasoria* (the other element of *declamatio,* which dealt with deliberative themes), the *controuersia* was an oratorical exercise designed originally to hone one's public-speaking skills, specifically for forensic practice, but which, in the early years of the Roman empire, had grown to become an art form in itself. Donald Clark has provided a satisfactory compact definition:

> The controversia, on the other hand, was a school exercise in the judicial oratory of the law courts. The student spoke on fictitious legal cases, prosecuting or defending a fictitious or historical person in a civil or criminal process. In the Roman schools the controversia was always considered as more advanced, more difficult, and more important than the suasoria.[1]

This is not the place for an exhaustive study of Roman declamation. All I wish to do here is highlight some of its characteristics in the second century, the age of the Second Sophistic, in order to provide a context in which to place *Aduersus Iudaeos.* After illustrating just how otiose and frivolous much second-century rhetoric had become, among the Africans just as much as anyone else, I shall suggest that the tenuous position of Christianity within the empire meant that Christian authors turned to rhetoric to help them in their struggle for survival rather than to demonstrate their dexterity in treating vacuous and trifling topics, as Second Sophistic orators employed it.

Most commentators on classical declamation repeat the complaints of some well-known Roman orators that the themes and settings of *controuersiae* generally had become quite fanciful and fictitious, and that those delivering them sought to demonstrate their skill and entertain their audiences because traditional opportunities to practice real forensic and deliberative oratory had diminished greatly, at least according to those thus sidelined.[2] Saying

---

1. Donald Lemen Clark, *Rhetoric in Greco-Roman Education* (New York: Columbia University Press, 1957), 213–14. See also Bonner, *Roman Declamation,* 54–58; and A. D. Leeman, *"Orationis Ratio": The Stylistic Theories and Practice of the Roman Orators, Historians and Philosophers,* 2 vols. (Amsterdam: Adolf M. Hakkert, 1963), 1:232–33.

2. E.g., Sen., *Controu.* 3.pr. (LCL 463.376–390), offers Cassius Severus's own explanation of why he, who was an outstanding forensic orator, was such a dismal declaimer. Also typical is Votienus Montanus's complaint in Sen., *Controu.* 9.pr.1 (LCL 464.208–10): "Qui declamationem parat, scribit non ut uincat sed ut placeat . . . Cupit enim se approbare, non causam." Suet., *Rhet.* 6 (LCL 38.422), reported C. Albucius Silus as suffering the opposite problem. Vipstanus Messalla is made to state, in Tac., *Dial.* 31 (LCL 35.312), concerning declamation: "nec ut fictis nec ullo modo ad ueritatem accedentibus controuersiis linguam modo et uocem exercerent"

something of substance generally gave way to saying nothing of importance, though said with class and eloquence. The subjects of these complaints tended to speak "on topics whose currency and reality were four or five hundred years removed from the realities of their own time."[3] Perry characterized the broader field of second-century literature as itself uninterested in reality and more concerned with escapism, the personal, the less than normal, and the otherworldly.[4] This was the age of the romantic novel, the triumph of prose over poetry, and the commentator over the innovator.[5] Van Groningen, writing on Greek literature of this century in particular, though perhaps not without relevance to that in Latin, finds a mechanical and school-based approach to writing, insincere use of emotion, an inner hollowness of intellectual content, and a fascination with the remarkable, exceptional, and trivial.[6]

The second century has been assigned to that complex of cultural phenomena known ever since Philostratus, a contemporary of Tertullian, as the Second Sophistic.[7] It sought to assert, among other things, as the essays edited by Simon Goldhill illustrate, a Greek cultural identity in a Roman political world.[8] The recent monographs by Anderson and Swain, to mention only

---

and in *Dial.* 35 (LCL 35.326–28): "quales, per fidem, et quam incredibiliter compositae! Sequitur autem ut materiae abhorrenti a ueritate declamatio quoque adhibeatur." Curiatius Maternus, in Tac., *Dial.* 36–41 (LCL 35.328–46), is made to comment on the changing political situation, although in a way that avoided criticizing the current political arrangement. Plin., *Ep.* 2.14 (LCL 55.124–26), also commented on the impact of declamation on forensic oratory. Yet, in *Ep.* 2.3 (LCL 55.84–86), Pliny could delight in the pleasure that declamation, artificial though it was, could give to those jaded by the realities of their oratorical lives. Quint., *Inst.* 2.10.2–3 (LCL 124.272), complained of declamation's degeneration. See Michael Winterbottom, "Quintilian and Rhetoric," in *Empire and Aftermath: Silver Latin II,* ed. T. A. Dorey (London: Routledge and Kegan Paul, 1975), 81; Graham Anderson, *The Second Sophistic: A Cultural Phenomenon in the Roman Empire* (London and New York: Routledge, 1993), 99; George A. Kennedy, *A New History of Classical Rhetoric* (Princeton, N.J.: Princeton University Press, 1994), 169–70; James J. Murphy, "The End of the Ancient World: The Second Sophistic and Saint Augustine," in *A Synoptic History of Classical Rhetoric,* 2nd ed., ed. James J. Murphy and Richard A. Katula (Davis, Calif.: Hermagoras Press, 1995), 205–7; Martin Lowther Clarke, *Rhetoric at Rome: A Historical Survey,* 3rd ed., rev. with new introduction by D. H. Berry (London and New York: Routledge, 1996), 100–108; William J. Dominik, "The Style is the Man: Seneca, Tacitus, and Quintilian's Canon," in *Roman Eloquence: Rhetoric in Society and Literature,* ed. William J. Dominik (London and New York: Routledge, 1997), 61; and Elaine Fantham, "The Contexts and Occasions of Roman Public Oratory," in *Roman Eloquence: Rhetoric in Society and Literature,* ed. William J. Dominik (London and New York: Routledge, 1997), 122–24.

3. B. E. Perry, "Literature in the Second Century," *CJ* 50 (1955): 297.
4. Ibid., 295.
5. B. A. van Groningen, "General Literary Tendencies in the Second Century A.D.," *Mnemosyne* series 4, 18 (1965): 43–45.
6. Ibid., 48–52.   7. Philostr., *V.S.* 481 (LCL 134.6).
8. Simon Goldhill, "The Erotic Eye: Visual Stimulation and Cultural Conflict," in *Being*

two, provide an overview of this movement.[9] Here I wish simply to outline one significant way rhetoric was used by those whom we place today under this ill-defined umbrella. While I run the risk of stereotyping and radical oversimplification, the points I make can all be defended as being valid, even if only partial.

With regard to sophistic oratory the interest tended to be epideictic declamation or eulogy, with speeches designed for public entertainment, often on ceremonial occasions.[10] This was the age of what we may call salon rhetoric: the development of skills designed to amuse and delight and be appreciated only by the aficionados and cognoscenti of the art. The power of oratory was to move and delight, provoke and deter, exhort, conciliate, inflame, calm, or allure.[11] Style was the arbiter of ability.[12] The recorded speeches of this age that survive tend to be archaic imitations of the past.[13]

The Second Sophistic was essentially a Greek experience, yet Anderson argues that Latin *virtuosi* orators were little different from their Greek counterparts.[14] Yet, by the end of the second century Latin literature had virtually disappeared, except for that by Christian writers like Tertullian and later Cyprian.[15] Russell explains this disappearance partly as the result of the failure to translate Greek literature into Latin.[16] Anderson finds that even Tertullian himself, when he advocated the use the archaic pallium instead of the toga in *De pallio*, employed what appear to be sophistic traits.[17] Yet, describing Tertullian as a Christian sophist can only ever be true superficially, I shall

---

Greek under Rome: Cultural Identity, the Second Sophistic and the Development of Empire, ed. Simon Goldhill (Cambridge: Cambridge University Press, 2001), 154–94.

9. Anderson, *The Second Sophistic;* and Simon Swain, *Hellenism and Empire: Language, Classicism, and Power in the Greek World AD 50–250* (Oxford: Clarendon Press, 1996).

10. Anderson, *The Second Sophistic,* 16.

11. Front., *De eloq.* 3.5 (LCL 113.76).

12. Front., *Ad M. Caes.* 2.3 (LCL 112.128): "Nihil ego umquam cultius nihil antiquius nihil conditius nihil latinius legi. O te hominem beatum hac eloquentia praeditum! O me hominem beatum huic magistro traditum. O ἐπιχειρήματα! O τάξις! O elegantia! O lepos! O uenustas! O uerba! O nitor! O argutiae! O kharites! O ἄσκησις! O omnia!"

13. Swain, *Hellenism and Empire,* 79–100, notes that an interest in the past, however fictionalized, was one way for a separate Greek identity to be maintained under Roman rule.

14. Graham Anderson, "The Second Sophistic: Some Problems of Perspective," in *Antonine Literature,* ed. D. A. Russell (Oxford: Clarendon Press, 1990), 94–96. Swain, *Hellenism and Empire,* 3–11, suggests the Second Sophistic was an elite, cultural reaction to the Greek lack of power in the Roman world.

15. D. A. Russell, "Introduction," in *Antonine Literature,* ed. D. A. Russell (Oxford: Clarendon Press, 1990), 1.

16. Ibid., 3–17.

17. Anderson, *The Second Sophistic,* 207–8.

argue.[18] There is little similarity between Tertullian and his fellow Latin-writing North Africans of the second century in the use they made of their shared educational background.

Juvenal tells us that Africa was the nursery of orators.[19] Susan Raven claims that as provincials overtook Italians in the intellectual life of the empire, the second century A.D. belonged to the Africans.[20] In the second half of the century the two outstanding Latin literary figures were both Africans skilled in rhetoric and oratory. Kennedy describes M. Cornelius Fronto, the African who moved to Rome and was tutor to future emperors, as the nearest Latin equivalent to the Greek Second Sophistic movement, stating that "Fronto and several of his contemporaries seem to want an analogous movement in Latin, imitating Greek subjects but turning back to early Latin models of diction. The result is archaizing."[21] In this he was different from many of his contemporaries, but this may be due to the fact that in Africa the developments in the Latin language in the imperial age, as exemplified by the literature of the first century A.D., never penetrated deeply.[22] Our knowledge of him derives mainly from his surviving correspondence.[23] Fronto, unique in many respects, was typical to the extent that his rhetorical interest was in epideictic oratory, the art of eulogy, in its most esoteric and trivial form. In his speech praising dust and smoke, he stated that giving pleasure was the chief purpose of oratory and that superficial topics must be treated as vitally important.[24] As Clarke stated: "There is nothing practical about his rhetorical teaching. His rhetoric is directed not to persuading but to pleasing; it is the art of elegant self-expression, which has lost touch with the world of politics and power."[25] In the next generation Apuleius became an orator of note, equally at home in Latin or Greek, as his *Florida* reveals. Best known as the author of *Metamorphoses,* as a person he is known through his *Apologia de*

---

18. Hence, although Horner, *Listening to Trypho,* 73–93, admittedly with some hesitation, sees Justin Martyr as a Christian sophist because he was a teacher and experimented with the dialogue genre, I would be more reluctant to make such an identification because I would hold that in other, more important elements, as I shall outline below, there was a great deal of difference between Christian writers, Justin included, and the sophists.

19. Juv., *Sat.* 7.148–149 (LCL 91.148).

20. Susan Raven, *Rome in Africa,* 3rd ed. (London and New York: Routledge, 1993), 122.

21. Kennedy, *A New History of Classical Rhetoric,* 198.

22. E. S. Bouchier, *Life and Letters in Roman Africa* (Oxford: Blackwell, 1913), 57–58, and Russell, "Introduction," 13.

23. Edward Champlin, *Fronto and Antonine Rome* (Cambridge, Mass.: Harvard University Press, 1980).

24. Front., *Laud. fum. et pul.* 3 (LCL 112.40).   25. Clarke, *Rhetoric at Rome,* 133.

magia. It was a typical product of the Second Sophistic: he portrayed himself as well read, highly educated, and quite capable of delivering a speech which was not only persuasive but entertaining.[26] His *Florida* is a collection of selections from orations he chose, not because they exemplified meaningful and important topics but because they were what he considered to be his most stylish and polished.

Aduersus Iudaeos as *Controuersia*

If we accept as accurate this admittedly anecdotal account describing declamation and eulogy as characteristic of second-century rhetoric, it would seem to suggest that Tertullian's *Aduersus Iudaeos,* if it were a *controuersia,* should be typical of its age, i.e., a composition based upon an unreal setting and dealing with fictitious matters. In other words, simply seeing Tertullian as a product of his time would lead one to conclude that the encounter between the Christian and proselyte Jew mentioned in its opening lines never took place (suggesting that such encounters by this time no longer took place). In that case the question of the readership of the pamphlet would be solved simply: it was written only for a Christian audience in order to help with matters of self-definition. This is a position I reject because, even though he was in some ways a man of his own age, in other ways Tertullian was quite distinct, even from fellow Africans like Fronto and Apuleius. I agree with Goldhill, who sees Tertullian as an example of the cultural clash that was taking place involving those on the fringe of empire who manipulated the educational system, and with Schwartz, who sees him as hostile to his literary environment.[27] In order to make my case I need to turn to the provisos offered by the same commentators mentioned earlier, who were complaining about the decline of rhetoric in their age, about what declamation could or should be like. I am not so concerned with eulogy and epideictic rhetoric because I shall argue that *Aduersus Iudaeos* is not concerned with praise and blame but with a forensic question: did a particular event that has ongoing consequences take place in the past?

---

26. Anderson, *The Second Sophistic,* 223–27.

27. Goldhill, "The Erotic Eye," 181–84; and Seth Schwartz, "The Rabbi in Aphrodite's Bath: Palestinian Society and Jewish Identity in the High Roman Empire," in *Being Greek under Rome: Cultural Identity, the Second Sophistic and the Development of Empire,* ed. Simon Goldhill (Cambridge: Cambridge University Press, 2001), 337.

Reading the *controuersiae* of the elder Seneca or of pseudo-Quintilian indicates that, although the topics chosen could be fanciful, this was not always the case. Topics could be based upon history or even upon actual laws. Winterbottom has put forward the view that declamation might not have been as remote from reality as some writers, ancient and modern, would have us believe.[28] His evidence is the Minor Declamations attributed to Quintilian. Bonner offers thirty-four pages of examples of Roman laws, on, among other things, murder, repudiation, treason, poisoning, and punishment of adultery, used by the elder Seneca, Quintilian, and others.[29] Bonner concluded:

Some of the "laws" used by the Senecan declaimers may well have been obsolete in their day, and revived merely for academic interest and learned dispute; but against this must be set a number of contemporary parallels, and the fact that our knowledge of the legislation of the early Empire is not great.[30]

While some traditionalists like Messalla completely rejected declamation, others, like Quintilian, thought that declamation could be useful if it actually prepared its students for real forensic situations.[31] The best way was to base the topics upon real cases or real laws and utilize real procedures.[32] Forensic oratory continued to be used in the law courts, yet the younger Pliny, in the first half of the second century, is not typical in the elegance of his speechmaking for such practical purposes.[33]

I am going to argue that Tertullian was a traditionalist like Quintilian in that he neither repudiated the existence of *controuersiae* nor engaged in the current fashion of indulging in wildly unrealistic themes in order simply to wax lyrical. He accepted that they could be useful to the extent that they were true to life. The encounter between the Christian and the proselyte Jew

28. Michael Winterbottom, "Schoolroom and Courtroom," in *Rhetoric Revalued: Papers from the International Society for the History of Rhetoric,* ed. Brian Vickers, Medieval and Renaissance Texts and Studies 19 (Binghamton, N.Y.: Center for Medieval and Renaissance Studies, 1982), 63.

29. Bonner, *Roman Declamation,* 97–131.

30. Ibid., 131. A few lines earlier he wrote: "nor indeed does it make sense that men who were living and debating in the greatest law-giving centre of the world should have needed their imaginations to conjure up imaginary statutes."

31. Quint., *Inst.* 2.10.8 (LCL 124.274–76): "Nam si foro non praeparat, aut scenicae ostentationi aut furiosae uociferationi simillimum est. Quid enim attinet iudicem praeparare, qui nullus est; narrare, quod omnes sciant falsum; probationes adhibere causae, de qua nemo sit pronuntiaturus? Et haec quidem otiosa tantum; adfici uero et ira uel luctu permouere, cuius est ludibrii, nisi quibusdam pugnae simulacris ad uerum discrimen aciemque iustam consuescimus?" On Quintilian as a traditionalist see Leeman, *"Orationis Ratio,"* 1:287–98.

32. Quint., *Inst.* 2.10.4 (LCL 124.272).

33. Fantham, "The Contexts and Occasions of Roman Public Oratory," 124.

was the real, historical situation. Tertullian declaimed on that topic, present-ing in *Aduersus Iudaeos* his own version of what should have been said by the Christian debater on that occasion but was not, and thus what could be said on such occasions in the future. Thus, his pamphlet is, I think, a *controuersia*, for he made no claim that this was the record of an actual speech. I would accept that the work is a literary fiction in that it was not delivered at that or any other real encounter, but it had an instructional or educative purpose in mind. All of this depends on whether one accepts my assertion that Tertul-lian was a traditionalist when it came to rhetoric. To offer some supportive argument let us turn to the subject of Christian rhetoric in the second cen-tury.

Second-Century Christian Rhetoric

If the criticisms of declamation apply to the Roman and Hellenistic worlds of the second century, such that the overwhelming sense is of an art lost in its own esoteric delights, I do not think they should be applied to Christians who had been trained in rhetorical schools. Like the advocates who contin-ued to use rhetoric, even if with rather lackluster application, I believe liter-ary Christians made use of rhetoric for very practical purposes. Christian-ity was not in a period of idleness and decline, with its intellectuals engaged simply in entertaining their fellow Christians. Christianity was an illegal sect and persecutions occurred, even though with variations in intensity and lo-cation. The original forensic and deliberative purposes of rhetoric (to plead one's innocence and to urge the state to change its policy) were very appro-priate and applicable to the Christian situation. This was a time when Chris-tians struggled to exist and justify their existence to themselves, Jews, and pagans alike. It makes sense then to understand Christian literature as con-cerned with themes that were vital, relevant, topical, and useful to their very existence. The need to be persuasive was a key concern to Christian intellec-tuals and, through them, classical rhetoric's traditional purpose was given a new lease on life.[34]

34. Philip E. Satterthwaite, "The Latin Church Fathers," in *Handbook of Classical Rhetoric in the Hellenistic Period, 330 B.C.–A.D. 400,* ed. Stanley E. Porter (Leiden: Brill, 1997), 693. See An-dreas Spira, "The Impact of Christianity on Ancient Rhetoric," in *Studia Patristica* 18, part 2, ed. Elizabeth A. Livingstone, papers presented to the ninth Oxford Patristics Conference, Oxford 1983 (Kalamazoo, Mich.: Cistercian Publications, 1989), 137–53.

This is especially true of Tertullian, as others have shown. Barnes states: "His erudition does not always show, because he was intent on effective use in argument rather than on empty display."[35] Fredouille goes even further:

Mais, comme écrivain chrétien, Tertullien se trouvait dans une position différente et, de ce point de vue, privilégiée. Il n'était pas soumis aux mêmes contraintes politiques et sociales; il se situait en marge des modes esthétiques; il assignait enfin à la littérature une tâche qui n'était plus la sienne depuis longtemps, celle d'être *utile,* par la transmission et la défense du message chrétien. En même temps qu'elle redonnait une inspiration nouvelle à la littérature, la proclamation de ce message plaçait les écrivains chrétiens, et Tertullien tout le premier, dans une situation assez comparable à celle des orateurs de la République.[36]

Averil Cameron, however, warns those who make such claims for a Christian revival of rhetoric to be aware that their presumptions that forensic and deliberative themes (as opposed to epideictic ones) were the proper use of rhetoric may come from too narrow a reading of the classical background.[37] Her points are well made, but I do not believe they negate my position. I think Tertullian would have agreed with the opinions of Tacitus, Pliny, and Quintilian about contemporary rhetoric's interest in declamation and eulogy. If there was too narrow a reading of the purpose of rhetoric, I want to include Tertullian as being equally guilty. As a highbrow traditionalist, he, like they, were out of step with the rest of their society, who found this popular entertainment most rewarding. Whether or not others were lamenting the decline of rhetoric was not an issue for Tertullian. All I want to argue is that he turned to *controuersia* for writing *Aduersus Iudaeos* and used it in a traditional way as a training exercise for declaiming on a historical theme, offering an improvement on what had been said on that actual occasion.

Tertullian utilized rhetoric for the practical purposes of making a persuasive case about the position of the Jews in God's disposition. It is a literary piece that seeks to persuade; it has a position to defend and alternatives to attack. The case rests not upon some highly improbable law but upon Scripture as a true and accurate record of God's past dealings with humanity, vital to the lives of Christians and Jews alike.

As will be clear in the course of the following chapters, Tertullian took the role of the defense advocate writing his case on behalf of his client. In

35. Barnes, *Tertullian,* 204.
36. Fredouille, *Tertullien et la conversion,* 172.
37. Cameron, *Christianity and the Rhetoric of Empire,* 81.

this case his client was God. If Tertullian was the defense advocate, then we need to know who the audience was, because in these matters, the audience was the judge. Whom was he trying to persuade? Knowing one's audience was a vital component for success. Literary theory about readers can be of some use in responding to this question.

Real, Imagined, and Intended Readers

We know from its opening lines, so the author would have us believe, that the writing of the pamphlet was occasioned by a dispute between a proselyte Jew and a Christian. We are not told whether the author was the Christian disputant, but one does gain the impression that he might well have been.[38] Tertullian (if we can accept at this early point that he was the author of at least the first half of the treatise, as most scholars are prepared to concede) wanted to give the impression that he was at least privy to the debate if not a participant. Also present had been each speaker's supporters, and their partisan interventions reduced the exchange to a shouting match. As a result Tertullian resorted to writing in order to settle the questions that had been debated.[39]

Was this work intended for a Jewish audience, real or imagined, in order to refute their points of view and point out the errors of their way, or even to convince them of the correctness of the Christian belief and to urge their conversion? Was it intended for a Christian audience, real or imagined, in order to demonstrate where Jewish thinking was astray, or to reclaim those who might have been too impressed by Judaism, or to help define what it was to be a Christian by way of contrast with what it was to be a Jew, or to help Christians in arguing better at other encounters? Was it written for pagans, real or imagined, interested in monotheism and confused with the choice between Judaism and Christianity, or for those pagans who denigrated Christianity as some deviant Jewish sect? There are a couple of different, though related, questions here. One is of audience or readership and the oth-

38. Barnes, *Tertullian*, 106, is convinced that he was.

39. Tert., *Adu. Iud.* 1.1 (CCSL 1339): "Proxime accidit: disputatio habita est Christiano et proselyto Iudaeo. Alternis uicibus contentioso fune uterque diem in uesperam traxerunt. Obstrepentibus etiam quibusdam <in> expertibus singulorum nubilo quodam ueritas obumbrabatur. Placuit ergo, uel quod per concentum disputationis minus plene potuit dilucidari, curiosius inspectis lectionibus, stilo quaestiones retractatas terminare."

er is of purpose. I believe that the rhetorical critical interest in readership will suggest the work's purpose, which, in turn, will be the best indicator of the historicity of the encounter described in its first lines.

Of course, even to ask questions about the historicity of the occasioning event, the purpose of the author in writing the pamphlet, and the identity of those who would have read it is to be interested in topics usually beyond the purview of modern literary criticism.[40] Yet these questions are important to my work. We are into the realm of classical rhetorical criticism. At least as early as Aristotle there was an explicit awareness among rhetoricians that one's audience determined one's success and not simply the validity of one's argument. Aristotle himself lamented the extent to which truth could be overridden by persuasive technique.[41] We now turn to the question of readership.

It will not be necessary here to investigate modern literary criticism's theories about readers in detail. Time and space only permit me to rely upon the generalized comments of others, yet they will be sufficient, I believe, to highlight the various possibilities when it comes to considering the readers of Tertullian's *Aduersus Iudaeos*. In introducing this material to a general audience interested in applying these insights to biblical studies, Mark Powell classifies both rhetorical criticism (a reader-centered, pragmatic approach) and narrative criticism (a text-centered, objective approach) as being interested in questions of readership. According to him, the first asks questions about the intended or actual readers and the second asks about the implied readers presupposed in the actual text.[42] The words of Vernon Robbins may

40. Kennedy, *A New History of Classical Rhetoric*, 5.

41. Arist., *Rh.* 1.1.10–12 (1354b–1355a) (LCL 193.6–12). On how Aristotle attempted to reconcile rhetorical proof with the other elements of persuasion, see Christopher Carey, "Rhetorical Means of Persuasion," in *Persuasion: Greek Rhetoric in Action*, ed. Ian Worthington (London and New York: Routledge, 1994), 34–43; Eckart Schütrumpf, "Some Observations on the Introduction to Aristotle's *Rhetoric*," in *Aristotle's "Rhetoric": Philosophical Essays*, ed. David J. Furley and Alexander Nehamas (Princeton, N.J.: Princeton University Press, 1994), 100–103; Jürgen Sprute, "Aristotle and the Legitimacy of Rhetoric," in Furley and Nehamas, eds., *Aristotle's "Rhetoric,"* 118–27; Eugene Garver, *Aristotle's "Rhetoric": An Art of Character* (Chicago and London: University of Chicago Press, 1994), 109–12; Jacques Brunschwig, "Aristotle's Rhetoric as a 'Counterpart' to Dialectic," in *Essays on Aristotle's "Rhetoric,"* ed. Amélie Oksenberg Rorty, Philosophical Traditions 6 (Berkeley: University of California Press, 1996), 45–51; and Robert Wardy, "Mighty Is the Truth and It Shall Prevail?" in Rorty, ed., *Essays on Aristotle's "Rhetoric,"* 58–81.

42. Powell, *What Is Narrative Criticism?*, 12–21. In addition, he mentions reader-response criticism (another reader-centered pragmatic approach), which is interested not in original readers (whether implied or intended) but in modern readers.

be helpful: "The phrase 'implied reader' designates the reader the text implies and the interpreter infers in relation to real readers and audiences both in the Mediterranean world and in the world of the interpreter today."[43] Yet, as Alan Culpepper observes, "already the population of readers is growing at an alarming rate. There are intended readers, implied readers, historical readers, model readers, mock readers, ideal readers, and an equal number of narratees. Definition is essential."[44] Here I shall offer my own sense of what the terms I shall be using mean.

The oral *controuersia* would be delivered in front of a real audience (those physically gathered to hear the exercise), yet the speaker could imagine his audience to be altogether different (a jury in some far distant land or in some far distant time, for example). A written *controuersia* could be read by anyone who actually picked it up or listened to someone reading it aloud, yet the author could imagine that he was addressing other readers altogether. Indeed, and here I depart from the summary given by Powell, the author could have intended his comments to be heard or read by yet another audience, who might not be the ones who actually heard it, read it, or were imagined as the hearers or the readers. In other words, unlike the modern literary critics described by Powell, I am distinguishing intended from real readers for, while the first group is entirely of the author's choosing, the second group is beyond the author's control.[45] The third group, the implied or imagined reader, is also a creation of the author. We discern this reader from within the text itself, whereas the intended reader usually is discerned only from taking extratextual information into account.

Aristides's oration in defense of oratory, a work written about fifty years before Tertullian's, is an appropriate illustration. He wrote as though addressing Plato directly and his imagined readers were Plato's contemporaries.[46]

---

43. Vernon K. Robbins, *The Tapestry of Early Christian Discourse: Rhetoric, Society and Ideology* (London and New York: Routledge, 1996), 22. On p. 23 he writes: "If they themselves [real readers] cannot understand the text, they create an image of a reader who the implied author imagined could read and understand the text."

44. R. Alan Culpepper, *Anatomy of the Fourth Gospel: A Study in Literary Design* (Minneapolis: Fortress Press, 1983), 205. He uses the term "authorial audience" for what I am calling "intended readers" and "narrative audience" for what I am calling "implied readers."

45. This group would include, incidentally, modern readers, in whom reader-response critics are interested.

46. Aristid., *Or.* 2.331 (LCL 458.474): "Φέρε γὰρ σὺ πρὸς τὸ βέλτιστον, ὦ Πλάτων, προὔστης Ἀθηναίων ἢ τινος ἄλλου δήμου τῶν ἐν τοῖς Ἕλλησιν ἢ τοῖς βαρβάροις ... οὐκ ἔχοις —ἂν εἰπεῖν· οὐδὲ γὰρ προὔστης ὅλως."

Yet he provided sufficient editorial comment to indicate that this was a literary fiction and that Plato was long dead.[47] He acknowledged that his intended readers were his own contemporaries, not Plato's. He intended that those
modern disciples of Plato who repeated his arguments against oratory (and
those who listened to those disciples) would be refuted (or convinced of the
correctness of Aristides's position). We can say nothing about the real readers.[48]

Aristides's oration may never have been delivered and may always have
been purely a literary piece, but with the other *controuersiae* that were actually delivered and then written down, and with the true forensic speeches of
someone like Cicero, for example, we are able to complicate this picture even
further. These would have had a real audience (those who heard a speech
delivered) and real readers (those who actually read the speech), and they
would not be the same group (given that the real readers include modern
readers). The intended audience and the intended readership would be those
Cicero wished to impress with his forensic abilities. In a real forensic case one
does not have an imagined audience or imagined readers.

With Tertullian's *Aduersus Iudaeos* I am not interested in what I have described as the real readers, those who have actually read the text, except to
the extent that they include the commentators whose works litter my notes
and bibliography. I am interested in the imagined readers and the intended
readers, those to whom the text itself is addressed and those whom Tertullian wanted to persuade. To whom does the work seem to be addressed? For
whom was the work actually written?[49]

Imagined Readers of *Aduersus Iudaeos*

Here I shall be concerned with what the text itself tells us about the reader, the imagined reader of narrative criticism. I am arguing that the imagined readers of this pamphlet are those who were at the earlier encounter

---

47. Ibid., 2.321 (LCL 458.464): "εἴ πως ἀναστάντες ἢ λαβόντες αἴσθησιν." Here and at 2.13–
14, Aristides justified this practice by identifying Plato himself as having created works "ἐν σχή-
ματι διαλόγων."

48. Other authors who refer to this work of Aristides, myself included, can be counted as
among the real or actual readers, but the full extent of that group over the centuries, of course,
is unknown.

49. The use of different tenses in these two questions captures something of the point that
Powell was making in distinguishing narrative criticism from rhetorical criticism.

between the Christian and the proselyte Jew. I wish to stress again, however, that Tertullian was not presenting us with the actual Christian input into that debate, nor was he pretending that this pamphlet was the record of that actual input. The proselyte Jew and the debate are not mentioned again in the remainder of the pamphlet. Although there is overwhelming evidence that Tertullian drew heavily on Justin's *Dialogus cum Tryphone,* he did not cast his work in that dialogue genre. There is no Trypho, no opponent. Instead, he was, in the words of John Gager, attempting "to clarify certain issues raised in the debate."[50] Some scholars have not appreciated this fact.[51] Taylor appears to allude to *Aduersus Iudaeos* as a dialogue when she writes: "Simon seems to assume that Tertullian would not have drawn attention to the fact that the Jew in his dialogue was a convert from paganism if this had not been a common occurrence."[52] The work is a position paper, not a dialogue, and there is a difference.

I suggest that Tertullian imagined his readers to be that same audience who heard the earlier encounter, *but at some possible future encounter.* This is the important point of qualification. In other words, Tertullian had said to himself: "If ever I were to get the opportunity (or another opportunity, if we believe that he was the Christian speaker at the first encounter) to put my case to that group, this is what I would say." Tertullian's work makes it clear that he was not pretending that this composition had ever been part

50. Gager, *The Origins of Anti-Semitism,* 164.

51. Schreckenberg, *Die christlichen Adversus-Judaeos-Texte,* 217: "Tertullians Auseinandersetzung mit der jüdischen Seite ist jedenfalls fast monologisch, und nur sporadisch erscheinen Andeutungen oder Rudimente eines Dialoges." George Foot Moore, "Christian Writers on Judaism," *HTR* 14 (1921): 198–99: "The occasion of the work, the author tells us, was a protracted discussion between a Christian and a convert to Judaism; but the argument is not conducted in the form of disputation." He believed that the pamphlet was claimed to be a record (and therefore one that was totally flawed) of that discussion.

52. Taylor, *Anti-Judaism and Early Christian Identity,* 15. Of course, she could simply mean "the Jew in the dialogue that occasioned the writing." However, I do not think this is what she means given what Simon himself wrote. Simon, *"Verus Israel,"* 283: "Tertullian likewise, at the beginning of his *Adversus Judaeos,* states that his treatise is intended to summarize and record an actual discussion in which a Christian and a proselyte engaged for an entire day." On this point Simon was quite wrong. Tertullian was clear: he intended to examine the issues that had arisen in the debate from a fresh perspective and to offer a better examination of the scriptural texts than had been possible on the day. This pamphlet is not the record of the earlier encounter. It would be better because, with the benefit of hindsight, he would be able to anticipate and counter, for any future encounter, the Jewish position that had been put forward on the day. Of course, while he revised and refined the Christian arguments, Tertullian worked from the presumption that the Jewish position itself had not changed in response to the Christian arguments and would remain static at future encounters.

of any real encounter. All he claimed was that it was written in response to an encounter. What he was providing was the template of the Christian arguments that could be used in such debates in response to the typical and entirely predictable arguments from the Jews. That, to me, distinguishes it from something like Cicero's speeches (the polished records of real forensic speeches) and identifies it as a *controuersia*. That also distinguishes it from the typical second-century declamatory *controuersia* and gives it a ring of authenticity.[53] The fact that an encounter is mentioned only in passing at the beginning would suggest to me that it probably did occur. Here I am in full agreement with Simon on this point. I would tend to think that if Tertullian were going to create a fictitious setting then he would want to get more mileage out of it than he did. That debate was over and, given its inconclusive result, best forgotten. Tertullian was interested in it to the extent that it revealed the typical, unvarying Jewish arguments that he could refute in the future.

A way of examining the question of readership is to consider the first-, second-, and third-person references in the pamphlet. According to my reading, there are a possible total of ten first-person singular references, if one considers all the manuscript variations. This does not seem to be very many, particularly in comparison with some of his other writings.[54] They are scattered throughout the work, even though the majority are from the second half.[55] This gives us information about the implied author, a term Robbins defines as "authors as they can be known through manifestations of their expressions through the text."[56]

Tertullian was not attempting to be more impersonal or removed in this

---

53. Tränkle, *Tertullian, "Adversus Iudaeos,"* xxiii: "Es ist müßig darüber zu streiten, ob ein solches Gespräch wirklich stattgefunden habe. Das kann geschehen sein." I disagree with him, though, that such a setting was only a *topos,* similar to "die Einkleidung platonischer oder ciceronianischer Dialoge."

54. E.g., Tert., *De test. anim.,* a work about one-fifth the length of *Adu. Iud.,* has thirteen first-person singular references; Tert., *De idol.,* a work about two-thirds the length of *Adu Iud.,* has fifty such references; and Tert., *Adu. Herm.,* a work only slightly longer than *Adu. Iud.,* has at least eighty-nine references to a singular first person.

55. Tert., *Adu Iud.* 2.7 (CCSL 2.1342): "contendo"; 4.11 (CCSL 2.1349): "putem"; 6.3 (CCSL 2.1353): "inquam" (this is found only in the early sixteenth-century editions of Rhenanus and is relegated to the critical apparatus by Kroymann); 7.8 (CCSL 2.1356): "dicam"; 9.3 (CCSL 2.1365): "puto" (= Tert., *Adu. Marc.* 3.12.3 [CCSL 1.523]); 9.6 (CCSL 2.1366): "credo" (= *Adu. Marc.* 3.13.3 [CCSL 1.524]); 9.29 (CCSL 2.1374): "fallor" (= *Adu. Marc.* 3.17.5 [CCSL 1.531]); 10.11 (CCSL 2.1378): "expecto" (= *Adu. Marc.* 3.19.1 [CCSL 1.533]); 10.15 (CCSL 2.1379): "uolo" (= *Adu. Marc.* 3.19.8 [CCSL 1.534]); 14.9 (CCSL 2.1394): "faciam" (= *Adu. Marc.* 3.7.7 [CCSL 1.517]. Kroymann preferred "faciamus" from the twelfth-century manuscript T).

56. Robbins, *The Tapestry of Early Christian Discourse,* 21.

work, for there are numerous first-person references in the plural that would seem to rule that out. Some of them are obviously what we may describe as the "literary plural." They are in clear evidence when Tertullian referred to other passages in his pamphlet and the references can only be to himself as author.[57] In other instances of his use of the plural he meant what he said—he claimed to speak on behalf of others (Christians)—and a plural subject was involved.[58] The remaining instances of first-person plural statements are less clearly distinguishable. Some seem to be euphemisms for the singular but with the implicit suggestion that he was not alone in holding these opinions.[59] Elsewhere Tertullian seems to identify himself with others but without entirely ruling out the possibility that he was only advancing a personal position.[60]

57. Tert., *Adu. Iud.* 1.7 (CCSL 2.1341): "ut supra memorauimus"; 2.1 (CCSL 2.1341): "conferamus"; "terminemus"; 3.11 (CCSL 2.1346): "supra quod ostendimus"; 4.6 (CCSL 2.1348): "sicuti iam praelocuti sumus"; 5.1 (CCSL 2.1349): "ostendimus"; 7.1 (CCSL 2.1353): "conseramus"; 8.2 (CCSL 2.1356): "quae inuestigabimus in Danielo"; "probabimus"; 8.15 (CCSL 2.1362): "uideamus"; 9.15 (CCSL 2.1368): "ut diximus"; 9.26 (CCSL 2.1372): "ut supra memorauimus"; 10.4 (CCSL 2.1375): "ut et supra de eo praedictum memorauimus"; 10.14 (CCSL 2.1379): "probabimus"; 10.16 (CCSL 2.1379): "ut supra ostendimus"; 11.10 (CCSL 2.1383): "quam supra memorauimus"; "quam euidenter exidimus"; 11.11 (CCSL 2.1383): "probauimus"; "ostendimus"; 13.1 (CCSL 2.1384): "probauerimus"; 13.8 (CCSL 2.1386): "ostendamus"; 14.12 (CCSL 2.1395): "sicuti iam praelocuti sumus."

58. Ibid., 1.3 (CCSL 2.1339): "habeamus" following a reference to the "gentes"; "et gentium, id est noster"; 1.5 (CCSL 2.1340): "noster" in reference to the "gentes"; 3.8 (CCSL 2.1346): "sed Iacob sequentis, id est populi nostri"; 3.9 (CCSL 2.1346): "id est inter nos, qui ex gentibus sumus uocati"; 3.10 (CCSL 2.1346): "qui igitur intelleguntur alii quam nos"; 3.12 (CCSL 2.1347): "quis autem populus . . . nisi noster"; 3.13 (CCSL 2.1347): "nos, qui non populus dei retro, facti sumus populus eius"; 5.1 (CCSL 2.1349): "id est populi nostri"; 7.1 (CCSL 2.1353): "in quem nos, gentes scilicet"; 9.22 (CCSL 2.1370): "quod sumus nos nationes"; 13.24 (CCSL 2.1390): "ex quo gentes nos."

59. Ibid., 3.2 (CCSL 2.1344): "consideremus"; 5.3 (CCSL 2.1350): "animaduertimus"; "inuenimus"; "legimus"; 6.2 (CCSL 2.1352): "praediximus" (which is misprinted in CCSL as "paediximus"); "debeamus"; 7.1 (CCSL 2.1353): "etiam tempora sunt nobis requirenda"; "recognouerimus"; 7.2 (CCSL 2.1354): "uidemus"; 8.7 (CCSL 2.1358): "animaduertamus"; 8.9 (CCSL 2.1359): "ostendemus"; "numerabimus"; "debemus"; 8.10 (CCSL 2.1359): "uideamus"; 8.11 (CCSL 2.1360): "uidemus"; 9.1 (CCSL 2.1364): "incipiamus"; 9.16 (CCSL 2.1369): "nostra interpretatio"; 9.18 (CCSL 2.1369): "uideamus"; 9.21 (CCSL 2.1370): "dicimus"; 9.29 (CCSL 2.1374): "dispungamus"; 13.1 (CCSL 2.1384): "praescribimus"; 13.9 (CCSL 2.1386): "legimus"; "recognoscimus"; 13.17 (CCSL 2.1388): "legimus"; 13.27 (CCSL 2.1391): "probamus"; "inueniamus."

60. Ibid., 2.3 (CCSL 2.1341): "recognoscimus"; 2.6 (CCSL 2.1342): "cognoscimus"; 2.9 (CCSL 2.1343): "intellegimus"; "adtendamus"; 2.10 (CCSL 2.1343): "adimamus"; 2.13 (CCSL 2.1344): "nobis ostenderet"; 3.6 (CCSL 2.1345): "uidemus"; "recognoscimus"; 3.8 (CCSL 2.1346): "intellegimus"; 4.2 (CCSL 2.1347): "intellegimus"; 4.3 (CCSL 2.1348): "dinoscimus"; 4.4 (CCSL 2.1348): "intellegimus"; 6.2 (CCSL 2.1352): "nobis incumbit"; 7.1 (CCSL 2.1353): "credamus"; 7.2 (CCSL 2.1353): "scimus"; 8.2 (CCSL 2.1357): "credamus"; 9.2 (CCSL 2.1365): "existimamus"; 9.8 (CCSL 2.1366): "nobis posita"; 11.11 (CCSL 2.1383): "proferimus"; 12.2 (CCSL 2.1384): "consideramus"; 13.1 (CCSL 2.1384): "nos errare"; 13.3 (CCSL 2.1385): "animaduertimus"; 13.12 (CCSL 2.1387): "sicuti nos"; "commorabamus"; 13.19 (CCSL 2.1388): "nobis scilicet"; 13.24 (CCSL 2.1389): "ad-

Those with whom he identified, or appeared to identify, were other Christians, certainly not Jews. Perhaps this ambiguity of number was exploited by Tertullian in order to give his arguments the appearance of wide support. Tertullian wanted whomever his imagined readers were to understand that he was not advocating anything novel or radical, but rather something traditional and widely shared among Christians.

In itself this use of the first-person plural cannot tell us whom the imagined readers were, for it would have been quite possible for Tertullian's imagined readers to be only Jews and for him still to have referred to "our people" or "we Christians" if he had the sense that he was writing on behalf of or as a representative of his fellow Christians to a hostile audience. So many first-person-plural references to Christians, however, give the impression that they were part of his imagined readership. Indeed, it suggests that they were a large contingent in this imaginary, future gathering—the majority, who were sitting right behind him. Clarity about this issue may be obtained from examining the second- and third-person references to Christians and Jews.

There are no second-person references with regard to Christians. This is not surprising given that Tertullian was a Christian and closely identified himself with other Christians. Never did he aim any of his pleading directly at the Christians among the imagined readers, as though he thought they needed to be convinced. At the same time, however, there seem to me to be some hints in his use of the first-person plural that he was making more than indicative statements. There is some suggestion, if not of persuading his imagined Christian readers, then at least of reinforcing in them shared positions ("we believe this, don't we?").

There are no third-person references with regard to Christians. Again, the close identification between author and Christians would tend to rule that out. All of this tells us that Tertullian included Christians in his imagined readership.

For further clarity we must turn our attention to the manner in which reference is made to the Jews. On the whole the Jews are referred to in the third person.[61] Some of these are clearly references to Jews in a past time,

---

probauimus"; 14.1 (CCSL 2.1391): "dicimus"; 14.11 (CCSL 2.1395): "intellegamus." One may well argue that some of the references in this note belong in the previous note and vice versa. However, the general point remains that sometimes Tertullian was referring more to himself and sometimes including others.

61. Ibid., 1.3 (CCSL 2.1339): "superbiat"; 1.7 (CCSL 2.1340): "prohiberentur"; 2.9 (CCSL 2.1343): "et Iudaeis certis temporibus datam"; 2.10 (CCSL 2.1343): "qui contendit"; 3.13 (CCSL

where a third-person reference would be expected. From the others we may be tempted to conclude that Tertullian did not imagine Jews among his readers. In other words, at first glance, it would appear that this was not designed as a work *to* the Jews but *about* the Jews. However, the matter is not so cut and dried, for we need to take into account the instances where Tertullian did address the Jews in the second person.[62] These references are sufficient to counter the claims of Efroymson, which are repeated by MacLennan, that Tertullian never addressed the Jews directly but only indirectly.[63]

Corssen had argued that there was a change of person with reference to the Jews from the first to the second half of *Aduersus Iudaeos*. He took this as an indication of the incompetence of the anonymous compiler, who could not be consistent in his usage.[64] Säflund, however, argues that changes of

---

2.1344): "fuerat cognitus"; 4.1 (CCSL 2.1347): "dicunt enim Iudaei"; 4.6 (CCSL 2.1348): "doceant"; 4.7 (CCSL 2.1348): "dicturi sunt Iudaei"; 4.10 (CCSL 2.1349): "eos operatos"; "fecerunt"; "expugnauerunt"; "reuocauerunt"; 5.3 (CCSL 2.1350): "et patribus eorum"; 6.2 (CCSL 2.1352): "patribus eorum"; 7.2 (CCSL 2.1353): "Iudaeos non refutare"; 8.13 (CCSL 2.1361): "exhibeant Iudaei"; 8.17 (CCSL 2.1363): "Iudaeis postea cessauerunt"; 9.1 (CCSL 2.1364): "dicunt Iudaei"; 9.2 (CCSL 2.1365): "dicunt"; 9.7 (CCSL 2.1366): "dicunt"; 9.16 (CCSL 2.1369): "conuincentur Iudaei"; 9.20 (CCSL 2.1370): "inquiunt", 11.9 (CCSL 2.1382): "In quo Iudaei non essent credituri"; 11.11 (CCSL 2.1383): "aduersus Iudaeos" (which Kroymann excluded from the text); "deducantur"; 13.1 (CCSL 2.1384): "filii Israel adfirmant"; "illis"; 13.5 (CCSL 2.1385): "secundum Iudaeos"; 13.15 (CCSL 2.1388): "coeperunt"; 13.16 (CCSL 2.1388): "eos"; 13.20 (CCSL 2.1388): "non possunt negare"; 13.24 (CCSL 2.1389–1390): "contendunt Iudaei"; "recognoscant"; "praedicabantur"; "despexerunt et interfecerunt"; "agnouerunt"; 13.25 (CCSL 2.1390): "apud illos"; 13.26 (CCSL 2.1390): "ab illis"; 13.27 (CCSL 2.1391): "perierunt"; "eis"; 13.28 (CCSL 2.1391): "praedicarentur Iudaei"; "eos"; 14.10 (CCSL 2.1394): "poterunt"; "decepti sunt"; "negari"; "ignorant."

62. Ibid., 3.1 (CCSL 2.1344): "inquies" (although the 1550 edition of Ghelen, based on the no longer extant *Codex Masburensis*, has "inquit"); 8.1 (CCSL 2.1356): "dubites"; "uideas"; 9.2 (CCSL 2.1365): "spectes"; 9.3 (CCSL 2.1365): "non negabis"; 9.5 (CCSL 2.1365): "inspicias"; 9.6 (CCSL 2.1366): "penes uos"; 9.8 (CCSL 2.1366): "gestitis"; "audetis"; "reuincimini"; 9.10 (CCSL 2.1367): "seruate"; 9.14 (CCSL 2.1368): "archontas uestras et populum uestrum"; 9.17 (CCSL 2.1369): "legis"; 9.20 (CCSL 2.1370): "agnosce"; "didicisti"; 9.21 (CCSL 2.1370): "disce . . . erroris tui"; "inquis"; 9.23 (CCSL 2.1371): "ipsi legitis"; 9.31 (CCSL 2.1374): "uos diffitemini"; "dicebatis"; 10.1 (CCSL 2.1374): "ambigitis"; 10.4 (CCSL 2.1375): "per uos"; 10.11 (CCSL 2.1378): "legistis"; "intellegatis"; "putetis"; 10.12 (CCSL 2.1378): "essetis dicturi"; 10.13 (CCSL 2.1378): "quaeris"; "tibi"; 10.14 (CCSL 2.1379): "ne putetis"; "cordis uestri"; 10.18 (CCSL 2.1380): "uos"; "interficeretis"; 10.19 (CCSL 2.1380): "captiuitas uobis"; 11.1 (CCSL 2.1380): "meritis uestris cladem uestram"; "respuistis"; 12.1 (CCSL 2.1384): "si audes negare"; "tibi"; 12.2 (CCSL 2.1384): "poteris" (although not found in the *Codex Trecensis*); 13.4 (CCSL 2.1385): "quod uobis, pro meritis uestris"; "terram uestram"; 13.11 (CCSL 2.1387): "uobis"; 13.29 (CCSL 2.1391): "redde"; 14.1 (CCSL 2.1391): "discite"; "erroris uestri"; 14.8 (CCSL 2.1393): "poteritis"; 14.12 (CCSL 2.1395): "cernitis"; "non audetis negare"; "si negaretis, statim uobis"; "nec poteritis"; 14.13 (CCSL 2.1395–1396): "potes"; "uides"; 14.14 (CCSL 2.1396): "negas."

63. David Efroymson, "Tertullian's Anti-Judaism and Its Role in His Theology" (Ph.D. diss., Temple University, 1976), 63; MacLennan, *Early Christian Texts on Jews and Judaism*, 138.

64. Corssen, *Die Altercatio*, 3–4.

person were common in ancient polemical literature.[65] Both Säflund and Tränkle point out that such changes of person occur in *Aduersus Marcionem* without the integrity of that work thereby being challenged.[66]

Almost all of these second-person references do indeed occur in the second half of the work. This is significant for it provides us with the opportunity to compare the parallels between *Aduersus Iudaeos* and the third book of *Aduersus Marcionem*. Many of the second-person references are repeated there,[67] although there are quite a number of second-person references in that part of *Aduersus Marcionem* that do not appear in *Aduersus Iudaeos* (or, if they do, they appear as third person).[68] There are even instances where second-person references in *Aduersus Iudaeos* are in the third person in *Aduersus Marcionem,* or are otherwise modified.[69] How may this be explained? *Aduersus Marcionem* was addressed to the followers of Marcion or to other Christians[70] and not to the Jews, and hence some of the specific references to the Jews in *Aduersus Iudaeos*

65. Säflund, *De pallio,* 160.

66. Ibid., 159–60; and Tränkle, *Tertullian, "Adversus Iudaeos,"* xv.

67. Tert., *Adu. Iud.* 9.2 (CCSL 2.1365) = Tert., *Adu. Marc.* 3.12.2 (CCSL 1.523); *Adu. Iud.* 9.3 (CCSL 2.1365) = *Adu. Marc.* 3.12.3 (CCSL 1.523); *Adu. Iud.* 9.5 (CCSL 2.1365) = *Adu. Marc.* 3.13.2 (CCSL 1.524); *Adu. Iud.* 9.10 (CCSL 2.1367) = *Adu. Marc.* 3.13.6 (CCSL 1.525) (although in the singular); *Adu. Iud.* 9.20 (CCSL 2.1370) = *Adu. Marc.* 3.14.7 (CCSL 1.527); *Adu. Iud.* 9.21 (CCSL 2.1370) = *Adu. Marc.* 3.16.3 (CCSL 1.529) (although the context—"cum partiariis erroris tui, Iudaeis"— makes it very clear that a different reader was being addressed, viz., Marcion and, by extension, his followers); *Adu. Iud.* 9.21 (CCSL 2.1370) = *Adu. Marc.* 3.16.4 (CCSL 1.529); *Adu. Iud.* 10.11 (CCSL 2.1378) = *Adu. Marc.* 3.19.1 (CCSL 1.533) (although all three in the singular); *Adu. Iud.* 10.12 (CCSL 2.1378) = *Adu. Marc.* 3.19.3 (CCSL 1.533) (although changed to "tibi insinuat, de dicturis praedicans Iudaeis"); *Adu. Iud.* 10.13 (CCSL 2.1378) = *Adu. Marc.* 3.19.5 (CCSL 1.533); *Adu. Iud.* 10.14 (CCSL 2.1379) = *Adu. Marc.* 3.19.6 (CCSL 1.534); *Adu. Iud.* 12.1 (CCSL 2.1384) = *Adu. Marc.* 3.20.2–3 (CCSL 1.535); *Adu. Iud.* 13.29 (CCSL 2.1391) = *Adu. Marc.* 3.23.7 (CCSL 1.541); *Adu. Iud.* 14.12 (CCSL 2.1395) = *Adu. Marc.* 3.20.2 (CCSL 1.535) (although in the singular); *Adu. Iud.* 14.13 (CCSL 2.1395–1396) = *Adu. Marc.* 3.20.10 (CCSL 1.537) (although "potes" has become "potest").

68. Tert., *Adu. Marc.* 3.13.1 (CCSL 1.524): "duceris"; "accipis"; and Tert., *Adu. Iud.* 9.4 (CCSL 2.1365): "inducuntur"; "accipiunt"; *Adu. Marc.* 3.13.6 (CCSL 1.525): "detraxisti"; *Adu. Marc.* 3.14.1 (CCSL 1.526): "conuinceris"; and *Adu. Iud.* 9.16 (CCSL 2.1369): "conuincentur"; *Adu. Marc.* 3.14.4 (CCSL 1.526): "habes"; *Adu. Marc.* 3.15.1 (CCSL 1.527): "uos"; *Adu. Marc.* 3.16.3 (CCSL 1.529): "inquis"; *Adu. Marc.* 3.16.7 (CCSL 1.530): "uobis"; "uos probare"; "poteritis"; *Adu. Marc.* 3.19.4 (CCSL 1.533): "in euangelio quoque uestro"; "intellegas."

69. Tert., *Adu. Iud.* 9.6 (CCSL 2.1366): "si penes uos"; and Tert., *Adu. Marc.* 3.13.3 (CCSL 1.524): "si penes"; *Adu. Iud.* 9.8 (CCSL 2.1366): "audetis"; and *Adu. Marc.* 3.13.4 (CCSL 1.524): "audent"; *Adu. Iud.* 9.8 (CCSL 2.1366): "reuincimini"; and *Adu. Marc.* 3.13.9 (CCSL 1.525): "reuincuntur"; *Adu. Iud.* 9.14 (CCSL 2.1368): "archontas uestras et populum uestrum"; and *Adu. Marc.* 3.13.9 (CCSL 1.525): "archontas Iudaeorum et populum ipsum"; *Adu. Iud.* 10.1 (CCSL 2.1374): "ambigitis"; and *Adu. Marc.* 3.18.1 (CCSL 1.531): "puto, diuersitatem temptatis inducere"; *Adu. Iud.* 10.18–19 (CCSL 2.1380) and 13.4 (CCSL 2.1385) do not appear in *Adu. Marc.; Adu. Iud.* 14.1 (CCSL 2.1391): "discite"; "erroris uestri"; and *Adu. Marc.* 3.7.1 (CCSL 1.516): "discat"; "errorum eius."

70. The same problem of readership occurs here. Was this work meant to be read by the

needed to be in a different person in *Aduersus Marcionem*. Given that the Marcionites accepted some version of the Christian gospel, Tertullian had more material from which to draw his arguments against them, as opposed to the material acceptable to the Jews from which he could have drawn arguments for *Aduersus Iudaeos*, hence the additional second-person references in *Aduersus Marcionem*. There were, as well, quite a number of arguments that Tertullian felt able to direct against them both. This is seen in the large number of occasions where a second-person reference occurs in both works.

Simply on the basis of this presentation of verbs and pronouns, no conclusion can be reached about the sequence of writing, although there is nothing here to prevent the view that I support, viz., that *Aduersus Iudaeos* was written first and then later used in parts of the third book of *Aduersus Marcionem*. It was obviously not a question of blind copying (nor of inferior copying), for there are some instances where a second-person reference in *Aduersus Iudaeos* has become third in *Aduersus Marcionem* and where some third-person references in *Aduersus Iudaeos* have become second in *Aduersus Marcionem*.

Further, it must be noted that some second-person references in *Aduersus Iudaeos* are singular while others are plural. The use of the singular suggests that Tertullian's imagined reader was the proselyte Jew, whom he pictured as being present in a further debate, but this time with Tertullian himself (or with him at his best, depending upon his participation at the first debate—the actual one). The use of the plural suggests that the Jewish supporters of their representative speaker were included among the imagined readers of this idealized and imaginary rerun.

How then do we explain why sometimes the Jews are referred to in the second person and others times in the third person? I would like to suggest that the answer to this tells us something important about Tertullian's intended readers of his pamphlet.

Intended Readers of *Aduersus Iudaeos*

By the intended readers of *Aduersus Iudaeos* I mean those people whom Tertullian himself wanted to read the work. Literary criticism alone, con-

---

followers of Marcion in order to refute their understandings or to persuade them to abandon them, or was it written for Christians in order to deepen their own self-understanding? It is not a question that needs to be resolved here.

cerned as it is with the world inside the text, cannot tell us everything about those to whom Tertullian was addressing his comments, yet it may point us in the right direction. When we confront the question of intended readers we are confronting the question of the work's purpose. Was it designed to convert Jews in Carthage to Christianity? Was it intended merely to beat them in argument? Did it seek to denigrate or vilify the Jews? Was it designed to help Christians gain a clearer self-identity by sharpening the differences between Christian and Jew, particularly for those Christians who were sympathetic to Jewish customs?[71] Was it directed at sympathetic pagans who were interested in monotheism?[72] Was it a piece of apologetic, intended to defend Christians before Jewish or even pagan opponents, or was it polemic, intended to dismiss the Jewish position in Christian or even pagan eyes?[73] I am going to argue that the work was intended first for a Christian readership, and through them for a Jewish audience, and that it could serve several purposes rather than merely one.

The fact that *Aduersus Iudaeos* was written in Latin would not have meant that Jews in North Africa could not have read it or have it read to them.[74] The

71. On this see Lloyd Gaston, "Judaism of the Uncircumcised in Ignatius and Related Writers," in *Anti-Judaism in Early Christianity*, vol. 2: *Separation and Polemic*, ed. Stephen G. Wilson, Études sur le christianisme et le judaïsme 2 (Waterloo, Ontario: Wilfrid Laurier Press, 1986), 33–36; and Murray, *Playing a Jewish Game*.

72. The last position is the one favored by Barnes, *Tertullian*, 106, and Gager, *The Origins of Anti-Semitism*, 164.

73. Although Mark Edwards, Martin Goodman, Simon Price, and Christopher Rowland, "Introduction: Apologetics in the Roman World," in *Apologetics in the Roman Empire: Pagans, Jews and Christians*, ed. Mark Edwards, Martin Goodman, Simon Price, and Christopher Rowland (Oxford: Oxford University Press, 1999), 1, distinguish apologetics from polemics, they recognize that some of the contributors to the volume they edited disagree. Tessa Rajak, "Talking at Trypho: Christian Apologetics as Anti-Judaism in Justin's *Dialogue with Trypho the Jew*," in Edwards et al., eds., *Apologetics in the Roman Empire*, 61, states: "It is hard to avoid the conclusion that the polemical element—what we might in crude terms call 'doing down the other side'—is intrinsic to defending one's own side in apologetic literature." She also points out that polemic could be directed at "a real opponent or a paper tiger." I accept this and so do not want my question above to imply that apologetics addressed real situations and polemics fictitious ones. According to Simon Price, "Latin Christian Apologetics: Minucius Felix, Tertullian, and Cyprian," in Edwards et al., eds., *Apologetics in the Roman Empire*, 105, who defines apologetics as literature formally addressed externally to outsiders regardless of who actually read it, Tert., *Adu. Iud.*, would classify as apologetic literature. However, Price does not even mention it.

74. William V. Harris, *Ancient Literacy* (Cambridge, Mass., and London: Harvard University Press, 1989), 3–42; Harry Y. Gamble, *Books and Readers in the Early Church: A History of Early Christian Texts* (New Haven, Conn.: Yale University Press, 1995), 1–41; and Keith Hopkins, "Christian Numbers and Its Implications," *JECS* 6 (1998): 207–13. Hopkins's article responded to the demographic calculations of Rodney Stark, *The Rise of Christianity: A Sociologist Reconsiders History* (Princeton, N.J.: Princeton University Press, 1996).

evidence from the cemetery epitaphs at Gammarth analyzed by LeBohec would seem to be conclusive proof that the Jewish community in Carthage in the second and third centuries was quite at home with Latin.[75] Some two-thirds of these epitaphs were written in Latin. Earlier, Caplan examined other Jewish African inscriptions, some quite possibly from this time, and they too were almost all written in Latin or Greek.[76] There were very few Hebrew inscriptions.[77] Perhaps Latin was the language all people in Carthage spoke.[78]

What suggests that the Jews could have been included among Tertullian's intended readers is the way in which he represents them in his work. As we shall see in the following chapters, he says very little about them.[79] Rather than conclude that he was not interested in contemporary Jews, my position is that he did not want to engage in personal invective but wanted to win a historical argument that had current relevance in determining the legitimacy of both Christianity and Judaism. As has been pointed out in other contexts, Tertullian could, to some extent at least, modify his views depending upon his intended readership. In works addressed to pagans he hid or glossed over intramural issues that, in works addressed to an exclusively Christian readership, he would otherwise have exploited. As Evans has suggested, we are not to harmonize the various utterances scattered throughout the corpus.[80]

75. Yann LeBohec, "Inscriptions juives et judaïsantes de l'Afrique romaine," *AntAfr* 17 (1981): 165–207; and LeBohec, "Juifs et Judaïsants dans l'Afrique romaine: Remarques onomestiques," *AntAfr* 17 (1981): 209–29. For comments about separate Christian cemeteries in Carthage see Éric Rebillard, "Les *Areae* Carthaginoises (Tertullien, *Ad Scapulam* 3,1): Cimetières, communautaires au enclos funéraires de Chrétiens?" *MEFRA* 108 (1996): 175–89.

76. Harry Caplan, "The History of the Jews in the Roman Province of Africa: A Collection of the Sources" (Ph.D. diss., Cornell University, 1921), 1–56.

77. Ibid., 54. J. B. Rives, *Religion and Authority in Roman Carthage from Augustus to Constantine* (Oxford: Clarendon Press, 1995), 217–18, suggests that the Jewish community in Carthage was a typical diaspora community, knowing little Hebrew. Leonard Victor Rutgers, *The Jews in Late Ancient Rome: Evidence of Cultural Interaction in the Roman Diaspora*, Religions in the Graeco-Roman World 126 (Leiden: E. J. Brill, 1995), 176–209, interpreting the Jewish funerary inscriptions from Rome, notes that Greek predominates until the third century and that Hebrew was generally absent. Cf. Gamble, *Books and Readers*, 2–7, who argues that even though Jews had a higher degree of literacy than other people in the ancient world, we should not conclude that literacy in one language (Hebrew) meant literacy in other languages. Perhaps one has to wonder at the degree of Jewish familiarity with Hebrew in Carthage by this time.

78. Gilles Quispel, "African Christianity before Minicius Felix and Tertullian," in *Actus: Studies in Honour of H. L. W. Nelson,* ed. J. den Boeft and A. H. M. Kessels (Utrecht: Instituut voor Klassieke Talen, 1982), 260.

79. Cf. the comments of Lieu, *Image and Reality,* 12.

80. R. F. Evans, "On the Problem of Church and Empire in Tertullian's *Apologeticum*," in

In addressing an audience already hostile, being too antagonistic would not have contributed to the admittedly limited scope for persuasiveness. This lack of hostility could suggest that Tertullian wanted Jews to know his work, if not directly then at least indirectly through the use made by Christians who read it in their own encounters with Jews.

May we notice any difference between *Aduersus Iudaeos* and book 3 of *Aduersus Marcionem* in this respect? If Tertullian's aim in the former was to be read by Jews, then we could expect him to have adopted a more conciliatory or less abusive tone than in a work for Christians in which Jews are mentioned. That Tertullian had a harsh attitude toward Jews and their faith in works addressed to Christian readers has been argued successfully and convincingly by Efroymson. He notes how Tertullian used the term "Jewish" in contrast with "Christian" as something to describe immorality, impatience, empty ritual, continual defilement, carnal practices, excess, ineffectiveness, and idolatry.[81] This is what one would expect, according to Evans.

We find such comments in Tertullian's statements in *Aduersus Marcionem* about the Jews being the source of poison for the heretics,[82] having wisdom taken from them,[83] being ignorant,[84] and being in error.[85] These statements are without direct parallel in *Aduersus Iudaeos*, even though occasionally he made similar comments in passages that are paralleled. It is just that there are more of them in *Aduersus Marcionem*. Although these anti-Jewish references in *Aduersus Marcionem* may not be particularly strident, they are harsher or more personal than what is found in *Aduersus Iudaeos*. There certainly is a vigorous disagreement in the latter work, but it remains at a theological level and, in comparison with *Aduersus Marcionem*, does not degenerate into personal abuse or snide comments. All of this suggests to me that this pamphlet was intended to be known by the Jews, if not directly as readers then at least indirectly as participants in future debates with better-prepared Christians.

Further, *Iudaeus* is a term that Tertullian used to designate a religious rather than an ethnic or racial group. What made them distinctive in his mind

---

Studia Patristica 14, ed. Elizabeth A. Livingstone, papers presented to the sixth International Conference on Patristic Studies, part 3, Oxford 1971 (Berlin: Akademie-Verlag, 1976), 28.

81. Efroymson, "Tertullian's Anti-Jewish Rhetoric," 26–35.

82. Tert., *Adu. Marc.* 3.8.1 (CCSL 1.518): "Desinat nunc haereticus a Iudaeo, aspis, quod aiunt, a uipera."

83. Ibid., 3.16.1 (CCSL 1.528): "et Iudaeis, quibus adempta est sapientia."

84. Ibid., 3.6.8 (CCSL 1.515): "Iudaicae ignorantiae."

85. Ibid., 3.6.2 (CCSL 514): "cum Iudaico errore."

was their belief, not their genetics. Recent scholarship has been concerned
with *Iudaeus* as a term of self-designation. Scholars, following Kraabel, argue
that the term and its Greek equivalent Ἰυδαῖος ought to be rendered as "Judaean" in English, indicative of geographic origin.[86] As Cohen points out,
Jewishness (or Judaeanness) was a subjective identity created by the individual, but one that entailed an ethnic-geographic group.[87] An outsider could become an insider (a proselyte) as a Judaean until the end of the second century
not so much through a conversion of belief or practice as through social acceptance, which was never total.[88] Kraemer has attempted to modify Kraabel
by adding to his theory the idea that the term may include a pagan adherent
to Judaism.[89] My interest is not with self-designation but with how a Christian like Tertullian classified and constructed Jews. Kraemer recognizes that
non-Jewish writers employed the term to refer to those born into Judaism
as well as converts. This is quite clear from the opening of our work, where
Tertullian writes that the proselyte Jew ("proselytus Iudaeus")[90] was "homo
ex gentibus nec de prosapia Israëlitum Iudaeus,"[91] i.e., that he was originally
an outsider but was now completely an insider. *Iudaeus* was a religious rather
than geographic term for Tertullian. Further, for Tertullian Jews were clearly
distinguishable from Christians in that they retained completely the covenant
with Moses and did not accept the covenant of Jesus.[92] Although Christianity might have had much in common with Judaism, it was what made them

86. A. Thomas Kraabel, "The Roman Diaspora: Six Questionable Assumptions," *JJS* 33
(1982): 445–64.

87. Shaye J. D. Cohen, *The Beginnings of Jewishness: Boundaries, Varieties and Uncertainties*,
Hellenistic Culture and Society 31 (Berkeley: University of California Press, 1999), 69–106.

88. Ibid., 140–74.

89. Ross S. Kraemer, "On the Meaning of the Term 'Jew' in Greco-Roman Inscriptions,"
HTR 82 (1989): 35–53.

90. I much prefer this to the term "Jewish proselyte," which seems to lack much sense at
all.

91. Tert., *Adu. Iud.* 1.2 (CCSL 2.1339): "the man . . . is from the Gentiles and is not a Jew from
the stock of the Israelites." (All translations of *Adu. Iud.* are my own and are from Dunn, *Tertullian*.)

92. I accept the argument of scholars like Alan F. Segal, *Rebecca's Children: Judaism and Christianity in the Roman World* (Cambridge, Mass., and London: Harvard University Press, 1986);
Daniel Boyarin, "Martyrdom and the Making of Christianity and Judaism," *JECS* 6 (1998): 590;
Boyarin, *Dying for God: Martyrdom and the Making of Christianity and Judaism* (Stanford, Calif.:
Stanford University Press, 1999), 11; and Boyarin, *Border Lines, 6*, that Christianity and Judaism
were still very much interrelated in the second century. The point I am making is that Tertullian, while providing evidence of that ongoing contact, I believe, wanted to assert that the two
were clearly distinguishable religious groups, one with a valid claim to legitimacy and the other without.

different that interested Tertullian. Boyarin's comment on this point, that the relationship between them until the fourth century should not be thought of simply in terms of "separations and partings" but "encounters and meetings" as well,[93] leads to the conclusion that perhaps Tertullian stressed the distinctiveness between the two so much because he experienced the encounters and meetings between them so frequently. That this distinctiveness was only on the religious level and that the pamphlet did not contain bitter invective could indicate that the Jews as Tertullian constructed them were among the intended readers of *Aduersus Iudaeos*.

There is no appeal to the Jews to embrace Christianity, so I do not think that this was Tertullian's purpose in writing this work. As noted, some of the second-person references call for the Jews to recognize their errors. What we find in this pamphlet is Tertullian the advocate not Tertullian the Christian missionary. He simply wanted to win his case by demonstrating that the Jewish position was wrong. What they did in response to that discovery was not his explicit concern. Occasionally in *Aduersus Iudaeos* he called upon the Jews themselves to accept his arguments. Perhaps Tertullian was self-assured (or even arrogant) enough to believe that his case was so watertight and so open-and-shut that any Jew who might get to hear his argument could not but be convinced that they had been wrong all along, and that any Jew who was not so convinced was just being obstinate. For this reason, such a verdict offered by a Jew who would stubbornly refuse to agree with Tertullian's presentation would not count in deciding the winner of the argument. The kind of argumentation that is to be found in *Aduersus Iudaeos* lays the foundation for this conclusion in that, throughout their history, the Jews had refused to listen to the truth when the prophets had announced it to them. That they would not listen to the truth as put by Tertullian should therefore not surprise anyone is the point at which Tertullian was hinting. Questions of their conversion were far from his mind.

Thus, Tertullian was much more concerned with winning the approval of an intended Christian readership, given that, as I noted in the previous section, there are so many first-person plural references that connect Tertullian with the imagined Christian readership and that the Jews are imagined as being hearers of Tertullian's arguments in a future debate, due to second-person references to them, yet are most often referred to in the third person.

---

93. Boyarin, "Martyrdom and the Making of Christianity and Judaism," 627.

I think Tertullian wanted to provide his fellow Christians in Carthage with solid information and debating points to use in the ongoing conflict with Jews.[94] He wanted his Christian readers to judge that his written work was a better Christian case than that which was heard at the debate.

In this instance I am arguing that there is a strong degree of Christian self-identification evident in this work. Other scholars would conclude from that that there were no real encounters between Jews and Christians, as we saw in the last chapter. I do not want to reach that conclusion, however. I think he intended this work to be read by Christians to give them a better sense of who they were and how they were different from Jews (in that they had superseded them) so that they could be prepared better for engaging with them in argument when they had the opportunity. Like Stroumsa, Carleton Paget, and Lieu, I do not think the controversy over contact between Christians and Jews need be reduced to an either-or decision. I too would suggest that a more inclusive and dynamic approach is better and more reflective of reality. This work was written primarily for a Christian readership in order to clarify their self-identity as well as prepare them for future encounters with Jews by providing them with Tertullian's own superior arguments. The Jews would hear the content of this pamphlet in those future encounters, and whether or not they accepted Tertullian's arguments was irrelevant. For his own success Tertullian merely needed to persuade his Christian readers.

I have not commented on the possibility that this work was addressed to pagans who were interested in choosing a monotheistic faith or who branded Christianity as an illegitimate offshoot of Judaism. All that needs to be said is that Tertullian could well have written the work with several simultaneous objectives in mind, these included, so it is a possibility I would not rule out.

Conclusion

Aduersus Iudaeos was written in the form of a *controuersia*, a scholastic form of forensic practice and skillful display, in which one set forth argu-

94. I agree with what Jack T. Sanders, *Schismatics, Sectarians, Dissidents, Deviants: The First One Hundred Years of Jewish-Christian Relations* (London: SCM Press, 1993), 52, says about Jus., *Dial.*, and would apply it to Tertullian: "In the *Dialogus* Justin certainly shows knowledge of Jewish-Christian debates, but his intended audience is rather Christian, to whom he provides ammunition for arguing with Jews." Cf. Rajak, "Talking at Trypho," 75–80, who argues that Justin's work was addressed principally to a Christian, not a pagan or Jewish, readership. She does not really entertain the more dynamic interpretation.

ments and dealt with the imagined arguments of an opponent. While many *controuersiae* could be based upon an entirely fictitious premise, some were based upon actual events and cases. Although many in the Graeco-Roman world of the second century engaged in such declamations as a leisure pursuit or form of entertainment, a Christian like Tertullian was more interested in their practical possibilities. He wrote in response to what he claimed to have been a real, recent debate between a Christian and a proselyte Jew but his literary production was not the record of that encounter. Rather, he wrote what the Christian participant should have said but did not or, more appropriately, should say on the next occasion. His pamphlet is not a dialogue and never pretends to be what was actually said at any such debate; it is an idealized template for future use. I am prepared to accept Tertullian at face value and believe that the original encounter between Christian and proselyte Jew took place.

Within the text we can discern an imagined readership consisting of those Jews and Christians who had witnessed that encounter. Tertullian imagines this mixed group being gathered together once again and this time listening to him as the Christian speaker (or perhaps listening to him a second time, if he was the one who spoke originally, but this time with a new and improved contribution). Within this imagined setting Tertullian most often spoke to the Christians about the Jews and sometimes he spoke directly to the Jews.

In terms of his intended readership, those to whom the work was actually directed in Tertullian's mind, it would seem that his comments were aimed at fellow Christians. He was preparing them for ongoing debates between Christians and Jews by offering them an already prepared version of the most persuasive arguments that could be used to prove that the Jews had been superseded by the Christians. He might not have intended Jews to read his work but I would think he certainly intended for them to hear his case, even if indirectly.

With these comments in mind we may now turn to the rhetorical analysis of the text itself in terms of its structure, its arguments, and its style.

CHAPTER THREE

⟨⟨⟨

Structure

To this point I have outlined the controversy concerning the integrity and authorship of *Aduersus Iudaeos* by summarizing scholarly opinion. Thus I have demonstrated that the controversy is the reason this text plays such an insignificant part in the debate about the relationship between Christians and Jews in the centuries after the destruction of the second temple in Jerusalem, and why this work was not considered in Robert Sider's examination of Tertullian's use of classical rhetoric.

My contention is that classical rhetoric provides particular insight into the nature of *Aduersus Iudaeos,* an insight that can contribute to the resolution of the controversy. In the previous chapter I pointed to the fact that *Aduersus Iudaeos* does not claim to be an account of an actual debate between a Christian and a Jew but is a literary production designed to demonstrate what the Christian participant should have said (or wanted to say but could not) and what any Christian participant in such encounters in the future ought to say. In this regard the pamphlet can be classified as a *controuersia,* a rhetorical forensic exercise. I argued that unlike his contemporaries Tertullian turned to *controuersia* not merely to delight or impress his readers with his skill but, because of Christianity's precarious status, to persuade them about the validity of his argument. A rhetorical approach asks questions about readership, and I put forward the view that while Tertullian imagined his work being heard by both sides in a future debate between Christians and Jews, he intended the work primarily for Christians in order to arm them for future encounters. This led me to conclude that we ought to take this work as evidence that such encounters still took place at the end of the second century, at least in North Africa.

This is the first time that this work has been analyzed rhetorically, along the lines pursued by Sider with regard to the rest of Tertullian's output. The conclusion that will be reached from an examination of its rhetorical structure, argumentation, and style in this chapter and the next two is that the pamphlet has an overall structural integrity that would indicate that whoever wrote the first half intended to write something that resembles closely what we find today in the second half. It is not a perfect rhetorical structure. Yet, rather than conclude that the elements of textbook rhetoric do not illuminate the pamphlet we have, I contend that its use helps us identify it not as the work of an inferior author who copied from Tertullian's *Aduersus Marcionem* but as an unrevised draft by someone who was trying very much to write according to rhetorical conventions, but whose effort was flawed. The work gives us a glimpse into the raw thought processes of an energetic writer trying to address too many ideas concurrently before the discipline of editorial revision forced a straightening out of his sometimes jumbled thoughts. Further, I would conclude that if Tertullian wrote the first half of *Aduersus Iudaeos* then, from a structural and stylistic analysis, he wrote the second half as well. A rhetorical perspective confirms the idea that Tertullian himself could have used much of the same material in both *Aduersus Iudaeos* and book 3 of *Aduersus Marcionem*. The coherence of the material structurally in *Aduersus Iudaeos* would suggest its temporal priority over book 3 of *Aduersus Marcionem*.

In this chapter I intend to consider what classical rhetoric may reveal about the structure of *Aduersus Iudaeos* in order to support the position I am advancing. My method is simple. After a few words about the standard patterns of rhetorical structure I shall present a summary of what Sider has observed about each part of a speech in Tertullian's other works, followed by comments on the rhetorical structure I have discerned in *Aduersus Iudaeos*. From this I shall suggest that we can believe that the structure of *Aduersus Iudaeos* is consistent with what Tertullian is known to have done elsewhere. Finally, I believe that rhetoric gives us a structure for *Aduersus Iudaeos* unlike that proposed by any other scholar, and one that helps us appreciate better the point at issue in the pamphlet and one that explains better the inelegancies of its second half.

Classical rhetoric typically divided a speech, especially a forensic one, into four, five, or six parts: *exordium* (or *prooemium*), *narratio, diuisio* (or *partitio*), *confirmatio* (or *probatio*), *refutatio* (or *confutatio* or *reprehensio*), and *peroratio* (or *conclusio*).[1] These basic parts were to be found in *controuersiae* as well, as the comments of the elder Seneca reveal.[2] The young Cicero, in the work that preserves what amounts to the instruction he received about the art of rhetoric, argued that in the composition of a speech the last thing an orator did was to work out what was to be said in the rest of one's speech apart from the point at issue and the main arguments.[3] While determining the finished structure might have been the orator's final task, for the modern analyst it tends to be the first. Once a structure of a treatise has been determined it is possible then to discern the point at issue and the individual arguments that have been employed.

Sider's Observations of General Structural Patterns in Tertullian

Sider has claimed that Tertullian was most attentive to the possibilities presented by structure, noting that it gives us access to the intricate pattern of his thought better than mere excerpts from his writings.[4] He examines how Tertullian used the classical tendency to symmetrical composition to construct balance between contrasting and parallel ideas not only in the contour of a work but in the arrangement of details. Although I shall argue that chronology rather than symmetry determines the structural thrust of *Aduersus Iudaeos,* his point about the importance of structure for interpretation remains valid. Of Tertullian's adherence to the rules of the parts of a speech, Sider wrote:

In Tertullian's use of this characteristic rhetorical structure, we must note three features in particular. First, we shall find that he employs the textbook pattern of structure with a degree of flexibility, omitting, transposing, and combining parts as the demand of rhetorical effectiveness suggested. Second, he brings to some of these parts a few basic features repeated so often as to become almost stereotyped. The *exordium,* for example, is developed with a great regularity on the basis of a central contrast or pejorative association. Third, his vigorous and abundant use of the pre-

---

1. *Rhet. Her.* 1.3.4 (LCL 403.8); Cic., *Inu. rhet.* 1.14.19 (LCL 386.38–40); Cic., *De or.* 1.31.143 (LCL 348.98); Cic., *Orat.* 15.50 (LCL 342.342); Cic., *Part. or.* 1.4 (LCL 349.312); Quint., *Inst.* 3.9.1 (LCL 124.514).

2. Bonner, *Roman Declamation,* 54, and Leeman, "*Orationis Ratio,*" 1:232.

3. Cic., *Inu. rhet.* 1.14.19 (LCL 386.40): "Quare cum iudicatio et ea quae ad iudicationem oportet argumenta inueniri diligenter erunt artificio reperta, cura et cogitatione pertractata, tum denique ordinandae sunt ceterae partes orationis."

4. Robert Dick Sider, "On Symmetrical Composition in Tertullian," *JTS* n.s. 24 (1973): 422.

munition allows us a special interest in that feature, an interest which is heightened when we observe that occasionally he will set a premunition in balance with an amplification to give his composition something of a symmetrical effect.[5]

It is worth stating that such a flexible approach to the parts of a speech is not the convenient fantasy of the modern commentator, enabling any piece of writing to fit the rhetorical mold, even if at first it does not seem to fit. On the contrary, rhetorical theorists like Cicero and Quintilian themselves were at pains to point this out. The sign of accomplished and mature orators was their ability to be creative and flexible in their approach to this standard pattern.[6]

The second point is that these major rhetoricians do not mention premunition as a separate part of a speech. In *De oratore* Cicero mentioned *praemunitio* as one of the *figurae,* those embellishments or adornments that gave polish to one's words, where one prepared briefly for what one was going to do next, anywhere it was relevant in a speech, by anticipating objections.[7] Bonner points out that *figurae* usually were no more than a few words, clauses, or sentences, not a whole section of a speech itself.[8] Sider knows this but argued that, in a few of Tertullian's treatises, it was expanded considerably.[9]

Exordium

Exordium in Tertullian

The *exordium,* according to Quintilian, was the opening of a speech, in which the orator sought to prepare his audience by making them well disposed toward the speaker, attentive, and ready to receive instruction.[10] It serves as a prologue through which an orator sought to establish rapport

---

5. Sider, *Ancient Rhetoric,* 22.

6. *Rhet. Her.* 3.9.17–3.10.17 (LCL 403.186–88); Cic., *De or.* 2.19.79–81 (LCL 348.256–58); 2.72.293 (LCL 348.420); 2.76.307–2.81.332 (LCL 348.432–50); Cic., *Orat.* 35.122 (LCL 342.396); Cic., *Part. or.* 5.15 (LCL 349.322); Quint., *Inst.* 4.1.43 (LCL 125.28); 4.1.72 (LCL 125.44–46); 4.2.4–5 (LCL 125.50–52); 7.1.3 (LCL 126.6); 7.10.5–9 (LCL 126.164–66).

7. Cic., *De or.* 3.53.204 (LCL 349.162); Cic., *Orat.* 40.137 (LCL 342.410). Quint., *Inst.* 9.1.30 (LCL 126.364); 9.1.43 (LCL 126.372) repeats these statements of Cicero. See also Quint., *Inst.* 4.1.49 (LCL 125.32); 9.2.2 (LCL 126.374); 9.2.16–17 (LCL 126.382–84).

8. Bonner, *Education in Ancient Rome,* 305.

9. Sider, *Ancient Rhetoric,* 34.

10. Quint., *Inst.* 4.1.5 (LCL 125.8): "Causa principii nulla alia est, quam ut auditorem, quo sit nobis in ceteris partibus accommodatior, praeparemus. Id fieri tribus maxime rebus inter auctores plurimos constat, si beneuolum, attentum, docilem fecerimus."

with his audience by commenting on himself, his audience, or the matter to
be discussed.

What are the general characteristics of Tertullian's use of the *exordium* according to Sider? In *Apologeticum* there is an appeal to the judges' responsibility to be fair and a contrast between Christians and criminals.[11] In *De resurrectione mortuorum* he linked his opponents with Jews and pagans and clearly
stated his position.[12] *Aduersus Praxean* opens with a denigration of his opponent by associating him with the devil.[13]

Sider notes Tertullian's ability elsewhere to be more adaptive and creative,
particularly in the interrelationship between the *exordium, narratio, partitio,*
and *propositio. De pudicitia* has a textbook *exordium* in which Tertullian sought
to arouse sympathy by showing the decline of modesty and, at the same
time, discredit his opponent by showing the lack of contrast between church
and world on this issue.[14] In *De praescriptione haereticorum,* Sider identifies an
exordium of fourteen chapters, and this in a work that is only forty-four chapters long.[15] A *partitio* opens *De carne Christi* and the *exordium* follows in the
first section, devoted to Marcion.[16] *De corona* has no *exordium* but opens immediately with the *narratio.*[17] The *exordium* of *Aduersus Marcionem* is conventional, in that Tertullian sought to win good will for himself and to castigate
his opponent by associating him with a barbarous country.[18] Finally, Sider argues that *Aduersus Valentinianos* consists only of *exordium* and *narratio,* and
that the *exordium* contains the usual technique of contrast and association.[19]

Exordium in Aduersus Iudaeos (1.1–3a)

This pamphlet contains a brief *exordium* at 1.1–3a. It contains the history
of events that led Tertullian to compose the work—the earlier debate between the Christian and the proselyte Jew. Although it contains a history it is
really the history of the work's evolution rather than the history of the topic
under discussion, and that is why it is not to be regarded as a *narratio.* This
can be illustrated by contrasting *Aduersus Iudaeos* and *De corona.* Both open
with very similar words: "Proxime accidit" in the first and "Proxime factum
est" in the second, which, as noted earlier, Sider identifies as the opening of

11. Sider, *Ancient Rhetoric,* 22–23.   12. Ibid., 23.
13. Ibid., 23–24.   14. Ibid., 24–25.
15. Ibid., 25–26.   16. Ibid., 27–28.
17. Ibid., 28–29.   18. Ibid., 29–30.
19. Ibid., 30.

the *narratio*.[20] Yet these words in *Aduersus Iudaeos* do not lead into a consideration of the topic itself, but of the origins of the pamphlet. In *De corona* the opening words do lead into the history of the very incident that becomes the topic for discussion—the refusal of a Christian soldier to wear an awarded military crown. In this regard the opening of *Aduersus Iudaeos* fulfills the same function as the first part of the *exordium* of *Aduersus Marcionem* (1.1.1–2) in explaining how the work came to be written.

The comparison with *Aduersus Marcionem* is instructive, for in the second part of the *exordium* as identified by Sider (1.1.4–6), we find the association of Marcion with the barbarity of his native land. There is nothing like this in the *exordium* of *Aduersus Iudaeos,* where Tertullian offered nothing derogatory about his opponent at all.

What type of *causa* would Tertullian have envisaged?[21] We may note that he did not spend time winning the favor of his readers or promoting his credentials. I think we may take this as yet another indication that his intended readers were mainly Christian, for in a *controuersia* intended for the Jews to read, where the matter would have been considered by them to be *admirabile,* one would expect him to have spent some effort in putting himself forward in the most positive light. This is something he did not do. He gives the impression that he believed that his readers were already well disposed toward him and receptive to his topic.

The only thing that Tertullian did to enhance his own position was to contrast the earlier debate, with its tug-of-war exchanges ("alternis uicibus contentioso fune"), its inordinate length ("uterque diem in uesperam traxerunt"), and its lack of logic ("per concentum disputationis minus plene potuit dilucidari"), with what this pamphlet promised to do, viz., "to settle the questions that have been reconsidered in writing, after a more careful examination of the texts."[22] In other words, Tertullian put himself forward as the

---

20. Tert., *Adu. Iud.* 1.1 (CCSL 2.1339); Tert., *De cor.* 1.1 (CCSL 2.1039).

21. Rhetoricians noted that there were different *causae* in a forensic speech and one would construct different *exordia* depending on the *causa* one faced. The matter could be honorable *(honestum)* if it was worthy of defense; difficult *(admirabile)* or discreditable *(turpe)* if it was not worthy of defense or if one was prosecuting the worthy; doubtful *(dubium)* or ambiguous *(anceps)* where the issue was unclear or mixed; petty *(humile)* where it was unimportant; or obscure *(obscurum)* if it was difficult to grasp or the judge was slow to understand. See *Rhet. Her.* 1.3.5 (LCL 403.10) (which listed only the first four); Cic., *Inu. rhet.* 1.15.20 (LCL 386.40–42); Quint., *Inst.* 4.1.40–41 (LCL 125.26–28).

22. Tert., *Adu. Iud.* 1.1. (CCSL 2.1339): "curiosius inspectis lectionibus, stilo questiones retractatas terminare."

person who could resolve what had earlier remained unresolved, in a complete, logical, and briefer fashion. By promising in an oblique manner to be rational rather than emotional, and focused rather than rambling, Tertullian wanted his readers to read him sympathetically. One point of interest is that Tertullian informs us that the argument is based upon texts. They were obviously passages from the Hebrew Scriptures.

We may note also the brevity of the *exordium*. There is something restrained about Tertullian's opening statements. This restraint continues in 1.3a, with the brief mention of the earlier opponent and Tertullian's quip that the Jews should not become conceited ("ne Israël adhuc superbiat") by appealing to an outdated piece of Scripture like Isaiah 40:15. Compared with the ways he characterized his opponents in other treatises, this was moderate indeed, indicative perhaps of the reality and relevance of that encounter. I suggest that the rest of the pamphlet does remain focused on the issues and does not descend into polemic, if, by this term, we mean personal invective.[23]

The *exordium* contains what amounts to the point that had been central to the earlier debate: could the Gentiles share in divine grace?[24] The point Tertullian wanted to make was that the person who had argued that they could not was himself a Gentile (or of Gentile origin).[25] Of course Tertullian was going to argue that the Gentiles could share in God's grace. Indeed, he would argue that they had replaced the Jews as the recipients of that grace. This central issue, the *propositio* from the previous debate, which would continue to be at the heart of this pamphlet, was repeated in 1.3a.[26]

---

23. Much depends upon how one defines polemic. Luke T. Johnson, "The New Testament's Anti-Jewish Slander and the Conventions of Ancient Polemic," *JBL* 108 (1989): 419–41, understands slander to be part of polemic, not just in the New Testament, but in ancient societies as a whole. David Rokeah, "Anti-Judaism in Early Christianity," *Immanuel* 16 (1983): 62, recognizes a difference between mutual rivalry and polemic, depending upon the degree of bitterness. Anthony J. Guerra, "Polemical Christianity: Tertullian's Search for Certitude," *The Second Century* 8 (1991): 109, simply used polemic in its more general sense of "controverting the positions of adversaries," in which case *Adu. Iud.* would be polemical.

24. Tert., *Adu. Iud.* 1.2 (CCSL 2.1339): "Nam occasio quidem defendendi etiam gentibus ibi diuinam gratiam."

25. The opponent could have responded to Tertullian that, although he had been born a Gentile, by becoming a Jew he was no longer Gentile and that Isaiah's statement still stood: the Gentiles count as nothing before God.

26. Tert., *Adu. Iud.* 1.3a (CCSL 1.1339): "posse gentes admitti ad dei legem."

Narratio

Narratio in Tertullian

According to Cicero, "narratio est rerum gestarum aut ut gestarum expositio."[27] In forensic oratory, telling the story of what had happened could be concentrated on persons or facts. It amounts to a summary presentation of the facts, which a speaker would then intend to support with proofs later in the speech.[28]

In *Apologeticum* Sider believes that there is no distinct *narratio* because there is no story to be told, but Tertullian employed one in the third chapter to describe how a good person could end up being accused falsely.[29] In *De resurrectione mortuorum* the *partitio* came before the *narratio,* while in *Aduersus Praxean* the placement is traditional.[30] The *narratio* of *De pudicitia* (1.6) occurs between the two parts of the *exordium.*[31] According to Sider, there is a *narratio* in *De praescriptione haereticorum* in the second half of the work where Tertullian's attention was turned to his prescriptive argument.[32] It has been noted earlier that *De corona* opens immediately with the *narratio.* In chapter 2 of the first book of *Aduersus Marcionem,* Tertullian developed a *narratio* by describing, in a historical narrative, how Marcion's heretical beliefs unfolded. Finally, in *Aduersus Valentinianos,* Sider states, the *narratio* runs from chapter 7 onward and that Tertullian used the *narratio* as his means of proof, as enunciated at 3.5.[33]

Narratio in *Aduersus Iudaeos*

In my doctoral dissertation and in some earlier published research into *Aduersus Iudaeos,* I put forward the idea that the *narratio* in this text occurs at 1.3b–7.[34] At the time I believed that this section of the pamphlet was con-

---

27. Cic., *Inu. rhet.* 1.19.27 (LCL 386.54).

28. See *Rhet. Her.* 1.8.12–1.9.16 (LCL 403.22–28); Quint., *Inst.* 4.2.1–132 (LCL 125.48–120).

29. Sider, *Ancient Rhetoric,* 23.   30. Ibid., 23–24, 27.

31. Ibid., 25.   32. Ibid., 26.

33. Ibid., 30. I am not convinced that the second half of Tert., *Adu. Val.,* is more than the *confirmatio* of a work that has no *narratio.* Quint., *Inst.* 4.2.79 (LCL 125.92), noted how closely related these two parts could be.

34. Geoffrey D. Dunn, "Tertullian and Rebekah: A Re-Reading of an 'Anti-Jewish' Argument in Early Christian Literature," *VChr* 52 (1998): 143; Dunn, "A Rhetorical Analysis of Tertullian's *Aduersus Iudaeos*" (Ph.D. diss., Australian Catholic University, 1999); Dunn, "*Pro Temporum Condicione:* Jews and Christians as God's People in Tertullian's *Adversus Iudaeos,*" in *Prayer and Spirituality in the Early Church,* vol. 2, ed. Pauline Allen, Wendy Mayer, and Lawrence Cross

cerned with outlining the history of God's promise to the Gentiles, which
was expressed in terms of the promise God made to Rebekah in Genesis
25:23. Since then it has been pointed out to me that this is a heavily argumentative passage, with positions being advanced in 1.4, 5, 6, and 7. In the light of
that I have suggested more recently that 1.3b–2.1a is the *partitio* and that there
is no *narratio* in *Aduersus Iudaeos*.[35]

Partitio

Partitio in Tertullian

The *partitio* or *diuisio* was that moment in a speech at which an orator indicated the question at issue and the approach he intended to take. According to *Ad Herennium* one attempted to achieve two things (in *De inuentione*
Cicero suggested that one attempted either one thing or the other): a discussion of where one agreed with one's opponent and where one disagreed, and
a *distributio*, which set forth the number of points to be discussed *(enumeratio)* and what they were *(expositio)*.[36] A century later Quintilian renamed the
partitio as *propositio*. For him the *partitio* was a characteristic of the structure
of a speech rather than any one part of a speech.[37] Although he considered
propositio to be part of *confirmatio* and maintained that it was not necessary
always to employ it (particularly when the question was obvious), Quintilian acknowledged the role of telling the audience the question about which
a decision needed to be made.[38] There could be several *propositiones* to be
decided or a *propositio* could consist of several parts and it could be framed
in a number of ways (supported or unsupported by a reason, seen from the
prosecutor's point of view or the defendant's, or expressed neutrally).[39] With
regard to what Quintilian defined as *partitio*,[40] his comments reveal that his

---

(Brisbane: Centre for Early Christian Studies, 1999), 317; and Dunn, "The Universal Spread of
Christianity as a Rhetorical Argument in Tertullian's *adversus Iudaeos*," *JECS* 8 (2000): 3.

35. Dunn, *Tertullian*, 65.

36. *Rhet. Her.* 1.10.17 (LCL 403.30); Cic., *Inu. rhet.* 1.22.31(LCL 386.62–64).

37. Quint., *Inst.* 3.9.2–3 (LCL 124.514); 4.4.1–4.5.28 (LCL 125.130–50).

38. Ibid., 4.4.2–4 (LCL 125.130–32); 4.5.22–24 (LCL 125.146–48). *Rhet. Her.* 2.18.28 (LCL 403.106–
8) mentions *propositio* as the first part of the complete argument in which one sets forth what
one intends to prove. This is the same as *expositio*, which the author had considered already as
part of *partitio* and which was the usual term he employed.

39. Quint., *Inst.* 4.4.5–8 (LCL 125.132–34).

40. Ibid., 4.5.1 (LCL 125.136): "Partitio est nostrarum aut aduersarii propositionum aut
utrarumque ordine collocata enumeratio."

understanding here was similar to what *Ad Herennium* had labeled *distributio:* the mentioning of the points that were to follow in the main body of the speech.[41]

It would seem to me that Sider has confused slightly how classical rhetoricians understood this part of a speech. His understanding of *propositio* is taken from Quintilian and his understanding of *partitio* from Cicero, without realizing that these are overlapping, not exclusive, terms:

The *propositio* attempted to set out the main point in dispute, or the essential point, or points, the speaker would make (*Inst.* iv.4.1–9); in the *partitio* the speaker either indicated how far he agreed with his opponent, and what remained in dispute, or set forth briefly the major divisions of his speech (*Inv.* i.22.31).[42]

As Sider sees it, a few pages later, *partitio* is the question and *propositio* is the position taken in relation to that question.[43] Such a clear-cut distinction is not found in the classical authors (nor, on close inspection, is it found in Sider's own statement quoted above).[44] As has been stated, Cicero used *partitio* to refer both to the stating of the question and the brief outline of the points to be made (the latter task having been named *distributio* in *Ad Herennium*), and Quintilian used *propositio* to mean the stating of the question and/or of the orator's position and limited *partitio* to the enumeration of the order of the points to be made.

Whatever varying terms the ancients and Sider used to refer to it, there was a segment in one's work where it was appropriate for an orator to state one or more of the following: the point at issue, one's position with regard to that point, and the topics one intended to discuss in relation to the point or one's position. I shall use the term *partitio* to refer to all three elements.

Sider makes it clear that Tertullian did use all these elements in his treatises. In *Apologeticum* he stated what the question was (2.5–7) and what his own position would be (2.13–14).[45] This is also present in *Aduersus Praxean.*[46] In *De pudicitia*, a *digressio* was placed between the *narratio* and the stating

41. Ibid., 4.5.9 (LCL 125.140).   42. Sider, *Ancient Rhetoric,* 21.
43. Ibid., 23.

44. Sider acknowledges on p. 21 that the *partitio* is more than just the question when he writes that it could also involve the setting forth of the major divisions of the speech, and he acknowledges that the *propositio* is more than one's position in regard to the question when he writes that the *propositio* could also set out the main point in dispute. His statement on p. 23 is therefore too simplistic.

45. Ibid., 21.
46. Ibid., 24.

of the question in 2.12–16.[47] According to Sider, in *De praescriptione haereticorum* there is a *propositio* in chapter 15 and a *partitio* in chapter 19.[48] Perhaps it would be more helpful and accurate to say that in chapter 15 there is a statement of Tertullian's own position[49] and a more general statement about the point at issue,[50] while in chapter 19 there is a statement about the topics he intended to cover in order to prove his position, which he restated.[51] *De carne Christi*, as has been noted, opens with the statement of the question and the topics with which he proposed to deal.[52] *Aduersus Marcionem* also has a statement of the disputed point and the position to be defended.[53]

Partitio in *Aduersus Iudaeos* (1.3b–2.1a)

All three elements of *partitio* as I have described them are found in *Aduersus Iudaeos*, although not all in one place. Since this pamphlet was designed as a response to and a rewriting of the earlier debate, the point at issue was the same for both.

I mentioned earlier that at 1.2, in the *exordium*, we find reference to the central point at stake in the earlier debate: could the Gentiles share in divine grace? The positive position the Christian debater took with regard to this question was then mentioned in 1.3a at the end of the *exordium*. In 1.3b–2.1a we find the *partitio* of this written text. Here the Christian position to be defended is drawn more sharply. Not only do the Gentiles share in divine grace, they have replaced the Jews as recipients of that grace.[54] The implicit question at the heart of the pamphlet then was whether or not the Gentiles had replaced the Jews as recipients of divine grace.

What of 1.3b–7, which once I had believed to be the *narratio* of the pamphlet? If the material found there is too argumentative to be a *narratio*, is

---

47. Ibid., 25.

48. Ibid., 26.

49. Tert., *De praescr.* 15.3 (CCSL 1.199): "Hunc igitur potissimum gradum obstruimus non admittendi eos ad ullam de scripturis disputationem."

50. Ibid., 15.4 (CCSL 1.199): "Si hae sunt illae uires eorum, uti eas habere possint, dispici debet cui competat possessio scripturarum, ne is admittatur ad eas cui nullo modo competit."

51. Ibid., 19.2 (CCSL 1.201): "Nam etsi non ita euaderet conlatio scripturarum ut utramque partem parem sisteret, ordo rerum desiderabat illud prius proponi quod nunc solum disputandum est: quibus competat fides ipsa, cuius sint scripturae, a quo et per quos et quando et quibus sit tradita disciplina qua fiunt christiani."

52. Sider, *Ancient Rhetoric*, 27.

53. Ibid., 30.

54. Tert., *Adu. Iud.* 1.8 (CCSL 2.1341): "Sic namque populus minor, id est posterior, populum maiorem superauit, dum gratiam diuinae dignationis consequitur, a qua Israël est repudiatus."

it also too argumentative to be a *partitio*? Quintilian noted that a *propositio* could be presented with an appended proof.[55] This is what I believe we find here in this section of *Aduersus Iudaeos*. It contains an explanation of how God's promise to Rebekah in Genesis 25:23 had been fulfilled, as well as references to Aaron and the golden calf from Exodus 32 and the sins of Jeroboam in 1 Kings 12:28; 14:15; 16:31. The promise to Rebekah was really a promise to the Gentiles, represented by her younger son, Tertullian argued. That promise had then been fulfilled by the failure of the Jews to live by God's grace and by the conversion of the Gentiles from their sinful ways.[56] The rest of this work was to be a more detailed exposition of how that promise was realized.

As it was God's promise rather than human reasoning that anchored the argument, it would seem that Tertullian was attempting to establish, right from the outset, an unassailable position, particularly for future debates with Jews. If his case derived from the word of God then how could the Jews argue against it? The promise to Rebekah was mentioned here because Tertullian was going to use it as the canon against which other scriptural passages had to be measured. The brief mention of Israel's failure was to be explored further in the *refutatio*. So rather than being an argument in itself, what we find in 1.3b–7 is a summary or, more accurately I think, the foundation of the arguments that are to follow in chapters 2 to 6. Having established in the opening chapter that such a promise was made to the Gentiles, its fulfillment would be the concern of the main body of proof. Presenting such material in one's *partitio* was an acceptable rhetorical practice.

Interestingly enough, in the usual conjectural forensic speech, the prosecution would argue that the defendant was responsible for some wrongdoing, and the defense would seek to establish that the defendant was not responsible. Tertullian wrote defending God, his client in this matter. There is a twist here, though. Rather than saying that God was innocent of having done something, Tertullian argued God's innocence because God had indeed done something, viz., made and kept a promise to the Gentiles through Rebekah. The Jewish charge against God—which, for the proselyte in the debate and for any Jew who would later argue on this topic, was not one to be held against God in any negative sense—was that God had done nothing to

---

55. Quint., *Inst.* 4.4.8 (LCL 125.134): "est ratione subiecta, ut Maiestatem minuit C. Cornelius; nam codicem tribunus plebis ipse pro contione legit."
56. Tert., *Adu. Iud.* 1.6–7 (CCSL 2.1340–41).

change having made a promise to the Jews alone. In one sense, then, it could be said that in fact the Jewish position was one of defending God, and the Christian position was one of alleging that God had done something, but that what God had done was admirable, not wrong. In other words, Tertullian could be said to be arguing that God was "guilty" of having done something good (replacing the Jews with the Gentiles in the divine disposition) or, conversely, innocent of the charge of having done nothing, because God had in fact done something by changing the divine disposition. All of this is a twist to the usual positions taken in a forensic debate. While there is interest in establishing whether a historical event (God's inclusion of the Gentiles as recipients of divine grace) had or had not taken place, the customary interest associated with a forensic focus in establishing guilt or innocence is not really present in *Aduersus Iudaeos*. This work is a debate in the rhetorical forensic style (concerned with the occurrence of events in the past) rather than a true forensic argument about someone's guilt or innocence with regard to that past event, hence its nature as a *controuersia*.

In 2.1a we find the final part of the *partitio*, the outlining of the points to be brought forward as proof to support the position taken with regard to the question at hand. It flows on immediately from Tertullian's statement of his own position in 1.8. Rather than spell out how many points he was going to make and what they were, he indicated merely that he was now about to "define by fixed limits the extent of the investigation itself."[57] This lack of detail is consistent with Quintilian's position of not having always to be too precise at the start of one's proof about what was going to follow.[58]

We may also note that in the course of the argumentation that follows, Tertullian provided occasional comment linking and summarizing sections.[59] As he moved from refutation to confirmation, he again repeated the point at issue, though this time in terms of a new law rather than a new people of grace,[60] and repeated his own position with regard to that question.[61] He was able to divide the issue into two: the first, about the cessation of the old law, had been treated already in the *refutatio,* and the second, about the com-

---

57. Ibid., 2.1 (CCSL 2.1341): "summam quaestionis ipsius certis lineis terminemus."

58. Quint., *Inst.* 4.5.4 (LCL 125.138).

59. Tert., *Adu. Iud.* 4.1 (CCSL 2.1347); 6.1 (2.1352).

60. Ibid., 6.2a (CCSL 2.1352–53): "ostendere et probare debeamus tam illam legem ueterem cessasse quam legem nouam promissam nunc operari."

61. Ibid., (CCSL 2.1352): "quoniam praedicatam nouam legem a prophetis paediximus [sic!]."

ing of the new law, would be treated next in the *confirmatio*. What may appear to be another refinement of the point at issue appears in 6.2b. In fact, it is the first of two questions that would shape the *confirmatio*: whether anyone was expecting a new law-giver. Cleverly, he identified this new law-giver as the one who suppressed the old law, sacrifice, circumcision, and Sabbath, the four points of the *refutatio* in 2.1b–6.1. The second question of the *confirmatio*, whether the promised law-giver had in fact come, was then raised and it would be central to the rest of the *confirmatio*.[62]

He drew together the two questions, which he had just mentioned, that would shape the *confirmatio* by once again repeating the point at issue and its relationship with the *refutatio*.[63] The first question of the *confirmatio*, about whether or not a new law-giver was promised, would not take long (7.2). The second question, about whether the promised law-giver had actually come, was divided into four: the time announced by the prophets for the coming of the Christ, whether he had come within that announced time, the prophecies about his coming, and the bringing of the new law.[64]

Thus, what may appear as a new point at issue in chapters 6 and 7 is the same as that found in the *partitio*, though spelled out in detail. Tertullian was providing some direction and refinement to this section of his essay, but this segment was but one element in establishing the overall point that grace now belonged to the Christians. The overall argument demanded that Tertullian establish two things: that the Jews had been disinherited and that the Gentiles had been installed because of their adherence to Christ, who was promised and who had come, as the new law-giver. This would be the subject matter of *refutatio* and *confirmatio*.

62. Ibid., 6.3 (CCSL 2.1353).

63. Ibid., 6.4 (CCSL 2.1353): "Et in primis definiendum est non potuisse cessare legem antiquam et prophetas, nisi uenisset is, qui per eandem legem et per eosdem prophetas uenturus adnuntiabatur."

64. Ibid., 7.1 (CCSL 2.1353): "Quod ipsum ut probari possit, etiam tempora sunt nobis requirenda, quando uenturum Christum prophetae adnuntiauerunt, ut, si intra ista tempora recognouerimus uenisse eum, sine dubio ipsum esse credamus, quem prophetae uenturum canebant, in quem nos, gentes scilicet, credituri adnuntiabamur, et cum constiterit uenisse, indubitate etiam legem nouam ab ipso datam esse credamus et testamentum nouum in ipso et per ipsum nobis dispositum non diffiteamur."

Refutatio

Refutatio in Tertullian

Variously named by the rhetorical writers as *confutatio, reprehensio,* or *refutatio,* it, together with its opposite *(confirmatio)* lay at the heart of forensic rhetoric.[65] The anonymous *Ad Herennium* presented the material on *confirmatio* and *confutatio* conjointly.[66] Although its author presumed that *confirmatio* would come first in a speech, he did recognize that, due to particular circumstances, the parts of a speech could be presented in a different order.[67] One advanced arguments in support of one's own position in the *confirmatio* and overturned the points made by one's opponent in the *refutatio.* The author recommended that one use the strongest arguments at the beginning and the end, and one's weaker arguments, bundled together to add to their impressiveness, in the middle.[68] Cicero observed that the purpose of *reprehensio* was to disprove or weaken the *confirmatio* of one's opponent and that the same method of reasoning for one applied also to the other.[69] In order to refute an argument one denied its assumptions, denied that the conclusions followed from the assumptions, demonstrated a fallacy in the line of reasoning, or came up with a stronger argument.[70] Attacking one argument at a time had the effect of demolishing the whole of one's opponent's arguments.[71] He too was aware that one could not always follow the theoretical order for the parts of a speech and that it was sometimes necessary to modify it depending upon requirements.[72] Quintilian made the point that in *refutatio* one had to make sure that one paid attention to the points that had been raised in one's opponent's *confirmatio* and then deny them, justify them, or trivialize them.[73]

Sider stated that Tertullian did not follow any particular sequence regarding confirmation and refutation, often making them inseparable.[74] In four works Sider notes that the *refutatio* follows the *confirmatio.* In *De resurrectio-*

---

65. *Rhet. Her.* 1.10.18 (LCL 403.32): "Nam cum adiumenta nostra exposuerimus contrariaque dissoluerimus, absolute nimirum munus oratorium confecerimus."
66. Ibid., 2.1.2–2.2.2 (LCL 403.60–62); 3.10.18 (LCL 403.188).
67. Ibid., 3.9.17–3.10.18 (LCL 403.186–88).   68. Ibid., 3.10.18 (LCL 304.188).
69. Cic., *Inu. rhet.* 1.42.78 (LCL 386.122).   70. Ibid., 1.42.79 (LCL 386.124).
71. Cic., *Part. or.* 12.44 (LCL 349.344).
72. Ibid., 5.15 (LCL 349.322); Cic., *De or.* 2.19.77–83 (LCL 348.256–258).
73. Quint., *Inst.* 5.13.4–10 (LCL 125.312–316).
74. Sider, *Ancient Rhetoric,* 30–31.

ne mortuorum, he proposes a parallel between the sequential exposition of Scripture and of rhetorical structure, in that Tertullian's arguments from the prophets and the gospels form the *confirmatio* (29–39) while the arguments from the Pauline epistles form the *refutatio* (40–51).[75] The same parallel is seen to operate in *De monogamia.*[76] A similar sequence of rhetorical structure, though without the scriptural parallel, is present in *De baptismo.*[77] Finally, in *De carne Christi,* Tertullian began his proof by refuting the three heresies he had mentioned in his introduction (2–16), before presenting his positive arguments for the humanity of Christ (17–21)—an inversion of the usual pattern.[78]

Refutatio in *Aduersus Iudaeos* (2.1b–6.1)

Proof in *Aduersus Iudaeos* begins with *refutatio* rather than *confirmatio.* Given that Tertullian planned this work to be an idealized version of the Christian input in an earlier debate, it is not surprising that the beginning of the body of the work should take the form of a rejoinder. Tertullian wrote as though he were speaking second in a debate, replying to the points that had been made by the proselyte Jew in that previous encounter, as though those same points, without alteration, would be made again in some imaginary future encounter. In that sense it makes little difference whether that debate was real or a literary concoction (even though I accept that it was real), because the Jewish position, for the sake of this work, was taken as a given. Part of the success of Tertullian's rhetorical strategy would depend on the extent to which the Jewish arguments were static and were believed by his Christian readers to be so.

The *refutatio* runs through 2.1b–6.1. In it Tertullian sought to counter the Jewish position that God's grace, call, or salvation had been given to the Jews alone. Four Jewish proofs for their position were then examined in order to demonstrate that their conclusions did not follow from the evidence they produced and that there were arguments from Scripture that they ignored. The four proofs were based on the law (2.1b–10a), circumcision (2.10b–3.6), the Sabbath (4.1–11), and sacrifices (5.1–7).[79] In each case Tertullian stated the Jewish position (2.1, 10; 3.1 [twice]; 4.1, 7; 5.3),[80] questioned it, and attempt-

75. Ibid., 31.
76. Ibid., 32.
77. Ibid., 32–33.
78. Ibid., 33.
79. See Dunn, "Pro Temporum Condicione," 321–22.
80. In Tert., *Adu. Iud.* 5.3 (CCSL 2.1350), though, it seems, on the basis of his use of *inueni-*

ed to refute it by pointing out inconsistencies derived from a comparison with other pieces of scriptural evidence, particularly the Pentateuch and the prophets. He challenged his Jewish opponents to respond to his refutation (2.10–11; 4.6), confident that they could not.

There are comments throughout that reveal Tertullian's structural thoughts about his four points. Having just completed his argument that the law existed prior to Moses, Tertullian made mention of both the Sabbath and circumcision at 2.10b, and then proceeded to discuss circumcision and how people had been graced by God, before and after Abraham, without being circumcised. Following this was the discussion about the Sabbath.

At 3.7–13 he linked the two counterarguments already presented (law and circumcision) to consider the fact that a new law and a new circumcision had been promised in Scripture for a new people by God. I have the sense that if Tertullian were to have submitted this work to the modern publishing process his editor would have asked for some revision at this point. The promise of a new law could have been inserted after 2.10 as part of the treatment on the law, for, although the section on the promise of a new Sabbath follows on immediately from 3.13 (4.1–5), that on the promise of a new sacrifice (5.1–3a) is separated. In other words, some revision could have seen the promises of replacement being treated in each of its four respective sections rather than having some of them grouped together and some of them not.

Only the discussion in chapter 5 about sacrifices does not seem to be prefigured in any of Tertullian's comments earlier in the *refutatio*, unless one counts the mention of Abel, who offered God sacrifices, was uncircumcised, and did not observe the Sabbath, as such a prefiguring.[81]

Although there are some other arguments to disprove the Jewish assertions about their own uniqueness and the Christians' lack of regard for their covenant with God, the one about the promise of a replacement law, circumcision, Sabbath, and sacrifices seems to be the central one. At the end of the *refutatio* Tertullian summarized what he had achieved, and his thoughts concern only this one point. They also reveal that the fourfold treatment did indeed provide the structure for these chapters:

---

mus, that he had to create a Jewish position he could then attack rather than repeat one he had heard from them.

81. Ibid., 2.12 (CCSL 2.1343).

Igitur cum manifestum sit et sabbatum temporale ostensum et sabbatum aeternum praedictum, circumcisionem quoque carnalem praedictam et circumcisionem spiritalem praeindicatam, legem quoque temporalem et legem aeternalem denuntiatam, sacrificia carnalia et sacrificia spiritalia praeostensa.[82]

What is interesting to observe is that this summary does not respect the order in which the material had been presented in the *refutatio*. Whether Tertullian did that deliberately in an effort not to appear too polished or whether it was accidental is unclear.

Confirmatio

Confirmatio in Tertullian

Much of what the rhetoricians wrote about *refutatio* was in the context of describing *confirmatio*. Here one presented the positive arguments that would persuade an audience to believe the case one was making. In presenting one's arguments Cicero suggested that the prosecutor would follow a chronological order of events while the defense had to take into account the mood of the audience and what the prosecution had argued already.[83] Quintilian's advice was not to present one's points in descending order from strongest to weakest.[84] We need not repeat what Sider said about how Tertullian presented his main body of proof.

Confirmatio in Aduersus Iudaeos (6.2–14.10)

The *confirmatio* of *Aduersus Iudaeos* commences at 6.2 with the repetition of the work's overall *partitio*—to prove that the old law had ceased, the promise of which he had investigated in the *refutatio*, and that the promised new law had come, which would occupy the *confirmatio*.

ostendere et probare debeamus tam illam legem ueterem cessasse quam legem nouam promissam nunc operari.[85]

---

82. Ibid., 6.1 (CCSL 2.1352): "It is clear that both a temporal sabbath has been shown and an eternal sabbath has been foretold. A circumcision of the flesh has been foretold and a circumcision of the spirit foretold beforehand. A temporal law and an eternal law have been announced. Carnal sacrifices and spiritual sacrifices have been foreshown."

83. Cic., *Part. or.* 4.14–5.15 (LCL 349.320–22).

84. Quint., *Inst.* 5.12.14 (LCL 125.304).

85. Tert., *Adu. Iud.* 6.2 (CCSL 2.1352–53): "it is incumbent upon us to show and prove that, as much as that old law has ceased, so too the promised new law now applies."

As has been noted, this repetition is itself repeated at the end of the chapter:

Et in primis definiendum est non potuisse cessare legem antiquam et prophetas, nisi uenisset is, qui per eandem legem et per eosdem prophetas uenturus adnuntiaba-tur.[86]

This sentence mentions the three major points of the pamphlet that Ter-tullian advocated: that the old law would come to an end, that there was the promise of a new law-giver, and that the new law-giver had come already. The first point was the *refutatio,* the second point was dealt with in summary fashion (7.2), and the third point was the heart of the *confirmatio.* This is a fur-ther explanation for why *refutatio* comes before *confirmatio* in this text, since Tertullian was following a chronological framework. The Jews believed that their covenant with God endured, so the first thing to do was to show that the old would cease before showing that the new one had started.

As I noted in the section on *partitio,* 6.2–7.1 is an introduction to the *confir-matio* and contains the two questions that would shape the unfolding argu-ment: whether there was a promise for the Christ to come,[87] and whether the Christ had indeed come.[88]

The *confirmatio* is at the very heart of the pamphlet, for the *refutatio* was dependent upon it. Tertullian stated this in 6.4. It would make no sense to argue that the old law had been replaced by the new if the new had not yet come. The coming of the new was proof that the promise that the old would cease had been fulfilled. Thus, the ending of the old law was not a question that Tertullian felt the need to answer. It was enough to prove that it had been promised, and it would be enough to prove that the new law had come. The logical and necessary conclusion would be therefore that the old law had indeed ceased.[89]

The second question is restated in 7.1[90] and then Tertullian provided an *ex-positio* or listing of the four topics he would cover in the *confirmatio* to prove

86. Ibid., 6.4 (CCSL 2.1353): "It especially ought to be understood that the ancient law and the prophets could not cease unless the one had come whose coming was announced through the same law and the same prophets."

87. Ibid., 6.2b (CCSL 2.1353): "Et quidem primum quaerendum, an expectetur nouae legis lator."

88. Ibid., 6.3 (CCSL 2.1353): "Nam etiam hic nouae legis lator . . . quaerendum, an iam ue-nerit necne."

89. Dunn, "The Universal Spread of Christianity," 5.

90. Tert., *Adu. Iud.* 7.1 (CCSL 2.1353): "Igitur in isto gradum conseramus, an qui uenturus Christus adnuntiabatur iam uenerit an uenturus adhuc speretur."

that the promised Christ had come: i) the times announced by the prophets
for the Christ's coming; ii) a demonstration that he had come within that
time; iii) the general prophetic theme of the coming of the Christ; and iv)
the connection between the coming of the Christ and the giving of the new
law:

Quod ipsum ut probari possit, etiam tempora sunt nobis requirenda, quando uenturum Christum prophetae adnuntiauerunt, ut, si intra ista tempora recognouerimus
uenisse eum, sine dubio ipsum esse credamus, quem prophetae uenturum canebant
. . . et cum constiterit uenisse, indubitate etiam legem nouam ab ipso datam esse credamus et testamentum nouum in ipso.[91]

The third topic differs from the first in that, whereas the first was concerned with the issue of time alone, the third would be concerned with more
general issues about the coming of the Christ. By linking the third topic to
the second by the relative pronoun, it could be suggested that Tertullian was
proposing to examine those two topics together, even though he would actually examine the first two topics together. It has to be conceded that this third
topic was not as clearly enunciated as a separate topic in the proof as were
the others.

In terms of the structure of the *confirmatio,* Tertullian proceeded to deal
with the four topics of the second question. The first argument, though, had
not been announced as one of those four topics; it appears without warning.
It has an almost *digressio*-like quality. Tertullian advocated that the Christ obviously had come because belief in his name had spread throughout the entire world (7.3–8.1a).[92] Again, in further revisions to his work one might have
expected that he would not have considered the fulfillment of the promise
of the coming of the Christ (proven through the universal spread of Christianity) in a very brief section about the very existence of the promise itself.
What he presented here anticipated what we are to find in later chapters of

91. Ibid.: "Now in order that the issue itself may be proved, the timing, in which the prophets have announced that the Christ was destined to come, ought to be investigated by us. This
is in order that, if we recognize him to have come during those times of your making, we may
without doubt believe him to be the same one whom the prophets prophesied would come . . .
And when it has been agreed that he has come, we may believe without a doubt also that the
new law has been given by him."

92. I have argued elsewhere that this digression is the result of Tertullian's use of Isaiah 45:1
as the only piece of evidence in his brief treatment of the first question, about whether a Christ
was promised, in 7.2. The passage gave him the opportunity to write on the topic of the universal spread of Christianity as proof that such a Christ was promised. See Dunn, "The Universal
Spread of Christianity," 7–8.

the pamphlet when he wrote about subsequent events (which is where, in fact, we do find a reappearance of this idea of the universal spread of Christianity).

The first topic of 7.1 (about the predictions of time) was taken up in 8.1b in terms of three things: the prophesied time when the Christ would be born, the time when he would suffer, and the time when Jerusalem would fall.[93] The prophecy of Daniel 9:21–27 was presented as the basis of those predictions (8.3–8). The second topic of 7.1 (about the fulfillment of the prophecies of time) follows. This was then dealt with in 8.9–15a, with regard to the time frame for the birth of the Christ, and 8.15b–18, with regard to the time of the passion of the Christ and the fall of Jerusalem.

Interestingly, having introduced the first of the four topics of the second question of the *confirmatio* in 8.1b about the prophecies of the time of the Christ, in 8.2 Tertullian restated his outline for the *confirmatio,* the original outline being in 7.1. It does seem a little sloppy that there is so much comment and outlining before the real proof gets under way. This is even more so since in 8.2 there is a revision of that original outline in 7.1, for now, instead of four topics, there are only three:

> Venturi itaque Christi ducis sunt tempora requirenda, quae inuestigabimus in Danielo; quibus computatis probabimus uenisse eum iam et ex temporibus praescriptis et ex signis competentibus et ex operationibus eius, quae proba<<bi>>mus et ex consequentibus, quae post aduentum eius futura adnuntiabantur, uti iam adimpleta omnia praecepta credamus.[94]

The new first topic includes the first two topics of 7.1. The second topic, about other matters, particularly those of action (signs and operations), is equivalent to the third general topic of 7.1. The last topic is no longer the connection between the coming of the Christ and the giving of the new law, but the events that unfolded as a consequence of his coming. They seem also to be expressed in more familiar rhetorical terms.

The third topic of 7.1 (the second of 8.2) about all the other matters prophe-

93. Tert., *Adu. Iud.* 8.1b (CCSL 2.1356): "Itaque requirenda tempora praedicta et futurae natiuitatis Christi et passionis eius et exterminii ciuitatis Hierusalem, id est uastationis eius."

94. Ibid., 8.2 (CCSL 2.1356–57): "And thus the times of the future coming of the Christ, the ruler, which we shall seek out in Daniel, must be considered. By having calculated these times we shall prove that he has come. Besides the ground of the fixed times, we will prove these things from relevant signs and from his activities, and from subsequent events that were announced as happening after his coming, in order that we may believe that everything anticipated now has been fulfilled."

sied about the coming of the Christ besides that of time, begins in detail from 9.1. As the first two topics had been discussed in relation to three issues—the birth of the Christ, the passion of the Christ, and the fall of Jerusalem—so too would the third topic be related to those same three issues: general prophecies about the birth of the Christ (9.1–31), general prophecies about the passion of the Christ (10.1–19a), and general prophecies about the fall of Jerusalem (10.19b–11.9; 13.8–29). In 13.1 we find support for Tertullian's having a twofold distinction in his mind: the prophecies and their fulfillment with respect to time (the birth and death of the Christ and the destruction of Jerusalem), and the prophecies and their fulfillment with respect to other themes (again relating to the birth and death of the Christ and the destruction of Jerusalem).[95]

Nevertheless, there are some problems with such a structure. The relation between the third topic of 7.1 and what unfolds from chapter 9 onward would have been clearer if Tertullian had indicated at the beginning of the latter chapter that he was intending to examine all the other matters about the prophecies of the coming of the Christ, with the exception of the already-dealt-with issue of time, as well as the passion of the Christ and the fall of Jerusalem. That he wrote only: "Incipiamus igitur probare natiuitatem Christi a prophetis esse nuntiatam"[96] seems to contradict his statement in 7.2 that establishing that there were prophecies about the coming of the Christ would not be necessary, unless one understands him to mean in 9.1 not that he intended now to prove that there were such prophecies but that he intended now to examine the content of those prophecies, which is what he went on to do. The use of "incipiamus igitur" would give some credence to a belief that there is something of a beginning of a new topic at this point.[97]

Further, as has been noted, 7.1 is not unambiguously explicit that the *confirmatio* would be divided into prophecies about the timing of the Christ and prophecies about other characteristics or qualities of the Christ, which is the way the text now divides, although such an intended structure may be discerned at least implicitly in 7.1.

---

95. Tränkle, *Tertullian, "Adversus Iudaeos,"* xlv, writes that it was "die Überraschung groß" to find 13.1 where it is. He suggests also that it belonged more appropriately at the beginning of ch. 9: "Dabei bildet das Zitat Mich. 5,1 in der Fassung, wie es bei Matth. 2,6 erscheint, den Ausgangspunkt, während in Kapitel 9,1 Es. 7, 13ff. dazu herangezogen war."

96. Tert., *Adu. Iud.* 9.1 (CCSL 2.1364): "Therefore, let us begin to prove that the birth of the Christ was announced by the prophets."

97. See Dunn, *Tertullian*, 84, where I am surprised, now that I look at my translation, that 9.1 does not start a new paragraph.

One could suggest that 10.1 reads as though it ought to belong to the *refutatio* ("De exitu plane passionis eius ambigitis, negantes passionem crucis in Christum praedicatam").[98] However, there is a difference between the arguments in the *refutatio* and the one here. In the *refutatio* Tertullian sought to counter Jewish arguments. Here he was responding to a Jewish *refutatio* of a Christian argument—that the Son of God had died upon a cross. It belongs to the *confirmatio* because Tertullian had, on the whole, excluded arguments about the Christ from the *refutatio* (there are the briefest of references at 3.8 and 4.4). It is only in the *confirmatio* that any prophecies were linked with Jesus as the Christ who was to come.

Another problem of even more concern is the seeming failure to deal with the fourth topic of 7.1, about the connection between the coming of the Christ and the giving of the new law. One could suggest that the use of "indubitate" at 7.1 made the second follow the first as a logical necessity and that Tertullian did not have to concern himself with it any further. Given how much he had written about the old law in the *refutatio* and had mentioned the new law at 6.2a, 2b, and 3, one would expect at least some further reference to this point or some acknowledgment that the circle had been closed. Can 9.18 be such a reference? Here Tertullian argued that the only sword with which Jesus was armed was the sword of the word of God, a sword with two edges: one the old law and the other the new. A little later he identified Jesus with Joshua linguistically (9.21) and contrasted Moses, the figure of the old law, with Joshua, the figure of the new law of grace: "idque non per Moysen, id est legis disciplinam, sed per Iesum, id est per nouae legis gratiam."[99] However, if this be the case, its location, in the middle of the general prophecies about the birth of the Christ seems rather strange, hardly the culminating point of the whole pamphlet. I think we have to conclude that this fourth topic makes no appearance in the actual body of proof. In a revision of the work one would expect either to see it make its appearance as its culmination, or to find its announcement in 7.1 removed. Indeed, the fact that it makes no appearance at 8.2 suggests that Tertullian had already deleted it in the revisions he was making as he wrote.

---

98. Tertullian, *Adu. Iud.* 10.1 (CCSL 2.1374): "Certainly you are disputing the issue of his suffering, denying that the passion of the cross was prophesied of the Christ."

99. Ibid., 9.22 (CCSL 2.1371): "and because this was going to be effected not through Moses—that is, not through the teaching of the law—but through Jesus, through the new law of grace."

In chapters 9 and 10 not only are there prophecies about the signs and operations of the Christ (excluding time), in these chapters Tertullian examined also the fulfillment of these prophecies. Thus, while considering the general prophecies about the coming of the Christ (9.1–31), he dealt with the ways in which they had been realized in Jesus: in 9.3 we find him mentioning Jesus as Emmanuel; in 9.8 he discussed the virgin birth; and in 9.10 the visit of the magi was proof of the fulfillment of the prophecy about the spoils of Damascus. All of these are arranged under several common rhetorical *topoi* such as name, family, character, and occupation. While considering the general prophecies about the death of the Christ (10.1–19a), he dealt with the fulfillment of those prophecies: in 10.4 with Jesus dying unjustly and on behalf of others; in 10.6 with Jesus dying at the hands of his brethren; and in 10.11 with Jesus dying on the tree. It would be natural to expect the general prophecies about the fall of Jerusalem to be treated the same way and this is what is found. We find a *praemunitio* in 10.1–5 where Tertullian considered the anticipated Jewish objection that Jesus was cursed by God because he was crucified.

Yet, a major structural problem of *Aduersus Iudaeos* occurs in these last few chapters. The discussion of the general prophecies about the fall of Jerusalem (10.19b–11.9 and 13.8–29), which is the third topic of 8.2, is split and for no immediately apparent reason. The material in the first half of chapter 11 is largely an extract from Ezekiel, and the section is concerned exclusively with prophecies about the fall. The argument in chapter 13 concerns how, given that Jerusalem had been sacked and the people removed from Judaea, the prophecies about the coming of the Christ could be fulfilled by no one else in the future. Why the material in 11.10–13.7 is between these two segments is not apparent.

The material in 11.10a seems to indicate that Tertullian had completed the task of the *confirmatio* and was now summarizing the argument. Indeed, 11.10b–11a is a repeat of what is found in 8.15. In the summary he mentioned how Christ, in his coming and his passion, had fulfilled all prophecies at the right time and that therefore the old law had ceased. However, Tertullian forgot to examine the fulfillment of the general prophecies about the fall of Jerusalem, even though its fall is mentioned in 11.11b. It is understandable that an author would occasionally like to summarize the results of their efforts before moving to a new section, but where this one occurs seems odd for the prophecies referred to in 11.10 were not those just repeated from Ezekiel and

Exodus in chapter 11 but those that had been presented in chapters 9 and 10. Perhaps 11.10–11a would have been better coming after 10.19a.

In 11.11b–12 Tertullian seems to return to the topic at hand—the fulfillment of those events that were prophesied to take place after the Christ had been on earth. One would expect him to have examined the fulfillment of the prophecies about the fall of Jerusalem, yet he did not. Instead he turned his attention to other events that were to take place in the aftermath of the coming of the Christ, such as the conversion of the Gentiles (12.1–2) and the impossibility that any other Christ could be born in Bethlehem, since no Jewish person was allowed to live there any more (13.1–7). This latter issue naturally was related to the fall of Jerusalem (13.4b), yet only after that did he return to the significance of the fulfillment of the prophecy about the fall of Jerusalem (13.8–29). Finally, he considered the last example of what was to follow after the coming of the Christ—the second coming of the Christ (14.1–10). These other matters had not been announced specifically any earlier in the pamphlet, although they do all fall under the third topic of 8.2. While the second coming was not yet a fulfilled event, the fact that there were two distinct comings meant that what had happened in Jesus was obviously related to the first coming, the one in humility.

This whole section 11.10–13.7 seems oddly placed and its relationship with the section that finished in 11.9 somewhat forced. The thoughts are jumbled and the material is in desperate need of a thorough editing. It needs to be re-ordered, to streamline it and polish the final presentation. It is as though Tertullian's train of thought has been interrupted by new ideas, which are then written down immediately without any regard for what this did to the plan he had outlined. Instead of considering only the fall of Jerusalem Tertullian expanded the number of examples used to illustrate the section on the events that were to take place after the coming of the Christ, but expanded them in such a way as to interrupt what he was saying about the fall.

Indeed, at first glance, even the section 13.11–23 does not seem to be connected with the material about the events that had taken place after the coming of the Christ. What we find in 13.11–23 seems to be a revisiting of the prophecies about the death of the Christ, particularly the symbolism of the cross, which was presented already in chapter 10. However, Tertullian only mentioned the cross again in order to demonstrate that following the death of the Christ would come the destruction of Jerusalem (13.10). The focus this time supposedly was on what followed his death, not the death itself, although admittedly this is not always clear. From 13.24 Tertullian drew together the points he was making about the events that had taken place after the coming of the Christ. The Jews were to suffer, while the Gentiles would inherit redemption (13.24). All of it was associated with the fact that Jerusalem and Judaea were no more and that therefore the Christ must have come already (13.25–29).

A second major structural problem, perhaps a more significant one, is to be found within these last few chapters: 11.11b–12.2a is repeated almost verbatim in 14.11–12a. It would appear that one of these two sections is an interpolation. There are arguments in support of each section being the interpolation. As has been noted above, 11.11b–12.2a is part of a section (11.10–13.7) that interrupts the flow of the presentation about the general prophecies of the fall of Jerusalem (11.1–9) and the fulfillment of those prophecies (13.8–29). As will be noted below, 14.11–14 lacks a number of characteristics of a *peroratio*. Neither passage appears to be entirely convincing in its present location.

As I have argued elsewhere and shall repeat below, I am more inclined to regard 14.11–12a as the interpolation.[100] There are several reasons why I would retain 11.11b–12.2a despite the difficulties it presents. First, even if one removed 11.11b–12.2a, that would still leave 11.10–11a and 12.2b–13.7 interrupting the material on the fall of Jerusalem. Yet 11.11b introduces what follows in 12.1–14.10 quite appropriately.[101] Perhaps one could explain the shift in direction that occurs after 11.10 as the result of Tertullian's having realized that the fall of Jerusalem was not the only event that was predicted to occur after the coming of the Christ, and that he needed to broaden the examples he was providing for the third topic announced in 8.2. If I were Tertullian's editor, I would suggest to him that 10.19b–11.9 would be better relocated to between 13.7 and 13.8, thereby keeping prophecies about the fall of Jerusalem together with his comments about the fulfillment of those prophecies. From the perspective of a rhetorical structure, the material at 10.19b–14.10 reads like a draft. We have access to something of the way Tertullian's thought processes seem to have worked. He had a plan in mind but in the course of writing, as new ideas occurred to him, he would interrupt himself and follow this new path, hope-

---

100. Dunn, "The Universal Spread of Christianity," 15–18. Here I can point to an undetected printing error on the last line of p. 15, which should read 12.2a instead of 12.12a.

101. Tertullian, *Adu. Iud.* 11.11b (CCSL 2.1383): "quae post Christum futura praecanebantur, quae scripta proferimus, ut ex hoc quoque paria iam in scripturis diuinis negari non possint, ut adimpleta cognoscantur."

fully to return to his original point at some later stage. So 11.11b–12.2a, while somewhat messy in terms of the unfolding structure of the work, is explicable in terms of that structure, whereas, as we shall soon see, 14.11–14 is not.

This explanation indeed makes some sense of these latter chapters of *Aduersus Iudaeos*. Structural consistency and integrity certainly is the aim of all essay writers, yet those who engage in the discipline of writing are very much aware that this does not happen always in the first attempt.

Some may argue that the case for discerning a rhetorical structure in *Aduersus Iudaeos* is considerably weakened by the unfinished nature of the work. This is a position I would not accept. Even within a draft one may detect the structure at which the author is aiming. The fact that the structure is not perfect does not mean that it is not there in some fashion. Further revision would have seen 6.2–7.1 rewritten in terms of the topics that were later announced in 8.2 and would have seen a reordering of the material that dealt with the third topic of 8.2 about subsequent events that incorporated the discussion on the fall of Jerusalem in a more coherent manner. However, we can still see what the structural intention was.

Peroratio

Peroratio in Tertullian

At the end of one's speech comes a conclusion *(peroratio* or *conclusio)*, in which an orator brings the presentation to an end and urges the audience to render a favorable decision. *Ad Herennium* stated that the *conclusio* consisted of three parts: a summary *(enumeratio)*, amplification *(amplificatio)*, and an emotional appeal for pity *(commiseratio)*.[102] Cicero named the three parts *enumeratio, indignatio* (a rousing of indignation), and *conquestio* (a rousing of sympathy or pity).[103] Later he would name only two divisions: *amplificatio* and *enumeratio*.[104] Quintilian had a simple division of the *peroratio*: it may deal with the facts of a case or some emotional aspect of a case.[105] In a forensic speech the conclusion was the final opportunity to drive home one's point in securing a conviction or acquittal and was a very important part of one's overall speech.

Sider suggests that Tertullian's proof, the main body of a treatise, was often framed by two smaller sections: the premunition, in which minor issues

---

102. *Rhet. Her.* 2.30.47 (LCL 403.144–46). 103. Cic., *Inu. rhet.* 1.52.98 (LCL 386.146–148).
104. Cic., *Part. or.* 15.22 (LCL 349.328). 105. Quint., *Inst.* 6.1.1 (LCL 125.382).

could be addressed or fundamental objections removed, and the amplification, which extended the proof by considering remaining objections.[106] In some works, like *Apologeticum, De monogamia, De resurrectione mortuorum,* and *Aduersus Praxean,* Sider contends that balance and symmetry were achieved through the exploration of the same or similar themes in both sections.[107] Reservations have been expressed already about seeing the *praemunitio* as an identifiable part of rhetorical structure. As with *amplificatio,* it was not so much a part of the structure of a speech for Latin rhetoricians as it was a tool to be employed in a speech.

With regard to the *conclusio* in particular, Sider notes that Tertullian was more often engaged in emotional climax than any summary of argument.[108] He mentions *De resurrectione mortuorum* and *De carne Christi* as contrasting examples. Barnes has suggested that in *Scorpiace* Tertullian presented a *peroratio* that served not only to draw that treatise to a conclusion but to continue the arguments found in earlier chapters.[109]

Peroratio in *Aduersus Iudaeos* (14.11–14)

In 14.11 is the briefest of summaries or, more accurately, a reminder of the *confirmatio:* having earlier investigated matters relating to Christ himself, proving that he was the one who fulfilled the prophecies of Scripture, what was just covered looked at matters in the time after Christ to see how they fulfilled what had been prophesied about them. It parallels 11.11b–12. If it was written by Tertullian himself, then he has repeated himself to a great extent. Perhaps, one could argue, this is an indication that he had begun to revise his initial draft and realized that the material at the end of chapter 11 would be better located after 14.10, but then never got around to removing it from the place of its initial appearance. My argument, which I shall develop in the appropriate place in the next chapter, is that 14.11–14 is an interpolation because it contains an interpretation of Psalm 2 that Tertullian himself did not make.

What this means is that there is no *peroratio* in *Aduersus Iudaeos.* This fact may explain why someone else decided to add some material, in an effort to provide a conclusion to the pamphlet. My understanding would be not that Tertullian failed to offer a rhetorically essential component because he was

---

106. Sider, *Ancient Rhetoric,* 34–38.   107. Ibid., 38.
108. Ibid., 38.
109. Timothy D. Barnes, "Tertullian's *Scorpiace,*" *JTS* n.s. 20 (1969): 110. See Dunn, *Tertullian,* 106.

not interested in utilizing rhetoric in writing this work, but that his task was abandoned before it was completed.

Summary of Rhetorical Structure

Most of *Aduersus Iudaeos* can be found to adhere to the general tenets of classical rhetorical theory in terms of structure, even though it remains only a draft document. The following chart illustrates the structure as I discern it.

Exordium   1.1–3a

Partitio   1.3b–2.1a

Refutatio   2.1b–6.1
—law   2.1b–10a
—circumcision   2.10b–3.6
—(promise of new law and new circumcision)   3.7–13
—Sabbath   4.1–11
—sacrifices   5.1–7
—conclusion   6.1

Confirmatio   6.2–14.10
—introduction (the two questions and the four topics of
   the second question)   6.2–7.1
—first question   7.2
—digression   7.3–8.1a
—second question   8.1b–14.10
   * first and second topics of 7.1 announced   8.1b
—(restatement of the second question in three new topics)   8.2
   * first topic of 7.1—prophecy about time (first topic of 8.2)
      —prophecy in Daniel 9   8.3–6
      —comments on time frame   8.7–8
   * second topic of 7.1—fulfillment of prophecy about time (first
      topic of 8.2)
      —coming of the Christ   8.9–15a
      —passion of the Christ/destruction of Jerusalem   8.15b–18
   * third topic of 7.1—general prophecies and their fulfillment
      (second topic of 8.2)
      —coming of the Christ   9.1–31
         introduction   9.1a

    topos of name   9.1b–3, 20b–25

    topos of achievements   9.4–6, 10–20a

    signs associated with birth   9.7–9

    topos of family   9.26–27

    topos of character/nature   9.28

    topos of occupation   9.29–31

  —passion of the Christ   10.1–19a

    praemunitio   10.1–5

    topos of manner   10.6–14a

    other aspects of his death   10.14b–19a

* third topic of 8.2—subsequent events

  —prophecy about fall of Jerusalem   10.19b–11.9

  —summary of third topic   11.10–11a

  —introduction to other subsequent events   11.11b–12

  —conversion of the Gentiles   12.1–2

  —loss of Bethlehem as birth place for the Christ   13.1–7

  —fulfillment of prophecy about fall of Jerusalem   13.8–29

  —the second coming of the Christ   14.1–10

Peroratio/ Interpolation   14.11–14

Comparison with Other Structural Arrangements of *Aduersus Iudaeos*

In order to demonstrate the importance of classical rhetoric to an understanding of this pamphlet, we can contrast the structure proposed above, which presents a clear understanding of the strategies and thinking involved in Tertullian's composition, with the structures that have been proposed by other scholars who have not been as interested in this influence. Some have simply noted the sequence of individual elements to be found in a reading of the text without trying to establish any connections between parts or an explanation for the sequence other than determining what might or might not be authentically Tertullian's. Others have been interested more in the relationship between passages of *Aduersus Iudaeos* and *Aduersus Marcionem* and have not been concerned with whether those parallel parts in *Aduersus Iudaeos* really fit within the context of that work itself. Such an extended contrast should highlight the significance of the rhetorical structural understanding of this controversial polemic.

While not interested in determining an overall structure for *Aduersus Iudae-os*, Kroymann did provide further comment about the work's integrity in his notes in the 1954 CCSL edition. The comments have a bearing on what structure he might have found within it. He suggested that 11.10–12.2 belong more appropriately right after 8.18 because it seemed to be an interpolation in its present location.[110] He also noted that the same material is repeated in two places (11.11b–12.2 and 14.11–12), as well as in *Aduersus Marcionem*.[111] On the basis of "sicuti iam praelocuti sumus" in 14.12, Kroymann believed *Aduersus Marcionem* to be the earlier material from which 14.11–14 was drawn, even though not by Tertullian himself.[112] Of the repeated material in *Aduersus Iudaeos*, that in chapter 11 is briefer than chapter 14.[113] The one in chapter 14 seemed to Kroymann to be an even worse imitation of the material in *Aduersus Marcionem* because of a number of inaccuracies, about which he said little.[114] His conclusion is clear: these two interpolations were not by Tertullian.[115]

A comparison between the three passages (*Adu. Iud.* 11.11–12.1; 14.11–12; and *Adu. Marc.* 3.20.1–4) does reveal a number of mistakes or inaccuracies, particularly in chapter 14. While all three passages refer to "quae post Christum futura,"[116] *Aduersus Marcionem* continues: "Nec <haec> enim dispositio expuncta inueniretur, si non ille uenisset, post quem habebat euenire."[117] This is similar to *Adu. Iud.* 11.12, although the latter is more awkward and less polished: "Ne<c haec enim expuncta inuenirentur>, nisi ille uenisset, post quem habebant expungi quae nuntiabantur."[118] In contrast, in chapter 14 we find: "ex dispositione diuina credantur expuncta. Nisi enim ille uenisset, post quem habebant expungi, nullo modo euenissent quae in aduentu eius futura praedicabantur."[119] Kroymann was correct in his suggestion that Tertul-

---

110. Kroymann, "[Q. S. F. Tertulliani]: *Aduersus Iudaeos*," 1382–83.
111. Ibid., 1395.   112. Ibid.
113. Ibid., 1383.   114. Ibid., 1395.
115. Ibid.

116. Tert., *Adu. Iud.* 11.11 (CCSL 2.1383) completed the clause with "praecanebantur"; 14.11 (CCSL 2.1395) with "praedicabantur"; and Tert., *Adu. Marc.* (CCSL 1.535) with "praecinebantur."

117. Tert., *Adu. Marc.* 3.20.2 (CCSL 1.535): "For the arrangement would not be found to be accomplished, if he had not come, after whom it had to happen." (My own translation)

118. Tert., *Adu. Iud.* 11.12 (CCSL 2.1383–84): "These things would not be found fulfilled in this manner, such that now they are proven, unless he had come, after whom the things that were being announced had to be accomplished."

119. Ibid., 14.11 (CCSL 2.1395): ". . . may be believed to have been accomplished by reason of the divine arrangement. In fact, in no way would the things have happened that were declared as following on his coming, unless he had come after whom they had to be accomplished."

lian himself would be most unlikely to have written "in aduentu" when the whole focus of the passage was "post aduentum."

Säflund noted how 11.11a is an almost verbatim repeat of 8.15. He saw this as a deliberate recapitulation by the author of an earlier point he had made rather than as an interpolation. Thus, he disagreed with Åkerman that this was a sign that the second half of *Aduersus Iudaeos* was by another hand.[120] He also considered the relationship between 11.11b and chapter 14 and *Aduersus Marcionem* 3.20.[121] He was prepared to accept that the material in chapter 14 was by Tertullian and that it was a deliberate repetition of the earlier material at the end of chapter 11, just as 11.11a was such a repetition of material in chapter 8.[122] Säflund suggested that what intervened between the end of chapter 11 and 14 was more information than Tertullian wished to include, of which he only became aware after he had begun to conclude his work at the end of chapter 11.[123] He seemed to suggest that the hasty conclusion in chapter 11 only remains in the pamphlet today because Tertullian "der endgültigen Abschleifung entbehrt."[124] Other than that, however, Säflund was not much interested in questions of the work's structure.

In terms of structure Schreckenberg provides only hints. That the material in *Aduersus Marcionem* that overlaps with *Aduersus Iudaeos* is considered to be "klarer und straffer" is a suggestion that the task of discerning a structure in *Aduersus Iudaeos* would encounter some difficulties, because that work has not enjoyed the benefit of revision.[125] He seems to suggest that *Aduersus Iudaeos* should be replete with all those jumbled, cluttered, half-thought-out ideas that leapfrog each other to create that abrupt and disjointed pattern found in the early drafts of most pieces of writing, which is what we do find. My argument goes one step further in suggesting that there are enough clues in what we have for us to reconstruct the structure of the work he envisaged.

---

120. Säflund, *De pallio*, 191: "Es ist allerdings auffallend, dass ein derart langer Abschnitt in leicht variierter und in stilistisch entwickelterer Gestalt in so kurzem Abstand wiederholt wird, und es deutet vielleicht darauf hin, dass die zweite Hälfte erst nach einem gewissen Zeitraum nach der ersten Hälfte verfasst worden sein mag: der Verfasser hat dabei ein grösseres Bedürfnis zum Rekapitulieren gehabt als der Leser."

121. Ibid., 192–202.

122. Ibid., 192.

123. Ibid., 206: "Als Tertullian sich dann veranlasst sah, seine Argumentation durch Anführung und Auslegung neuer Bibelstellen zu ergänzen—d.h. derer, die sich in Kap. 13–14 finden—wiederholte er den ursprünglichen Abschluss mit gewissen Umstilisierungen."

124. Ibid., 207.

125. Schreckenberg, *Die christlichen Adversus-Judaeos-Texte*, 217.

Indeed the rhetorical structure I have proposed helps us assess Schrecken-berg's claims about repetitions in the second half of the work.[126] He does not classify any of the material from 13.1 onward as being an interpolation, mere-ly a repetition or revision in the course of writing. How much of 13.24–14.13, though, is a repetition of 10.17–12.2, and how much of 13.1–23 is a repetition of chapters 9–12? Certainly, there is no dispute about the fact that 11.11b–12.2a is repeated almost verbatim in 14.11–12a, but I have argued that chapters 13 and 14 fulfill a different purpose than the several previous chapters and so Schrecken-berg's assertion cannot remain unchallenged. One measure of repetition is a comparison of the scriptural arguments Tertullian used in both sections.

No piece of Scripture cited or referred to in 10.17–11.11a (we can omit 11.11b–12.2a) is found in 13.24–14.10. On this basis it is clear that 13.24–14.10 is not a repetition of 10.17–11.11a. As I have shown, 10.17–11.11a examines sever-al matters: the suffering of the Christ (10.17–19—how the death of Jesus ful-filled the prophecy that the sun would grow dark in the middle of the day, a section that fits naturally with the rest of chapter 10), and prophecy from Ezekiel about the destruction of Jerusalem (11.1–9). The section 13.24–14.10 also examines several matters: that those things prophesied to occur after the coming of the Christ had indeed occurred, not only the destruction of Je-rusalem, associated with the conversion of the Gentiles (13.24–29), but how the life and death of Jesus was proof that the first of the two comings of the Christ had now taken place (14.1–10). They are separate and distinct topics. Yet Schreckenberg is right to notice that the idea of the conversion of the Gentiles occurs in both 12.1–2a and 13.24–26 and the fall of Jerusalem is dis-cussed in both chapters 11 and 13. The structure I propose shows, in the sec-ond instance, how this was part of a more extensive pattern throughout this pamphlet of Tertullian discussing first the prophecy about something and then its fulfillment.

The same kind of analysis could be conducted on chapters 9–12 and 13.1–23. Mention has been made above of the fact that much of 13.11–23 seems concerned not with the fall of Jerusalem but with the death of the Christ, the topic indeed of chapter 10. It cannot be denied that there is a certain de-gree to which this is true, but Tertullian did that in order to reach a different conclusion in each place. The material on the death of Christ establishes a connection between that event and the fall of Jerusalem (13.10). Even though

126. Ibid.

what we find in this part of chapter 13 is not actually a repetition of the arguments in chapter 10, it has to be admitted that much of it is a continuation of
the arguments found in the earlier chapter and that, in an extensive revision
of the work, some of this material would have been better relocated to that
earlier chapter.

So Schreckenberg is right to see flaws in the unfolding of the arguments
in the last chapters of *Aduersus Iudaeos,* although I do not think that what we
find, with one notable exception, are repetitions so much as the technique of
distinguishing material on prophecy from its fulfillment (in the case of the
fall of Jerusalem) or additional arguments that are not located where they
would best appear.

We do find evidence that some scholars are aware of the influence of
rhetoric on the structure of *Aduersus Iudaeos,* yet this is not a theme they develop at any great length. Eric Osborn seems to recognize that what comes
before chapter 6 is the *refutatio* since it deals with "the deficiency of the Jewish claim" and that what follows is the positive proof that the Christ had
come.[127] Fredouille, likewise, is not overly interested in the work's structure,
going only so far as to note a basic twofold division, with chapter 6 as belonging more to the first part than to the second.[128] MacLennan accepts Sider's
point that classical rhetoric influenced Tertullian's writings and yet does not
acknowledge any such influence in the two-part structure he offered for this
particular work. According to MacLennan, *Aduersus Iudaeos* consists of the
first eight chapters, which attempt to prove that Israel had turned from God,
and the last six chapters, which attempt to prove that messianic promises in
the Old Testament had been fulfilled in Jesus.[129]

In contrast, Aziza provides a much more detailed structure for this text.[130]
At its heart is, he believes, a three-point plan that is derived from a chronological perspective that binds the whole work together: the time before
the Christ (2–6), the time of the Christ (7–10), and the time after the Christ
(11–13), together with an introduction (1) and conclusion (14).[131] Aziza has not

127. Eric Osborn, *Tertullian: First Theologian of the West* (Cambridge: Cambridge University
Press, 1997), 118.

128. Fredouille, *Tertullien et la conversion,* 261: "La 1re partie de l'*Aduersus Iudaeos* (chap. 1–6)
est consacrée à l'abrogation de la loi; la 2e partie (chap. 7–14), à la réalisation des prophéties et à
la cristologie."

129. MacLennan, *Early Christian Texts on Jews and Judaism,* 118.

130. Aziza, *Tertullien et le judaïsme,* 265–71.

131. Ibid., 105.

considered the work rhetorically as such. For him, chapter 1 is simply an introduction consisting of several parts: the controversy (1.1–2), the promise of
God to Abraham (1.3), Christianity and Judaism (1.4), their relationship (1.5),
Jewish idolatry and Christian faithfulness (1.6–7), and the abandonment of
Israel (1.8). Merely calling this an introduction does not convey the importance of these opening lines as presenting the central question at issue that
we have seen the rhetorical structural analysis yields. Further, we have noted
that chapter 14 hardly serves as an adequate conclusion.

The main section of the work here presented as *refutatio* corresponds rea-
sonably closely with Aziza's first main section: "le caractère temporaire de
l'ancienne loi" (2–6). Aziza focuses on the Mosaic law as being the overarching theme of this section, seeing circumcision and the Sabbath as two of the
precepts of the law ("les pratiques de la loi") as mentioned in 1.9 and 4.10.
Rather than seeing this whole section as being about the law in general (2)
and in particular (3–5), my position is that the *refutatio* is made to appear as
though dealing with four separate themes. This position is supported by the
conclusion at 6.1. Aziza entitles chapters 8 to 10 "Christologie." One could
not disagree with him that the figure of the Christ is central. However, by
describing the second section as "le Christ" and the third as "après le Christ"
he ends up with a problem. Throughout Aziza's second section Tertullian
mentioned events that should not have been considered until the third section (8.1, 16–18). Nor does Aziza explain successfully the difference between
the two blocks of material about the predictions of the birth of the Christ
(8.3–14 and 9.1–31), other than that one centers on prophecies in Daniel and
the other on prophecies in Isaiah (in which case 8.15–18 seems to be an un-
warranted intrusion). The rhetorical analysis offered above explains and de-
fends more successfully than does Aziza the view that these chapters do form
a single unit. Aziza rejects the idea that there is any ineptitude in chapter 13,
because he does not believe that Tertullian went back to discuss the passion
in a section on events after the passion.[132] The point he makes is that events
that were to take place after the death of the Christ were prefigured through
the symbolism of the cross.[133]

132. Ibid., 106: "Mais la pensée, jusqu'alors logique, de l'apologiste ne s'arrête pas là:
l'évocation de la crucifixion du Christ déclenche, chez le chrétien, un véritable élan mystique.
Les épisodes de la Passion revivent à un rythme accéléré dans deux paragraphes (22 et 23) qu'on
comprendrait mal—et qu'on comprend en général mal—à cette place, si justement ils ne corre-
spondaient pas à un mouvement irrationel de l'écrivain."

133. Ibid., 270.

Tränkle has noted that abrupt transitions and repetitions make it difficult to determine the structure of this work.[134] In considering the structure of the work, occasionally he pointed out rhetorical features,[135] but did not provide it with a rhetorical structure. He recognized that it has an "eigentliche Streitfrage," which appears at the beginning of chapter 2, and which is about "die Gültigkeit des jüdischen Gesetzes."[136] A little later he restated that this was the central idea and stated that it was so for the first half of the work.[137]

I have argued that Tertullian was interested in a broader question than that of the validity of the Jewish law; he was interested in the admission of Gentiles to divine grace (1.2–3) at the expense of the Jews (1.8). Tränkle believes that the law was the overarching theme and that circumcision, Sabbath, and sacrifices are each examples "der einselnen Gesetzbestimmungen."[138] Thus he thinks that 3.10 is a "plötzliche Zurückwendung" to the theme of the law and finds this "doch verwunderlich."[139] He sees it as sudden and surprising, I think, only because he was not reading these chapters as a *refutatio* that find their culmination in 6.1 with the statement that the old law, circumcision, Sabbath, and sacrifices were temporary or physical only and that the new would be eternal or spiritual (a clear statement by Tertullian that he had considered four themes not just one theme under three headings). Tränkle argues that Tertullian's presentation in the early chapters was so unsystematic and unplanned that the author was creating the structure as he went along, regardless of any resultant inconsistency.[140]

I would agree with him that the end of 3.13 is "etwas planlose Weitergleiten des Gedankengangs"[141] because of the way in which the treatment of the law and circumcision have been mingled in 3.7–12. However, it does show that Tertullian regarded law and circumcision as two equal themes and that he kept his *partitio* (showing that the Gentiles had replaced the Jews as God's people) very much in mind.

Tränkle notes how 6.2 seems to announce the rest of the work, but how the rest of the work does not always match that plan. At 7.2 Tertullian takes

134. Tränkle, *Tertullian, "Adversus Iudaeos,"* xi.
135. Ibid., xxiii—the suggestion that the setting was a *topos;* the recognition of this work as a *praescriptio;* xxiv—that the question at the beginning of ch. 2 was rhetorical.
136. Ibid., xxiv.   137. Ibid., xxvi.
138. Ibid., xxviii.   139. Ibid.
140. Ibid., xxx: "Die skizzenhafte Unfertigkeit scheint hier fast mit Händen zu greifen und bei näherem Zusehen glaubt man zu erkennen, wie sich die Gedanken des Autors erst allmählich während der Niederschrift formten."
141. Ibid., xxviii.

up the investigation of a promised new law-giver only in a dismissive way.[142] Chapter 8 begins the proof of the times announced for the appearance of the Christ, as had been foreshadowed in 7.1, but in such a way as to outline again where the work was heading. Tränkle sees the comments of 8.2 determining anew that structure: "ex temporibus praescriptis, ex signis competentibus, ex operationibus eius" and "ex consequentibus quae post aduentum eius futura adnuntiabantur." I have suggested that we should see only three topics in 8.2 not four, as I join "signa" and "opera" together as one topic.

Even though he agrees with Säflund that what is found in chapter 8 had been announced in chapter 7, Tränkle thinks it would be going too far to argue that this proves completely that the work is of a unified design.[143] It is noted that the theme of the birth of the Christ occupies 9.1–27 and that of his life and death 10.1–19; Tränkle links this back to what was mentioned in chapter 7 and to the theme "ex signis competentibus et ex operationibus eius" of 8.2, all of which suggests the authenticity of at least the first part of the second half of the pamphlet, because chapters 9 and 10 are where they should be.[144]

Tränkle notes the way in which 11.11–12.2 appears to be a summary of chapters 7–10.[145] Finally, he was well aware of the correspondence between 1.11–12.2a and 14.11–14 and suggests that the latter was designed to replace contradictions found in the ideas Tertullian was putting forward and that 13.24–14.14 was designed to replace 10.17–12.2.[146]

Thus Tränkle divides *Aduersus Iudaeos* into two parts: one dealing with the law and the other with the new law-giver.[147] This is roughly similar to my argument about the main body of the work containing *refutatio* and *confirmatio*. The second part itself consists of two issues according to Tränkle: to show that the Christ had come (which occupied chapters 7 and 8) and to show that the circumstances of his life fulfilled what had been announced by the prophets. Tränkle finds several versions of the treatment of the second issue surviving in *Aduersus Iudaeos*. For him 13.1–23 was the oldest and most connected with chapter 8. A newer and fuller treatment occurs in chapters 9 to 12, although the intensity of Tertullian's writing declined over these chapters so much that the final part was rewritten, which we now have as 13.24–

142. Ibid., xxxi.   143. Ibid., xxxiii.
144. Ibid., xxxvi: "Dieses Vorgehen ist ganz folgerichtig."
145. Ibid., xliv.   146. Ibid., li–lii.
147. Ibid., lii.

14.13.[148] This last section, "eine unfertige Skizze," was not by Tertullian or at least not published with his will and knowledge during his lifetime.[149] Even though the plan may not be unified, this does not mean that the work is not Tertullian's. *Ad nationes,* an indisputably authentic work, is one, like *Aduersus Iudaeos,* that survives in an incomplete form: ideas not integrated, deviations from plan, contradictory arguments, and repetitions. Tränkle suggests that *Aduersus Iudaeos* be regarded as authentic but incomplete.[150]

Conclusion

What I have argued in this chapter is that *Aduersus Iudaeos* can be analyzed structurally from a classical rhetorical perspective. This would suggest, as Sider has done, that Tertullian was quite familiar with, and observant of, the rules of that discipline, although in a creative way. This work contains the major elements of rhetorical structure.

A rhetorical perspective helps the modern reader appreciate the central purpose of the work, which Tertullian made clear in his *partitio:* that God had replaced the Jews with the Christians as the people of divine favor. A realization that the work was written by one trained in the art of rhetoric helps us keep in mind that the author was attempting to convince and persuade through argument and debate. Tertullian set out not to present factual information but to win a case. Facts were useful insofar as they supported the desired position, and they were presented in such a way as to be at their most convincing. As Aristotle observed long before, facts sometimes were the least convincing thing for persuading certain types of people.[151]

Discerning a rhetorical structure for the work also helps address the questions of its unity and integrity. My analysis establishes that *Aduersus Iudaeos* does have an overall unity, at least in general terms. Its author provided a number of summary comments throughout that indicate he had an overall plan for the entire pamphlet. The second half of the work is generally consistent with the plans announced in the first half. There are some sections, though, where that plan does not seem to have worked. However, rather than concluding that this is a sign of interpolation or that it is proof that classical rhetoric cannot provide us with a total explanation for the present form

148. Ibid.
150. Ibid., xxxvi.

149. Ibid.
151. Arist. *Rh.* 1.1.12 (1355a) (LCL 193.10).

of *Aduersus Iudaeos,* I would conclude that what we have today is a work in progress, fixed in form before its completion. The author revised his plan as he wrote (this is clear when we contrast 6.2–7.1 with 8.2, both sections incidentally within the first half of the work) and addressed some sections out of sequence (the mess that is 11.10–13.7 being the most obvious example). A revision of the work, which never occurred, would have seen most of these problems eliminated. What the present state of *Aduersus Iudaeos* reveals is an author striving to present a coherent rhetorical argument but failing to be perfect on the first attempt.

The *refutatio* aimed at convincing its readers that God had indeed made promises that the old law would one day be replaced. The *confirmatio* aimed at persuading those who read it that those promises had been fulfilled in the person of Jesus and the events that followed him. He fulfilled those prophecies and now, because of circumstances, no one else could possibly be the one promised long ago by God. Only sections 14.11–14 cannot be worked into the rhetorical framework successfully and I shall contend, in the next chapter, that it is an interpolation.

On the basis of my research thus far, it has been argued here that, given the work's structural unity, if we accept that Tertullian composed the first half of *Aduersus Iudaeos,* then there is no reason to reject his hand in the second half (with the exception of the brief interpolation at the end). The parallel material in *Aduersus Marcionem* 3 is accepted by scholars without question as being authentically Tertullian's. That it also appears in *Aduersus Iudaeos* does not mean that it has been copied by someone else. Tränkle's argument that Tertullian used the material from the second half of *Aduersus Iudaeos* in his later *Aduersus Marcionem,* after some revision, seems entirely suitable and satisfactory.

In comparison with the comments offered by other scholars about the structure of *Aduersus Iudaeos,* a rhetorical analysis not only discerns a detailed plan to the work, but it explains, as no one else has yet done, the connections and relationships between the various structural elements in a coherent way. It even explains the failure of its author always to carry out that overall plan. This comparison reveals the uniqueness of this present research into the rhetorical influences in the composition of *Aduersus Iudaeos.*

Having considered its rhetorical structure, we may now turn in the next chapter to the various arguments used throughout the work.

CHAPTER FOUR

ΩΩ

Argumentation

Having identified a rhetorical structure for *Aduersus Iudaeos* in the previous chapter, we may now consider the arguments by which Tertullian put forward his case that the Christians had replaced the Jews as God's people. I shall begin by outlining in general terms the elements of rhetorical argumentation. They are not only complex but extensive, and although the individual elements are to a great extent common across the rhetorical theorists, their grouping for the sake of presentation varied considerably. My purpose here is to sketch the significant types of rhetorical argument particularly for non-specialists in classical rhetoric so that they may be familiar with the technical terms that appear in the body of the chapter.

A brief summary of Sider's observations on Tertullian's method of rhetorical argumentation in the rest of his works will follow in order to highlight Tertullian's breadth of application and to indicate that what we find in *Aduersus Iudaeos* is typical of someone like Tertullian who was well versed in the art of rhetoric.

In the third section, by far the longest of the chapter, I shall examine the rhetorical arguments found in *Aduersus Iudaeos*. I intend to identify and comment on the arguments as they appear in each of the sections of the pamphlet, noting the rhetorical strategies Tertullian employed. My purpose is to illustrate the ways in which he constructed his case and to demonstrate the overall unity of the text, despite the weaknesses that are evident in its construction. Part of the way of discovering how Tertullian constructed his arguments is to note how he treated those arguments derived from other sources, such as earlier Christian writers like Irenaeus and Justin Martyr. As well, I shall make occasional asides describing how an opponent could have responded to some of the arguments Tertullian advanced in *Aduersus Iudaeos.*

Classical Rhetoric on Argumentation

Latin-writing rhetoricians described the creation of the arguments that would be persuasive in presenting proof for their point of view as *inuentio.*[1] It has to do with the method employed by orators in gathering and using material from the facts of a case that would have the desired probative and persuasive effect. These rhetoricians considered *inuentio* under the various parts of a speech, which often was different from the way Aristotle presented it. As Barwick commented, post-Aristotelian handbooks of rhetoric arranged their material on *inuentio* either according to the parts of a speech (the old method employed by the technographers) or according to the functions of the orator (as had Aristotle).[2] The author of *Ad Herennium* generally followed the Aristotelian division, yet, as Solmsen noted, he (and Cicero in *De inuentione*) dealt with it under the section on parts of a speech.[3]

Ever since the appearance of the theory of *stasis* with Hermagoras in the middle of the second century B.C., perhaps the most important feature of

1. *Rhet. Her.* 1.2.3 (LCL 403.6): "Inuentio est excogitatio rerum uerarum aut ueri similium quae causam probabilem reddant."; Cic., *Inu. rhet.* 1.7.9 (LCL 386.18) (the same definition is repeated verbatim); Cic., *De or.* 1.31.142 (LCL 348.98); 2.27.114–2.35.151 (LCL 348.280–306); Cic., *Part. or.* 2.5 (LCL 349.312); Quint., *Inst.* 3.3.1–15 (LCL 124.382–390).

2. Karl Barwick, "Die Gliederung der Rhetorischen TEXNH und die Horazische Epistula ad Pisones," *Hermes* 57 (1922): 1–5.

3. Friedrich Solmsen, "The Aristotelian Tradition in Ancient Rhetoric," *AJPh* 62 (1941): 48. See also Harry Caplan, trans., *[Cicero]: Ad C. Herennium. De Ratione Dicendi (Rhetorica ad Herennium),* LCL 403 (Cambridge, Mass.: Harvard University Press, 1954), xviii. Cf. Eckart Schütrumpf, "Non-Logical Means of Persuasion in Aristotle's Rhetoric and Cicero's *De oratore,*" in *Peripatetic Rhetoric after Aristotle,* ed. William W. Fortenbaugh and David C. Mirhady, Rutgers University Studies in Classical Humanities 6 (New Brunswick, N.J.: Transaction, 1994), 103–4, who argues that *Rhet. Her.,* in placing the parts of a speech in *inuentio,* is actually in the Aristotelian spirit. He argues that Aristotle considered style and structure as well as proof to be ἔντεχνον. This is based upon Arist., *Rh.* 3.1.7 (1404a) (LCL 193.348). Yet what we see in 3.1.1 (1403b) (LCL 193.344) and 1.2.2–3 (1355b–1356a) (LCL 193.14–16) is a distinction between artificial proofs, which must be invented, and both style and structure. Hugh Lawson-Tancred, trans., *Aristotle: The Art of Rhetoric,* Penguin Classics (Harmondsworth: Penguin, 1991), 18; George A. Kennedy, *Aristotle, "On Rhetoric": A Theory of Civic Discourse* (Oxford: Oxford University Press, 1991), 13–22; and Forbes I. Hill, "Aristotle's Rhetorical Theory. With a Synopsis of Aristotle's *Rhetoric,*" in *A Synoptic History of Classical Rhetoric,* 2nd ed., ed. James J. Murphy and Richard A. Katula (Davis, Calif.: Hermagoras Press, 1995), 52–55, believe that *Rh.* 3.1.1 provides the basic structure for the whole treatise.

inuentio was the determination of what kind of issue was at stake.[4] Assembling one's arguments depended upon the type of issue *(constitutio* or *status)* involved. Nadeau notes that all Latin systems of rhetoric utilized the Hermagoran *stasis* system in varying degrees.[5] *Ad Herennium,* for example, reduces the number of *stases* or *constitutiones* to three: conjectural *(coniecturalis),* legal *(legitima),* and juridical *(iuridicalis).*[6] According to the author of this text, the first issue dealt with questions of fact and was divided into six parts whereby one attempted to argue for the guilt or innocence of the accused: probability (including motive and manner of life), comparison (eliminating or including others as alternative suspects), signs (opportunity: place and time, etc.), presumptive proof (the accused's activities before and during the incident and other evidence left after the incident), subsequent behavior (reactions of the accused), and confirmatory proof (the use of witnesses, torture, rumor, etc.).[7] The second issue, the legal, was also divided into six parts and usually concerned the interpretation of texts: letter and spirit, conflicting laws, ambiguity, definition, transference (competence), and reasoning from analogy (similarity with other laws in cases not covered by existing laws).[8] The final issue, the juridical, concerned the circumstances that might excuse or justify the act having been committed. This was divided into two parts: absolute (where the act is claimed to be right or wrong according to the laws of nature, statute, legal custom, previous judgments, equity, and agreements) and assumptive (when considered from other perspectives: plea for mercy, exculpation, shifting responsibility, shifting guilt, and lack of viable alternatives).[9]

In his youthful *De inuentione,* Cicero presented all four Hermagoran *stases* or *constitutiones:* disputes about facts *(coniecturalis),* disputes about definitions *(definitiua),* disputes about the quality of an act *(generalis),* and disputes about correct procedures *(translatiua).*[10] The fact that Cicero introduced the *stases* at this point (at the beginning of *inuentio*) rather than as divisions of *confirmatio,* as did *Ad Herennium,* is evidence to Wisse that Cicero's work was

---

4. See Ray Nadeau, "Classical Systems of Stases in Greek: Hermagoras to Hermogenes," *GRBS* 2 (1959): 53–71; Antoine Braet, "The Classical Doctrine of *status* and the Rhetorical Theory of Argumentation," *Ph&Rh* 20 (1987): 79–93; and Malcolm Heath, "The Substructure of *Stasis-*Theory from Hermagoras to Hermogenes," *CQ* n.s. 44 (1994): 114–29.

5. Nadeau, "Classical Systems of Stases," 54.

6. *Rhet. Her.* 1.11.18 (LCL 403.34).

7. Ibid., 2.2.3–2.8.12 (LCL 403.60–80).

8. Ibid., 1.11.19–1.13.23 (LCL 403.34–42); 2.9.13–2.12.18 (LCL 403.80–90).

9. Ibid., 1.14.24–1.15.25 (LCL 403.42–48); 2.13.19–2.17.26 (LCL 403.90–104).

10. Cic., *Inu. rhet.* 1.8.10 (LCL 386.20–22).

less contaminated with post-Aristotelian alterations than was the anonymous handbook.[11] The first *constitutio* in both Cicero and *Ad Herennium* is much the same and there is a great deal of similarity between *Ad Herennium's constitutio iuridicalis* and Cicero's *constitutio generalis.* The latter's *constitutiones definitiua* and *translatiua* resemble two of the subdivisions in the former's *constitutio legitima.*[12] Perhaps the most striking difference between these two texts is that Cicero separated these four *constitutiones,* as cases involving general reasoning,[13] from cases that involved the interpretation of a document, which is where he considered the matters of ambiguity, letter and spirit, conflict of laws, reasoning by analogy, and definition.[14] In the later *De oratore* Cicero had Antonius distinguish them not as general and particular reasoning, but, following Aristotle, as artificial and inartificial proof.[15] The first had to be thought of by the orator himself while the second, found in documents, oral evidence, and statute law, only had to be handled by the orator.[16] In *De partitione oratoria* Cicero would refer to *argumenta remota* and *insita.*[17]

Kennedy sees in Quintilian, who wrote 150 years later, an admission that he felt there was nothing left in rhetoric to develop and he had only to select from the existing body of theory.[18] Quintilian first presented the material on *status* or *constitutio* (the two Latin terms he used to translate the Greek *stasis*)

---

11. Jakob Wisse, *Ethos and Pathos from Aristotle to Cicero* (Amsterdam: Adolf M. Hakkert, 1989), 86–87. Solmsen, "The Aristotelian Tradition," 49, described Cic., *De or.,* as the only major work to escape such contamination. When rhetoricians considered *inuentio* under the parts of a speech, it was incorporated under *confirmatio.* Carole Blair, "Contested Histories of Rhetoric: The Politics of Preservation, Progress and Change," *QJS* 78 (1992): 403–28, would consider the word "contamination" as evidence that Solmsen was operating from an influence studies approach. Indeed, I am sure she would consider *Quellenforschung* (in this case, the reconstruction of the original handbook based on extant handbooks) as the epitome of influence studies. If her critique of this approach is true it could go some way toward explaining why *Rhet. Her.* and Cic., *Inu. rhet.* traditionally have been "looked down at" because of their "deviation" from the Aristotelian source. Murphy, "The Codification of Roman Rhetoric," 111, speaks instead of the Roman contribution as being codification.

12. Interestingly, Cicero's *constitutio definitiua* considers how one defines an act (*Inu. rhet.* 2.17.52–2.18.56 [LCL 386.212–18]), while the matter of *definitio* that most closely resembled the section in *Rhet. Her.* 1.12.21 (LCL 403.38) and 2.12.17 (LCL 403.86–88) was, in Cicero, limited to definition in documents (*Inu. rhet.* 2.51.153–154 [LCL 386.320–22]).

13. Cic., *Inu. rhet.* 2.4.14–2.39.115 (LCL 386.178–284).

14. Ibid., 2.40.116–2.51.156 (LCL 386.284–324).

15. Solmsen, "The Aristotelian Tradition," 186–87, noted that in *Inu. rhet.,* unlike *De or.,* Cicero did not follow the division into artificial and inartificial proofs.

16. Cic., *De or.* 2.27.116–17 (LCL 348.280–82).

17. Cic., *Part. or.* 2.5–7 (LCL 349.312–16).

18. George A. Kennedy, "An Estimation of Quintilian," *AJPh* 83 (1962): 132.

apart from comments on the parts of a speech. He accepted that there were three *status (coniecturalis, qualitatis,* and *finitiuus)* concerned with conjecture, quality, and definition, and one *quaestio legalis,* which dealt with letter and spirit, contradictory laws, syllogism, and ambiguity (competence being usually able to be considered under one of the other headings).[19] At other times he wrote of four *generales status,* divided into three *rationales status* and one *legalis status.*[20] The particulars of the latter could be used in all three of the rational bases. After having considered the parts of a forensic speech in books 4 to 6, Quintilian returned to the *status* in more detail in book 7, under the heading not of *inuentio* but of *dispositio.* The construction of a speech was determined by the question at issue.[21]

In writing about confirmatory proof, one of the six divisions of the *constitutio coniecturalis,* the author of *Ad Herennium* mentioned the *loci communes,* the topics used as building blocks for constructing arguments.[22] In this context they were stock and standard commonplaces used to argue in favor of or against the use of witnesses, torture, rumor, etc.[23] There were also *loci* to be employed to argue for or against using the divisions of the *constitutio legitima:* there were typical points an orator would make to support the letter or the spirit of the law, whatever was more appropriate.[24]

In *De inuentione* Cicero wrote about *loci* in his section on *confirmatio.* He referred to "quaedam silua atque materia universa" from which arguments are drawn.[25] These consisted of attributes either of the person (name, nature, manner of life, fortune, habit, feeling, interests, purposes, achievements, accidents, and speeches made) or of the action (coherent with, connected with—place, opportunity, time, occasion, manner, facilities—adjunct to, and consequent upon).[26] These *loci* were presented in more detail in the second book.[27] There were other *loci* to be used with other *constitutiones.*

In book 5 of *Institutio oratoria* Quintilian considered artificial and inartificial proofs. In the latter category he placed decisions of previous courts,

19. Quint., *Inst.* 3.6.66–79 (LCL 124.442–50).   20. Ibid., 3.6.86 (LCL 124.452–54).

21. Ibid., 7.1.1–7.10.17 (LCL 126.4–172).

22. On the topics in classical rhetoric see Jan M. van Ophuijsen, "Where Have the Topics Gone?" in *Peripatetic Rhetoric after Aristotle,* ed. William W. Fortenbaugh and David C. Mirhady, Rutgers University Studies in Classical Humanities 6 (New Brunswick, N.J.: Transaction, 1994), 131–73.

23. *Rhet. Her.* 2.6.9 (LCL 403.72–74).   24. Ibid., 2.9.13–2.10.14 (LCL 403.80–84).

25. Cic., *Inu. rhet.* 1.24.34 (LCL 386.68–70).   26. Ibid., 1.24.34–1.28.43 (LCL 386.70–82).

27. Ibid., 2.4.14–2.16.51 (LCL 386.178–212).

rumors, torture, documents, oaths, and witnesses.[28] When considering the *artificales* Quintilian was more Ciceronian than Aristotelian, adopting the distinction between thing and person rather than special and common topic.[29] All proofs must be either necessary, probable, or possible.[30] They were obtained through signs, arguments, or examples.[31] Arguments could employ *loci,* and Quintilian provided the usual list of them associated with people[32] and things.[33] Arguments were to be constructed as enthymemes, a form, usually an abbreviated form, of the logical syllogisms.[34] In book 6 Quintilian would go on to consider the role stirring the emotions played in securing persuasion.

In his historical survey of classical rhetoric George Kennedy mentions that there were hundreds of handbooks on rhetoric written in antiquity.[35] In choosing to comment briefly upon *Ad Herennium,* Cicero, and Quintilian I am not suggesting that these were the writers who influenced Tertullian's own rhetorical education. What these easily accessible authors demonstrate is that most of the building blocks of argumentation were the same and where rhetoricians differed was in their grouping of those blocks into a system. My interest shall not be in determining which school of rhetoric influenced Tertullian but in offering comment on how he utilized those building blocks to construct *Aduersus Iudaeos.* A summary of what Sider wrote with regard to argumentation in Tertullian's other works will assist in showing the extent to which *Aduersus Iudaeos* is characteristic of Tertullian's rhetorical pattern of argumentation.

---

28. Quint., *Inst.* 5.2.1–5.7.37 (LCL 125.158–90).   29. Ibid., 5.8.4 (LCL 125.192).
30. Ibid., 5.8.6 (LCL 125.192–94).   31. Ibid., 5.9.1 (LCL 125.194).
32. Ibid., 5.10.23–31 (LCL 125.212–18).   33. Ibid., 5.10.32–52 (LCL 125.218–28).
34. Ibid., 5.10.1–8 (LCL 125.202–206). On the enthymeme in classical rhetoric see James H. McBurney, "The Place of the Enthymeme in Rhetorical Theory," *Speech Monographs* 3 (1936): 49–74; Thomas M. Conley, "The Enthymeme in Perspective," *QJS* 70 (1984): 168–87; Scott Consigny, "Dialectical, Rhetorical and Aristotelian Rhetoric," *Ph&Rh* 22 (1989): 281–87; M. F. Burnyeat, "Enthymeme: Aristotle on the Logic of Persuasion," in *Aristotle's "Rhetoric": Philosophical Essays,* ed. David J. Furley and Alexander Nehamas (Princeton, N.J.: Princeton University Press, 1994): 3–55; and M. F. Burnyeat, "Enthymeme: Aristotle on the Rationality of Rhetoric," in *Essays on Aristotle's "Rhetoric,"* ed. Amélie Oksenberg Rorty, Philosophical Traditions 6 (Berkeley: University of California Press, 1996), 88–115.
35. Kennedy, *A New History of Classical Rhetoric,* 19.

Sider's Observations on Tertullian's Arguments

Sider states that he will be satisfied with the "conventional patterns which persisted over the centuries."[36] In considering Tertullian's method of arguing, Sider focuses on his forensic treatises, devoting chapters 4 to 6 to them (while both deliberative and epideictic themes are handled together in chapter 7, a brief chapter of only eleven pages), and he divides those treatises into three groups corresponding to their central issue or *stasis* (the conjectural in chapter 4, the qualitative in chapter 5, and the definitive in chapter 6). At the same time, within those chapters, he examines some of the common *topoi* that could be used in rational argument. The rhetorical rules for the interpretation of written documents were very helpful in commenting upon Scripture.[37] He would use scriptural passages as useful material for constructing conjectural arguments.

Sider has noted that, when investigating matters of fact, Tertullian employed both artificial and inartificial proofs. In *De testimonio animae* he attempted to offer the soul as a witness that was cross-examined to offer evidence that there is but one God. What Tertullian was attempting to do was establish confidence in the reader of the treatise that his witness was reliable and trustworthy.[38] Even to claim the soul as capable of being a witness was something of a rhetorical sleight of hand by Tertullian.

Apologeticum offers some examples of pure defense conjecture:[39] the charges brought against the Christians involving Thyestean banquets and incest were false, as there was no evidence from signs or witnesses, only rumors. This was dealt with in chapter 7, which dealt with inartificial proofs.[40]

36. Sider, *Ancient Rhetoric*, 12. On such a statement see Juv., *Sat.* 15.110–12 (LCL 91.296); D. A. Russell, "Rhetoric and Criticism," *G&R* 14 (1967): 134; Clark, *Rhetoric in Greco-Roman Education*, 66; Elaine Fantham, "Imitation and Evolution: The Discussion of Imitation in Cicero *De Oratore* 2.87–97 and Some Related Problems of Ciceronian Theory," *CPh* 73 (1978): 2; Donald C. Bryant, "Rhetoric: Its Function and Scope," *QJS* 39 (1953) (reproduced in *The Province of Rhetoric,* ed. Joseph Schwartz and John A. Rycenga [New York: Ronald Press, 1965], 7); and George A. Kennedy, *New Testament Interpretation through Rhetorical Criticism* (Chapel Hill and London: University of North Carolina Press, 1984), 6.

37. Sider, *Ancient Rhetoric*, 63.

38. Ibid., 43–44.

39. Even though Paul Keresztes, "Tertullian's *Apologeticus*: A Historical and Literary Survey," *Latomus* 25 (1966): 124–33, argues that *Apol.* is deliberative, Sider counters that forensic themes do appear. Cf. Louis J. Swift, "Forensic Rhetoric in Tertullian's *Apologeticum*," *Latomus* 27 (1968): 864–77; and Dunn, *Tertullian*, 40.

40. Quint., *Inst.* 5.9.1–16 (LCL 125.194–202), considered the conclusive and irrefutable evi-

In chapter 8 are the artificial proofs, using the *loci* or *topoi* of motive, ability, nature, means, and past action to argue that the charges were impossible. Chapter 9 throws the charges back against the accusers. The second lot of charges involving sacrilege and treason were handled not using the conjectural method but that of quality: the action was admitted and then justified.[41]

The first book of *Aduersus Marcionem* is divided by Sider into definitional, conjectural, and qualitative parts. In chapters 8 to 21, the conjectural part, the arguments derive from the *loci* of cause and effect, place, past deeds, means, ability, manner, and time.[42] Particularly striking are Tertullian's arguments against the existence of the Marcionite god from the *locus* of cause and effect. There is nothing in creation, he argued, that points back to such a god and, if there is no effect, it follows that there is no cause. The third book makes use of signs.[43] This is the book that parallels closely, at least in chapters 7 and 13 to 20, *Aduersus Iudaeos*. Sider mentions chapter 13, which corresponds with the first part of chapter 9 of *Aduersus Iudaeos*, where Tertullian supported the probative nature of a sign by demonstrating its uniqueness.

In *De carne Christi* Tertullian's opponents denied that Christ had human flesh. He examined God's motive and will from the point of view of the deliberative *loci* of advantage, honor, and necessity in both *refutatio* and *confirmatio*.[44] Sider sees three conjectural *loci* of desire, ability, and cause in *De resurrectione mortuorum*.[45]

Sider suggests that rhetorical theory "provided Tertullian with two particularly useful sets of rules" when it came to the use of Scripture in argument.[46] One set of rules concerned the legal question of how to interpret a written document and the other concerned the artificial proofs of the conjectural method. This latter method was particularly apt when both sides of the debate appealed to Scripture as a source of evidence in questions of fact.[47] What Sider notes is that, starting with Scripture as raw material, Tertullian used that information to construct rhetorical arguments. Reference is made to *De carne Christi* and the fourth book of *Aduersus Marcionem*.

dence of signs as inartificial proof, and the evidence of signs that did not lead to necessary conclusions as artificial proof.

41. Sider, *Ancient Rhetoric*, 45–49.
42. Ibid., 49–54.
43. Ibid., 54–55.
44. Ibid., 55–63.
45. Ibid., 63.
46. Ibid.
47. Ibid., 64.

Sider indicates the presence of qualitative arguments in *Apologeticum*, in the chapters dealing with sacrilege (10 to 28) and treason (29 to 45), in chapters 22 to 27 of the first book of *Aduersus Marcionem*, and in the second book as well.[48]

Tertullian was also well able to use what Quintilian described as legal questions when using Scripture, such as resolving ambiguity in a text or resolving conflict between the letter and spirit of a written document. Sider refers to book 4 of *Aduersus Marcionem*, *De resurrectione mortuorum*, *De pudicitia*, *De monogamia*, and *De praescriptione haereticorum* for other instances of Tertullian's use of Scripture.[49]

With these general comments in mind about the rhetorical theory of argumentation and about how Sider sees Tertullian making use of this theory, attention may now be turned to the argumentation in *Aduersus Iudaeos*.

Argumentation in *Aduersus Iudaeos*

By way of general introduction, it needs to be stated with regard to the pamphlet as a whole that the facts of this case, from which Tertullian derived his information and constructed his arguments, come from the Hebrew Scriptures (the Old Testament) more than from any other source. This is not surprising given that the point at issue found in the *partitio* was the question of whether or not the Gentiles were admissible to God's grace or law (and whether or not the Gentiles had replaced the Jews as God's people), and that the position Tertullian took with regard to that question (they were admissible and had replaced the Jews—1.3a, 8), involved the correct interpretation of those scriptural passages. Thus, there was little need for him to look elsewhere for source material from which to produce arguments.

It is not surprising, therefore, in a work that outlines what the Christian contribution to a debate between Jews and Christians ought to have been (and should be in future such encounters) to find few references or allusions to the New Testament. It would be a foolish orator who, in seeking to persuade, employed arguments based upon facts that those who needed to be persuaded would rule inadmissible. This is entirely consistent with the suggestion that Tertullian composed this work for an imagined readership of

48. Ibid., 76–84.
49. Ibid., 88–100.

both Jews and Christians. It is also consistent with the suggestion that the intended readers were Christians who were having doubts or feeling under pressure about being able to explain their position to pagans, Jews, or Judaizing Christians.[50] However, if the intended readers were pagans who, because of an interest in monotheism, were deciding between Judaism and Christianity, one would have expected Tertullian to have made more use of the New Testament to highlight the positive appeal of Christianity and more use of philosophy and other arguments from non-Christian culture. Indeed, to base one's arguments on the Hebrew Scriptures would be what one would expect Jews to have demanded of Christians in debates with them.[51]

Exordium (1.1–3a)

One should not expect too much argumentation in an *exordium*. This is the case here. Rather than attempting to secure the goodwill of his readers by presenting himself as a person of dispassionate logic and a seeker after the truth instead of effective argument (itself a rhetorical ploy), what we find in the *exordium* in 1.2 is an argument based upon person, one of the *loci communes*. In particular it is an argument from nationality.[52] What Tertullian argued was that the former opponent was a proselyte Jew, a Jew of Gentile origin and "not a Jew from the stock of the Israelites."[53]

Tertullian seems to have recognized a distinction between one's religious identity as a Jew and one's geographic or political origin as an Israelite,[54] if we understand him in this sentence to be distinguishing those Jews of the stock of Israel from those Jews not of the stock of Israel.[55] As Cohen points

50. Guerra, "Polemical Christianity," 116.

51. M. F. Wiles, "The Old Testament in Controversy with the Jews," *SJT* 8 (1955): 115–16.

52. Cic., *Inu. rhet.* 1.24.35 (LCL 386.70–72); 2.9.29 (LCL 386.190); Quint., *Inst.* 5.10.24 (LCL 125.214).

53. Tert., *Adu. Iud.* 1.2 (CCSL 2.1339): "nec de prosapia Israëlitum Iudaeus."

54. I have noted (Dunn, *Tertullian*, 166, n. 4) my reluctance to use terms like "nation" and "race" to translate *natio* and *gens*. The question of how modern terms like "race" and "ethnicity" can be applied to the situation in late antiquity, as raised recently by Denise Kimber Buell, "Rethinking the Relevance of Race for Early Christian Self-Definition," *HTR* 94 (2001): 449–76; "Race and Universalism in Early Christianity," *JECS* 10 (2002): 431–32; and *Why This New Race? Ethnic Reasoning in Early Christianity* (New York: Columbia University Press, 2005), is a complex one and cannot be discussed here, but deserves further study.

55. The alternative interpretation would be that he is arguing that one could not be a Jew at all if one was not from the stock of Israel. I accept the first interpretation based on the fact that at the start of the pamphlet (1.1 [CCSL 2.1339]) Tertullian described the previous opponent as "proselytus Iudaeus."

out, it was only in the second half of the second century that *Iudaeus* came to
have a religious meaning (Jew) instead of an ethnic-geographic meaning (Judaean).[56] As Tertullian would make clear in chapter 13, his own position was
that *Iudaeus* could no longer have a geo-political meaning but only a cultural-
religious one.[57] That the Jews would accept proselytes (and he was not concerned about the extent to which converts were truly accepted) was an indication for Tertullian that Gentiles were not, as a matter of principle, excluded
from inclusion among God's people, a point he believed the Jews themselves
would have had to concede. Hence Isaiah 40:15, which probably had been
used as a major point in the earlier encounter, did not apply.[58] Tertullian's argument from nationality stated that even the Jews admitted that no person
necessarily was excluded from inclusion within God's people.

There could well be a Jewish response to Tertullian's argument. It would
have to do with definition of terms. When Tertullian described the former
debater as being "ex gentibus," he was using that word, it could be argued,
differently from the way it is used in Isaiah 40:15. Tertullian used it to mean
that person's religious origins—the contrast would be to being a Jew. What
Isaiah stated was about Gentiles as a term of broader ethnic-geographic
identification (which certainly included but was by no means limited to a
religious identification)—the contrast would be to being a Judaean. While
Tertullian argued that the proselyte always retained something of his Gentile
origins, what Jewish readers of *Aduersus Iudaeos* could claim was that, to interpret Isaiah 40 correctly, one would have to assert that Gentiles could not
be Jews. Thus, by understanding the word in Isaiah in a different way than
what it actually meant (and by not acknowledging this difference or, in other
words, by not entering into the question of definition), Tertullian wanted to
turn this piece of Scripture against the Jews.

Tertullian pointed out that the argument from nationality was a sign
("praerogatiua").[59] From this point on, the previous debater (and all contem-

---

56. Cohen, *The Beginnings of Jewishness*, 70. His position is a little more subtle in that he also
adds those who moved into the geographic area (but who, in the years of the dispersion of its
former inhabitants, did not embrace the ethnic or religious identity of the former occupants).
They are not relevant to this study.

57. Could one suggest that Tertullian believed that "Iudaeus" as an ethnic term, as Cohen
understands it, no longer had a geographic connotation as a key feature but had changed to
have a religious connotation as a key feature?

58. Tert., *Adu. Iud.* 1.3 (CCSL 2.1339).

59. Tränkle, *Tertullian, "Adversus Iudaeos,"* xxiii, makes the point that this seemed to be a ref-

porary Jews) disappears from the pamphlet. He had served his purpose in
providing the first argument of the pamphlet. Only Jews from either the recent past or from biblical times were discussed. Instead of concluding that
Tertullian was not interested in addressing contemporary issues in the relationship between Jews and Christians, I am making the case that Tertullian
refrained from constructing arguments from person and concentrated on arguments from events. His promise to avoid personal abuse and to stick to the
question was going to be fulfilled. The only negative comment about the previous debater was to refer to his pride in using Isaiah 40:15 against the Christians.[60]

Partitio (1.3b–2.1a)

If the proselyte turned to Isaiah 40:15 in the debate to support his position that the Jews alone were God's chosen people, Tertullian could not only
offer an alternative explanation in his pamphlet, he could go one further
and turn to Genesis 25:23 to argue that God had promised the Gentiles that
they would supersede the Jews as recipient of God's grace. Tertullian seems
to have placed one extract from Scripture up against another, as an orator
would do with conflicting laws.[61] What made Genesis 25 more authoritative
than Isaiah 40? Tertullian did not say. Perhaps he could have claimed that the
words in Genesis were directly from God to Abraham, while what is found
in Isaiah are simply the words of the prophet. Tertullian's silence is perhaps
understandable given that in response to Tertullian one could have used the
topos or *locus* that, since Isaiah is later than Genesis, it supersedes the earlier
passage, not the other way around.

In making use of Genesis 25:23 Tertullian had first to clear up any ambiguity in what the passage meant. Rebekah's twins had typological significance,

---

erence equivalent to the inartificial proof found in the decisions of previous courts *(praeiudi-
cia)* (Quint., *Inst.* 5.1.2 [LCL 125.156]) or matters of competence *(praescriptio)* (Quint., *Inst.* 3.6.72
[LCL 124.444–46]): "Die formale Bedeutung dieses Gedankens ist klar: Es handelt sich um ein
praeiudicium, eine *praestructio* oder *praescriptio*—hier heißt es 1,2 *hinc habuit praerogativam.*"

60. Tert., *Adu. Iud.* 1.3 (CCSL 1.1339): "ne Israël adhuc superbiat." Interestingly, here Tertullian seems to have identified the proselyte with Israel, something that would be strictly excluded given the way he has used his terms earlier. Perhaps, given the way he has dismissed the
proselyte from being an effective spokesperson for the Jewish position, Tertullian was now going to concern himself only with those from the stock of Israel. Quint., *Inst.* 4.1.10 (LCL 125.10)
stated that pride was an impression to be avoided. Ascribing it to one's opponent was meant to
attack his character.

61. *Rhet. Her.* 2.10.15 (LCL 403.84); Cic., *Inu. rhet.* 2.49.144–147 (LCL 386.312–16); Quint., *Inst.*
7.7.1–10 (LCL 126.142–48).

as God's interpretation to Rebekah about her condition as reported in Genesis itself indicated. The question was about which twin represented which people, for God's promise was that the younger twin would overcome the elder. There was a standard rhetorical treatment with regard to the ambiguity of texts.[62] One could look at a passage in its context, consider the wider context, point to the difficulties raised by one's opponent's interpretation, argue for what is more honorable, necessary, or expedient, or appeal to what the author could have written if the intention was as one's opponent argued.

For Tertullian, the elder twin, Esau, represented the Jews and the younger twin, Jacob, represented the Christians. He appealed, as it were, to the wider context of what we find in biblical literature and to the historical fact that the Jews appeared before the Christians did, and concluded that the Jews had to be the elder of the two peoples.[63] Yet, in offering this interpretation, Tertullian did not acknowledge that there was any ambiguity or contrary opinion. Tertullian wanted nothing to cast a shadow over what he offered. Resolving ambiguity in a text's interpretation while not even hinting at the fact that any ambiguity exists seems designed to make his position more convincing than it otherwise would be and to make his interpretation appear to be beyond dispute. By contrast, in *De pudicitia*, where he offered the same interpretation of who was represented by Rebekah's twins, Tertullian did so by acknowledging that, in the context of interpreting who was represented by the two sons in the parable in Luke 15, there was an alternative to his own explanation about the parable's referents.[64] I have suggested that Tertullian's lack of explanation about the Genesis passage in *De pudicitia* could be attributed to the fact that *De pudicitia* was written after *Aduersus Iudaeos*.[65] The same suggestion about the priority of *Aduersus Iudaeos* could also be made with regard to *Aduersus Marcionem* 3. Since, at *Adu. Marc.* 3.24.8–9, Tertullian did not need to prove the connection between Jacob and the Christians[66] and Esau and the Jews, suggests that *Aduersus Marcionem* came later.

---

62. *Rhet. Her.* 2.11.16 (LCL 403.84–86); Cic., *Inu. rhet.* 2.40.116–2.41.121 (LCL 386.284–88); Quint., *Inst.* 7.9.1–15 (LCL 126.152–60).

63. Tert., *Adu. Iud.* 1.5 (CCSL 2.1340).

64. Tert., *De pud.* 8.3–9.22 (CCSL 2.1295–99). The reference to Gen. 25:23 is at 8.8 (CCSL 2.1295–96).

65. Dunn, "Tertullian and Rebekah," 121–22. See also Eric Osborn, "The Subtlety of Tertullian," *VChr* 52 (1998): 362–63.

66. Tert., *Adu. Marc.* 3.24.8 (CCSL 1.543): "Iacob, qui quidem posterioris et praelatioris populi figura est, id est nostri."

I have examined this section of *Aduersus Iudaeos* in some detail elsewhere, where I have argued that this identification of the Jews with the elder twin and the Christians with the younger is first found not in Paul, *Barnabas,* or Justin Martyr, but in Irenaeus.[67] Hence, I would have to disagree with Tränkle, who suggested that Tertullian's typology was dependent upon a common tradition going back to Romans 9:12.[68]

The fact that this passage of Scripture is placed within the *partitio* of the work means that it is not just another piece of evidence in the overall case, but is the lynchpin of the argument: have the Gentiles (at least those who were Christian) replaced the Jews as God's people?

For the remainder of the *partitio* (1.6–2.1a) Tertullian offered argument derived from the *locus* of motive, one of the *loci* related to actions or events.[69] Why would God have made this promise to the Gentiles? The answer is that the Jews turned away from God and turned to the worship of idols (exemplified by Exodus 32:1–4, where the people of the exodus asked Aaron to fashion them a god and he provided them with the golden head of a calf ["bubulum caput"]; by 1 Kings 12:25–33, where Jeroboam the king set up more golden calves; and by 2 Kings 17:7–17, where the whole history of the kingdoms of Israel and Judah was one of idolatry).[70] By contrast, those pagans who had abandoned their worship of idols and had turned to the God whom the Jews rejected were to be those who would replace the Jews as the recipients of divine grace.[71] Jewish unfaithfulness and Christian fidelity provided the motive for God's prophetic announcement to Rebekah. The rest of the pamphlet would be devoted to investigating this claim in greater detail.

Refutatio (2.1b–6.1)

Tränkle suggests that the ideas mentioned in *Adu. Iud.* 1.3b–8, about Jews being prior to Christians, were ignored in the following section and that Ter-

67. Dunn, "Tertullian and Rebekah," 124–41. Boyarin, *Dying for God,* 134, misunderstands what I write on p. 122 by being selective in what he quotes. He claims I argue that this typological interpretation was unique to Tertullian, whereas what I wrote was that my argument about the priority of *Adu. Iud.* over *De pud.* "would achieve a degree of certainty if it could be shown that the typological interpretation of the twins . . . was unique to Tertullian." Further along in my article I do consider Iren., *Adu. haer.* 4.21.3 (not 4.11.3 as reported by Boyarin).

68. Tränkle, *Tertullian, "Adversus Iudaeos,"* lxxv.

69. Cic., *Inu. rhet.* 1.26.37 (LCL 386.74); Quint., *Inst.* 5.10.33–36 (LCL 125.218–20). *Rhet. Her.* 2.2.3 (LCL 403.62) listed motive simply as one of the two subheadings under probability, one of the six divisions of the *constitutio coniecturalis.*

70. Tert., *Adu. Iud.* 1.6–7a (CCSL 2.1340).   71. Ibid., 1.7b (CCSL 2.1341).

tullian resumed a discussion about the law, which had been suspended at 1.3a.[72] He seems to imply a disjointed or incoherent structure in this part of the pamphlet. I have suggested already that seeing a transition from *partitio* to *refutatio* makes better sense of these chapters. As I have discussed the *refutatio* in detail elsewhere,[73] here I wish only to outline the rhetorical arguments Tertullian used in the construction of these chapters.

The Jewish position, as understood and presented by Tertullian, was that the covenant between God and Israel endured and that all who wished to be considered God's people had to observe the requirements of that covenant. The notion proposed by Tertullian to counter that position was that God was free to reform the covenant depending upon prevailing circumstances.[74] He sought to defend the notion by examining the law, circumcision, the Sabbath, and sacrifices in the light of what could be construed as proof from both the Hebrew Scriptures and the events of more recent history, in order to demonstrate that God was free to reform the covenant by making it universal and inclusive, which God had done. Just as the Jewish rabbis developed Midrash partly in response to the threat of Christianity,[75] Christian authors like Tertullian entered into the debate about the interpretation and meaning of Scripture to develop arguments.

In essence, this *refutatio* was an extended debate about the conflict between the spirit and the letter of the law, for which there were standard rhetorical strategies, as we have noted. The Hebrew Scriptures provided evidence of conflicting statements made by God. There was the establishment of the law with one people on the one hand, and the announced divine intention to establish a law with all peoples on the other. Closely involved with this will be questions of establishing divine motive and manner of life.

The first section of the *refutatio* deals with the law, in particular the giving of the law by God and the keeping of the law by people (2.1b–10a). This is an action and in considering actions the rhetoricians offered a number of *loci*. Cicero had written about four topics relevant to this question (coherent attributes like motive; performance attributes like place, time, occasion, manner, and facilities; adjunct attributes like comparison with other actions; and con-

---

72. Tränkle, Tertullian, "Adversus Iudaeos," xxiv.

73. Dunn, "Pro Temporum Condicione," 315–41.

74. Tert., Adu. Iud. 2.10 (CCSL 2.1343): "Nec adimamus hanc dei potestatem pro temporum condicione legis praecepta reformantem in hominis salutem."

75. Jacob Neusner, What Is Midrash? (Philadelphia: Fortress Press, 1987), 45.

sequence attributes like definition, agents, nature, and following events).[76] Tertullian mentioned those he wished to investigate: "omnibus gentibus eandem legem dedit, quam certis statutis temporibus obseruari praecepit quando uolit et per quos uolit et sicut uoluit."[77] Thus, we should expect to find arguments about motive, time (both the time when the law was given and the length of time for which the law was to be observed), subsequent results (who was affected by the giving of the law?), and manner (how was the law given and to be observed?).

Tertullian began by questioning the motive of God in giving the law only to the Jews, as they alleged God did. If God created the whole universe and all people, why would God give the law to only one people, the Jews (2.1b)? To make the point, Tertullian employed an invalid induction that because proselytes had access to the law all people must have access to it (2.2a).[78] He offered God a motive for wanting to give the law to all people: God is good and equitable. This is an argument from degree: if God is good and the giving of the law is a good thing, then it would make sense to argue that God would be more likely to give the law to more people than just the Jews.[79]

Next Tertullian considered the matter of time: when did God give the law? A reading of the Hebrew Scriptures reveals, according to Tertullian, that the law was given "in the beginning of the world itself" to Adam and Eve.[80] How was this law given and to be kept? The law given to Adam was an embryonic form of the written law later given to Moses (2.2b–6). Adam and Eve are typological figures for all humanity. Thus, all people were to keep the law, not just the Jews. Indeed, Noah, Abraham, and Melchizedek had kept the law naturally before it received its written form with Moses (2.7–9a).

The implication was that the Gentiles, like the patriarchs, were keeping the original, natural law rather than the derivative, written law. Of course, one could imagine the Jewish argument, in support of the "letter of the law," that the written law improved the inferior, original law, and that the law of

---

76. Cic., *Inu. rhet.* 1.26.37–1.28.43 (LCL 386.74–82).

77. Tert., *Adu. Iud.* 2.2 (CCSL 2.1341): "[God] gave the same law to all clans and, at certain definite times, directed it to be kept when, by whom, and as [God] wished."

78. As I argued elsewhere (Dunn, *"Pro Temporum Condicione,"* 321, n. 24), the most Tertullian could conclude from that would be that God gave the law to Jews and to *some* other people. Further, a Jewish response to Tertullian's pamphlet could have argued that their understanding was that, for anyone else to have access to God's law, they had to cease being Gentile and become a Jew.

79. Quint., *Inst.* 5.10.97 (LCL 125.254).

80. Tert., *Adu. Iud.* 2.2b (CCSL 2.1341): "in principio mundi ipse."

Moses cancelled any previous natural law. Tertullian's response, from the spirit of the law, was that the original law was superior.[81] If God could add to the unwritten law to create the written law, then God, as its author, was free to make changes to the written law, even to bring it to an end (2.6–7). Again, in terms of manner, the argument here is that the law of Moses was given temporarily (2.9).

The argument about promises of a new law, made through the prophets in the time after the giving of the law to Moses, makes only the briefest of appearances at this point in the pamphlet (2.9). In 2.4b–5, just when he was reaching the high point of his brief contrast between the primordial law given to Adam and Eve and the written law given to Moses, Tertullian digressed and described how Adam and Eve had failed to obey that primordial law. This adds nothing to Tertullian's argument; in fact, it detracts from it. Highlighting the failure of those two to keep the primordial law could be taken by a skilled opponent as an argument in support of the necessity (and superiority) of the law given to Moses, even though that law too would be broken. As I have pointed out elsewhere, Tertullian was the first Christian writer we know who interpreted Genesis in this fashion, arguing that the new law of Christ was a restoration of the universal law given to Adam and Eve, as a replacement for the particular written law given to Moses.[82]

The second section of the *refutatio* deals with circumcision and runs from 2.10b to 3.13. Once again Scripture was scrutinized to supply evidence that God's real intention was revealed earlier than when the Jewish practice of circumcision was instigated. What Tertullian wanted to point out was that the important attribute of Adam, Abel, Noah, Enoch, Melchizedek, Lot, and even Abraham himself was that they pleased God without being circumcised (2.11–3.1). We may classify this as an argument from nature, one of the attributes of persons.[83] Even though Abraham was circumcised eventually, Tertullian was able to point out that he was pleasing to God before then. Circumcision was the sign not the cause of salvation. Even the evidence of Exodus 4:24–26 about the circumcision of the son of Moses was countered.

81. Ibid., 2.9 (CCSL 2.1343): "ut non iam ad Moysei legem ita adtendamus, quasi ad principalem legem, sed ad subsequentem."

82. Dunn, *"Pro Temporum Condicione,"* 323–25. On p. 325 I wrote: "Only in *Adversus Iudaeos* is there the argument that the old law was replaced because, as its author, God had that freedom and because, as was shown in Adam and Eve, God had always intended a universal law. This makes this chapter of *Adversus Iudaeos* original in Christian anti-Judaic literature."

83. Cic., *Inu. rhet.* 1.24.35 (LCL 386.70–72).

If circumcision was so important, Moses would have ensured it happened at the appropriate time. What Tertullian overlooked was that God's anger was precisely because of Moses's failure.

Behind these arguments is the implicit combination of other arguments: from possibility (if God changed things once—from non-circumcision to circumcision—then God has every right to change things again), and from priority (Adam, not Moses, is the typological figure in whom God's intention for all humanity was revealed). Thus the uncircumcised Adam is held out as a figure of enduring relevance, while the circumcised son of Moses cannot be used as a universal precedent (3.2).

Circumcision was no longer a sign of salvation but a sign by which the Romans could keep the Jews out of Jerusalem because it had become a sign of this people's rebellion against God (3.4–6). Signs, like arguments, were to be used rhetorically as a means of proof. The only question would be whether the new sign of circumcision was to be taken as irrefutable or probable proof.[84] The final circumcision argument is derived from what one has said in the past.[85] This was where Scripture provided a wealth of information. Tertullian could turn to Jeremiah 4:3–4 and 31:31–32 to put forward the view that God had promised to replace physical circumcision with a spiritual one (3.7).

The material on the Sabbath (4.1–11) follows. The same array of arguments as in the section on circumcision was employed, though in something of a reverse order. The first section examines God's past utterances and actions in Genesis 2:2–3, Isaiah 1:13, Ezekiel 22:8, and Isaiah 66:23, to indicate that God had promised an eternal Sabbath. This would be different from the temporal Sabbath observed by the Jews, or rather, because the Jews had violated the Sabbath there needed to be a new one (although Tertullian called it an eternal one) that all people would observe.[86] The Sabbath God had announced at the creation of the world, obviously earlier than the temporal Sabbath of the Jews, had a priority (4.1–5). The argument that the Jewish Sabbath was temporal was that the Jews themselves could point to its coming into existence with Moses. For Tertullian, this meant that if something has a beginning it must have an end. By contrast, the proper understanding of

---

84. Quint., *Inst.* 5.9.1–16 (LCL 125.194–202).

85. Cic., *Inu. rhet.* 1.35.36 (LCL 386.74); Quint., *Inst.* 5.10.28 (LCL 125.216).

86. Tertullian's argument that there must be an eternal Sabbath rather than a new Sabbath seems rather forced. I would note that I am mistaken in my translation of "expuncta" in 4.1 (Dunn, *Tertullian*, 75). It should read "accomplished" rather than "cancelled."

the Sabbath was that it would be eternal. The Jewish understanding of what the Sabbath entailed (rest from work) was obviously not God's understanding since Joshua must have worked on a Sabbath day in the capture of Jericho (Jo 6:3–5, 15–20), and the Maccabees fought on the Sabbath (1 Mc 2:38, 41) (4.7–11). In the midst of all this is the familiar cavalcade of pre-Mosaic characters (Adam, Abel, Enoch, Noah, Abraham, and Melchizedek). Rather than from their personal qualities, the argument was drawn from their past behavior: none of these individuals observed the Jewish Sabbath (4.6). Once again, the implicit presumption is that what was older was closer to God's actual intentions than what came later.

The fourth and final part of the *refutatio* deals with sacrifices (5.1–7). As with the section on circumcision, the contrast here is between the physical and the spiritual. The passage in Genesis 4:3–11, 14 is interpreted typologically along the same lines as Genesis 25:23 was: Cain, the elder son, whose sacrifice was rejected by God, represents the Jews, while Abel, the younger son, whose sacrifice was accepted by God, represents the Christians. What is worth noting, though, is that Tertullian did not interpret this scriptural passage to mean that God never accepted Jewish sacrifice, which would seem to be the most natural way to apply the typology, but rather that Jewish sacrifice was physical and Christian sacrifice spiritual (5.1–3a). This seems an unlikely conclusion to draw, and it is justified by Tertullian who again constructed arguments from God's past utterances, as found in Scripture (Mal 1:10–11; Ps 95[96]:7–8; 50[51]:19; 49[50]:14; Is 1:11–13), to show that God rejected the earthly sacrifices of the Jews, limited to one land, and indicated that spiritual sacrifices to be offered everywhere were acceptable (5.3b–7). We find here rhetorical arguments concerned with actions, like manner and place.[87]

Guerra suggests that Tertullian's arguments in this part of his pamphlet, even though circuitous, are barbed—particularly his argument about the Mosaic law being in embryonic form in the command given to Adam and Eve.[88] Yet one still finds a lack of personal invective in Tertullian's *refutatio*. Perhaps the suggestion that Tertullian was walking a fine line between demonstrating that the Jews had too limited a view of God's activity and intentions and were unfaithful in keeping God's commands, on the one hand, and, on the other, rejecting any value at all in the Hebrew Scriptures as had Marcion,

---

87. Cic., *Inu. rhet.* 1.36.38 (LCL 386.74–76); 1.37.41 (LCL 386.78–80); Quint. *Inst.* 5.10.37 (LCL 125.220); 5.10.48 (LCL 125.226).

88. Guerra, "Polemical Christianity," 116.

helps explain why Tertullian was not nearly as vehement with the Jews in the text as one might expect.[89] Tertullian certainly believed in the superiority of Christianity over Judaism and was not reluctant to point out Jewish error and lack of understanding, but to me his comments here have more the tones of academic difference of opinion.

Confirmatio (6.2–14.10)

As was pointed out in the previous chapter, 6.2 is an important passage in determining the rhetorical structure of *Aduersus Iudaeos*. Tertullian was aware that in the *refutatio* he had managed only to establish, as far as he was concerned, that there was a promise that the old covenant would come to an end. He had a twofold task to accomplish in the *confirmatio:* to prove that the old covenant had indeed come to an end (in other words, that such a promise had been fulfilled), and to prove that the new covenant had been established. He did not need to prove these two things separately, for to prove the second would, of logical necessity, prove the first. Indeed, if the new were in operation then the old must have ceased. So one of the principal aims of the *confirmatio* was to demonstrate that the new covenant was in operation. Tertullian did not even allude to the theoretical possibility of the two being in operation concurrently, i.e., of the old covenant's enduring. This is a point that a critic or opponent of Tertullian might have raised with regard to his logic. If Tertullian himself were ever aware of this possibility, it would seem that he hoped his readers were not. Another aim of the *confirmatio* was to demonstrate that the one who would bring that new covenant had materialized, for to be able to show that this person had come would also mean that one could show that the new covenant had come. Thus, even as he announced that the *confirmatio* would be concerned with proving that the new covenant or new law was in operation (6.2), the focus shifts immediately to the question of whether the new law-giver had come:

Nam etiam hic nouae legis lator, sabbati spiritalis cultor, sacrificiorum aeternorum antistes, regni aeterni aeternus dominator quaerendum, an iam uenerit necne, ut, si iam uenit, seruiendum sit illi, si necdum uenit, sustinendus sit, dummodo manifestum sit aduentu eius comprimi legis ueteris praecepta et oriri debere nouae legis exordia.[90]

89. Efroymson, "The Patristic Connection," 105, goes further than I in suggesting that Tertullian did employ invective against the Jews in this work.

90. Tert., *Adu. Iud.* 6.3 (CCSL 2.1353): "For I ought to ask as well whether this proposer of the new law, the establisher of the spiritual sabbath, the high priest of the eternal sacrifices, the

This was sound oratorical practice. In commenting upon what he defined as *partitio* (the enumeration of the *propositiones* to be treated), Quintilian noted that it was unnecessary to divide an argument into parts if, in proving one point, all the others were also proven as a matter of necessity.[91]

Before being able to illustrate that the new law-giver had come, there was the need to show that one had been promised (6.2b). As has been noted in the previous chapter, this first question about whether such a new law-giver was even expected was dealt with swiftly (7.2a). One has the impression that, within the overall rhetorical structure of the pamphlet, Tertullian's claim that the Jews would not disagree that a new law-giver was promised, belongs to the *partitio,* where one sets out the extent to which there was agreement or disagreement with one's opponent.[92] By delaying it until this point Tertullian seems to have achieved a couple of things. First, it reinforces the impression he was attempting to instill in his readers that he was a reasonable person. After having spent several chapters pointing out where he considered the Jews misunderstood God's intentions and promises, by turning his attention, albeit briefly, to where they agreed (or, at least, where he claimed they agreed with each other),[93] he helped reinforce the impression of reasonableness and fairness. It also legitimized the entire *refutatio.* In a very subtle way, by claiming that the Jews too expected a new law-giver and by linking the coming of the new law-giver with the establishment of a new law, Tertullian hinted at the ultimate argument of his *refutatio:* since the Jews themselves expected a new law, they themselves provided the best proof against their own position that their "old" law was God's ultimate and final intention.

Isaiah 45:1 was cited as an example of such Jewish acceptance that a new law-giver would come (7.2). I have noted elsewhere how this piece of Scripture could only function as an example of the expectation of a new law-giver

---

ruler of the eternal kingdom, has arrived yet or not, because, if he has come already he ought to be served, and if he has not yet come it should be endured until it is evident from his coming that the precepts of the old law are suppressed and that the introduction of the new law ought to arise." The necessary connection between the coming of the new law-giver and the establishment of the new law is seen further in 7.1 (CCSL 2.1353): "et cum constiterit uenisse indubitate etiam legem nouam ab ipso datam esse credamus et testamentum nouum in ipso et per ipsum nobis dispositum non diffiteamur."

91. Quint., *Inst.* 4.5.9–11 (LCL 125.140–42).

92. *Rhet. Her.* 1.10.17 (LCL 403.30); Cic., *Inu. rhet.* 1.22.31 (LCL 386.62–64).

93. Here one is reminded of the characteristically rhetorical insight of Quint., *Inst.* 4.5.5 (LCL 125.138): "Interim uero etiam fallendus est iudex et uariis artibus subeundus, ut aliud agi quam quod petimus putet."

because of the textual transformation of κύρῳ into κυρίῳ, something Tertullian inherited in his scriptural source.[94] From here Tertullian ought to have turned to the second major question of the *confirmatio*: determining whether or not the promised Christ had come, under the four topics announced in 7.1, beginning with that of time. However, that task does not start until 8.1b. As I mentioned in the previous chapter there is a digression at 7.3 –8.1a.

That digression was occasioned by Isaiah 45:1 with its mention of the Gentiles hearing the Christ. Tertullian discussed the conversion of the Gentiles in the time after Jesus. In the scheme announced in 7.1, this matter ought to have been treated later. In conjectural matters one of the *topoi* or *loci* about things was subsequent time.[95] The spread of Christianity was a subsequent action that must demonstrate that the Christ had come. In developing this *topos* (7.2–5) Tertullian cited Psalm 18(19):5 as the proof that such a thing was expected, and Acts 2:9–10, 5 as the historical evidence that such an expectation had been fulfilled. It is interesting to note that in 7.4, with the addition of the Gaetulians and Moors to the list of nations found in Acts 2, Tertullian has inserted an African perspective to this New Testament passage. I have commented elsewhere on what makes this first interpretation in early Christian literature of Acts 2 unique.[96]

The last part of the argument in this *digressio* about the universal spread of Christianity involved the general *topos* of contrast, comparison, or dissimilarity (7.6–8.1a).[97] Unlike any other great figure from the past (Solomon, Darius, Pharaoh, Nebuchadnezzar, and Alexander the Great are mentioned), or any group of people (Germans, Britons, Moors and Gaetulians, and even Romans), the reign of Christ knows no limits. The implication is that he must be the promised new law-giver, for only that individual could reign over the whole world and beyond. Osborn seems to suggest that this is the major proof Tertullian offered.[98] Richard Hanson has drawn attention to 7.6, where Tertullian made comment about his interpretative approach to Scripture, ac-

---

94. Dunn, "The Universal Spread of Christianity," 7.

95. Quint., *Inst.* 5.10.45–46 (LCL 125.224). *Rhet. Her.* 2.5.8 (LCL 403.70) considered subsequent behavior of the person, rather than subsequent events.

96. Dunn, "The Universal Spread of Christianity," 10–11. While Acts itself refers to foreign Jews from a variety of locations being present in Jerusalem, Tertullian took the passage to mean foreigners from a variety of locations and Jews being present in Jerusalem.

97. *Rhet. Her.* 2.4.6 (LCL 403.66); Cic., *De or.* 2.40.169–170 (LCL 348.318–20); Quint., *Inst.* 5.10.73 (LCL 125.240).

98. Osborn, *Tertullian,* 118.

knowledging that Isaiah 45:1 could be understood in a spiritual ("spiritaliter") and in a more literal sense ("attamen etiam propria specie sunt adimpleta").[99] This accords with Tertullian's common approach of playing down the allegorical in his treatises (largely, I would argue, because his opponents made so much use of it, not because he himself was ideologically opposed to it).[100]

As has been noted already, the body of the *confirmatio*, the longest part of *Aduersus Iudaeos*, concerned the four topics related to the questions of whether the Christ had come (7.1), four topics that would be reworked in 8.2 into three. In the first version, the first two topics concerned time (the prophecies about the time of the birth and death of the Christ and the destruction of Jerusalem, and the fulfillment of those prophecies), which, in the second version, was the first topic. In rhetoric time was an important issue. The author of *Ad Herennium* saw it as a sign, which was one of the six conjectural topics.[101] The young Cicero in his early notebook observed that time was one of the topics concerned with the nature of the act, one of the three divisions he listed for the conjectural issue.[102] Questions of time would occupy 8.1b–18.

Elsewhere I have written at some length analyzing chapter 8 of *Aduersus Iudaeos*,[103] a chapter that Säflund described as "recht umständlich."[104] The witness Tertullian provided to give evidence about what God had said in the past about prophecies of the coming of the Christ and the destruction of Jerusalem was Daniel 9:1–2a, 21–27 (*Adu. Iud.* 8.3–6). Only briefly did he treat Daniel as a written text needing clarification to remove ambiguity (8.7–8), which was one of the tasks in the juridical or legal issue, but, on the whole, he treated the text as a source of evidence for the conjectural question of time. In offering his interpretation of the prophetic time frame in Daniel, Tertullian proposed one that was unique in early Christian literature. He drew two periods of time instead of three from the prophecy of the seventy

99. R. P. C. Hanson, "Notes on Tertullian's Interpretation of Scripture," *JTS* n.s. 12 (1961): 275. Cf. Karlfried Froelich, *Biblical Interpretation in the Early Church,* Sources of Early Christian Thought (Philadelphia: Fortress Press, 1984), 10, who talks of typological allegory and allegorical typology as being characteristic of second-century biblical interpretation.

100. Geoffrey D. Dunn, "Tertullian's Scriptural Exegesis in *de praescriptione haereticorum,*" *JECS* 14 (2006): 141–55.

101. *Rhet. Her.* 2.4.7 (LCL 403.66–68).

102. Cic., *Inu. rhet.* 1.26.39 (LCL 386.76); 2.12.40 (LCL 386.200).

103. Geoffrey D. Dunn, "Tertullian and Daniel 9:24–27: A Patristic Interpretation of a Prophetic Time-Frame," *ZAC* 6 (2002): 330–44; and Dunn, "*Probabimus venisse eum iam*: The Fulfillment of Daniel's Prophetic Time-Frame in Tertullian's *Adversus Iudaeos*," *ZAC* 7 (2003): 140–55.

104. Säflund, *De pallio,* 191.

weeks: the first of sixty-two and a half weeks and the second of seven and a half weeks.[105] The possibility for such an interpretation arose from the fact that the Greek texts of Daniel (Theodotion and the Old Greek) were misinterpretations of the Hebrew original (preserved accurately, I have argued, in the Masoretic Text) and, being misinterpretations, they contain inconsistencies that could be exploited by later commentators, such as Tertullian, to construct very different interpretations, depending upon which of the inconsistencies one relied on most.[106] By exploiting the confusion in the text, Tertullian was able to invert the time periods (which made him a unique interpreter of this passage of Daniel) and to argue that events like the birth of the Christ and the destruction of the temple occurred not at the end points of the periods of time but within those periods.[107]

Having provided his own textual version, Tertullian set out a detailed calculation of the time frame with regard to the prophecies of the birth of the Christ (8.9–10), and the death of the Christ and destruction of Jerusalem (8.15b–16), and indicated how the birth (8.11–15a) and death (8.17–18) of Jesus best matched those requirements. This is precisely what the rhetorical *topoi* of time and occasion enabled an orator to achieve: to make a connection between a person and an event that best suited their position.

Tertullian's arguments—that the Christ was to appear and die (and that Jerusalem was to be destroyed) at particular times, and that Jesus appeared and died (and that Jerusalem was destroyed) at precisely those times—are intricate, their very complexity and detail intended obviously to overwhelm an opponent. It is possible to refute Tertullian's arguments, but it requires some involved analysis of textual variants in Daniel, which would not have been possible at the time, and chronological examination of ancient ruling dynasties.[108] The overall aim of Tertullian, though, is clear. He intended to show

105. This reading of Tertullian is supported by Reinhard Bodenmann, *Naissance d'une Exégèse. Daniel dans l'Eglise ancienne des trois premiers siècles*, Beiträge zur Geschichte der biblischen Exegese 28 (Tübingen: J. C. B. Mohr [Paul Siebeck], 1986), 347.

106. Thus in 8.7 Tertullian could refer to the whole seventy-week period, which would seem to suggest that his text of Dan 9:25 in 8.5b should refer to seventy weeks and not just sixty-two and a half (which is closer to what Theodotion did), yet the period of time covered in Dan 9:25 extends not to the destruction of the temple but to the coming of the Christ, in which case it must only be a reference to sixty-two and a half weeks and not the seventy. See Dunn, "Tertullian and Daniel 9:24–27," 338–40. Bodenmann, *Naissance d'une Exégèse*, 344, notes what is found in Theodotion, but does not discuss the fact that there is room for debate about Tertullian's actual text of Dan 9:25 in 8.5b.

107. Dunn, "Tertullian and Daniel 9:24–27," 342–43.

108. See Dunn, "Tertullian and Daniel 9:24–27," 330–44; and Dunn, *"Probabimus venisse eum*

to Jewish opponents that their continued waiting for the arrival of a messiah was ridiculous, because the prophecy in Daniel proved, at least in the way he read it, that the messiah would be born during the reign of Augustus (in 3 B.C. to be precise, according to Tertullian) and would die (in A.D. 29) before the destruction of the temple, which had to be the one that occurred under Vespasian. Now that that time had elapsed, if Jesus, the one who best fulfilled the time requirements, were not the messiah then it was too late for there ever to be one, for the opportunity had passed. The same "closed window of opportunity" argument would reappear in 13.1–3 in a *topos* on place. That Jesus lived at the right time was the first argument that he was indeed the new law-giver.

Time and opportunity were not sufficient to clinch the case. Tertullian needed to look at other characteristics of the new law-giver, particularly as expected through prophetic announcements. Arguments about persons and their activities were, as we know, at the heart of conjecture. So, from chapter 9 onward Tertullian was engaged in the third topic announced in 7.1: other prophetic themes. This was the second revised theme of 8.2: signs and operations of the new law-giver. As I have not considered these chapters elsewhere, it is appropriate to consider them in a little more detail here.

Quintilian listed birth as the first attribute of a person worth exploring.[109] Tertullian was interested in proving that, in respect to his birth, Jesus was the one who fulfilled the other prophecies that were believed to apply to the birth of the new law-giver, on more grounds than just the one about the time of his birth.

According to Isaiah 7:13–15 and 8:4, the promised one would be born of a virgin, would be called Emmanuel, and would receive the wealth of Damascus and the plunder of Samaria (9.1a). Tertullian's position was that Jesus was the one who fulfilled those conditions. These pieces of Scripture determine the *topoi* he was going to explore in this chapter. The Jewish position could be repeated from the earlier encounter: Isaiah did not refer to a virgin, Jesus was never called Emmanuel, and he was never a warrior who received spoils and plunder. Tertullian here was refuting the Jewish *refutatio* of earlier Christian arguments. Thus, even though I believe that the second half of the pam-

---

iam," 140–55, for just such a detailed examination of those issues. The omission of figures like Ptolemy VI and Claudius may well have been a deliberate attempt to squeeze too many years into a defined but smaller period allowed by the prophecy.

109. Quint., *Inst.* 5.10.24 (LCL 125.214).

phlet is overwhelmingly *confirmatio* (as the first half was overwhelmingly *refutatio*), this does not mean that Tertullian did not sometimes jump between the two tasks.

It is to be noted that the argument from the *topos* of birth, in this case the virgin birth, appears only briefly in the introduction in 9.1a. It reappears in 9.7–9, a little disconnected from its immediate context. Here it is appropriate to note how Tertullian has treated the sources from which he derived this argument, particularly to notice how he has recast them to fit his rhetorical structure. Ever since Matthew, the prophecy to Ahaz about the birth of a son had been read by Christians christologically and as proof for the virgin birth (Mt 1:23). It is not surprising to see this passage from Isaiah 7 quoted on a number of occasions in early Christian literature, including by Tertullian himself in several works.[110] What is interesting to note is that in a number of these examples Isaiah 8:4 is added after Isaiah 7:14.[111] Indeed, Skarsaune argues that such a combination, with Isaiah 8:4 interpolated for Isaiah 7:16, was part of a *testimonium* that Justin, unaware of the interpolation, quoted and from which his argument in *Dialogus* 77 was derived.[112] What he suggests is that Justin's argument depended on a Jesus-Hezekiah polemic and that Justin's aim was to demonstrate the miraculous nature of the virgin birth of the messiah.[113] After announcing his intention in chapter 43 of proving that Isaiah did not refer merely to a young woman or the birth of Hezekiah, Justin began his proof of the virgin birth as being a necessary part of the coming of the messiah in chapter 63 and continued it from chapters 66 to 85 (with digressions in chapters 67–70, 72–75, and 79–82). According to Skarsaune, chapter 77 is the high point of Justin's argument and he was able to reject Hezekiah as the object of the prophecy on the basis of the interpolated Isaiah 8:4,

110. Ign., *Eph.* 18 (long version) (Lightfoot 3.264); Jus., *1 Apol.* 33.1; Jus., *Dial.* 43.5–6, 8 (PTS 47.141–42); 66.2 (PTS 47.183–84); 67.1 (PTS 47.184–85); 68.6 (PTS 47.188); 71.3 (PTS 47.193); 84.1 (PTS 215); Iren., *Adu. haer.* 3.16.3 (FC 8/3.192); 3.19.2 (FC 8/3.240); 3.21.1 (FC 8/3.252–254); 4.33.11 (FC 8/4.270); Tert., *De carn.* 17.2 (CCSL 2.904); 21.2 (CCSL 2.911); 23.1 (CCSL 2.914); 23.6 (CCSL 2.915); Tert., *De res.* 20.3 (CCSL 2.945); Tert., *Adu. Marc.* 3.12.1 (CCSL 1.523) (= *Adu. Iud.* 9.1 [CCSL 2.1364]); 3.13.4 (CCSL 1.524) (= *Adu. Iud.* 9.7 [CCSL 2.1366]); 4.10.7 (CCSL 1.563).

111. Jus., *Dial.* 43.6 (PTS 47.141); 66.2 (PTS 47.183–84); Iren., *Adu. haer.* 4.33.11 (with Is 8:3 rather than 8:4, and reversed) (FC 8/4.268–270); Tert., *De res.* 20.3 (CCSL 2.945); Tert., *Adu. Marc.* 3.12.1 (CCSL 1.523). For Is 8:4 on its own: Iren., *Adu. haer.* 3.16.4 (FC 8/3.194); Tert., *Adu. Marc.* 3.13.1 (CCSL 1.524); 3.13.8 (CCSL 1.525); 4.20.4 (CCSL 1.595).

112. Oskar Skarsaune, *Proof from Prophecy: A Study in Justin Martyr's Proof-Text Tradition. Text-Type, Provenance, Theological Profile,* Supplements to *Novum Testamentum* 56 (Leiden: E. J. Brill, 1987), 32–34.

113. Ibid., 200–202.

which would require superhuman achievement by an infant, thus ruling out Hezekiah but not Jesus.[114] What is interesting to note is that Tertullian was going to be more interested in the comments about Emmanuel than in the miraculous birth.

Skarsaune also considers the relationship between Justin and Tertullian. Here I digress to consider his reading of Tertullian. While it would appear that Tertullian has borrowed from Justin, Skarsaune argues that the positions of the two are different and that Tertullian's position was a response to a statement of Marcion rather than being taken from Justin.[115] Justin reported his Jewish opponents as denying that Isaiah 7:14 and 8:4 had messianic implications.[116] Tertullian's opponents accepted (or are made to appear as though they accepted) that the prophecy did refer to the messiah but that Jesus could not be that messiah. On the basis of "Christo qui iam uenit" in *Adu. Iud.* 9.1, Skarsaune goes further and claims that Tertullian's opponent in *Aduersus Iudaeos* was Marcion.[117] But it must be conceded, I think, that neither Jews nor Marcion would have said "Christo qui iam uenit." Even though put onto the lips of the opponent, it reveals the thinking of Tertullian. In other words, I think that here we find a degree of slackness in Tertullian's writing, in that he did not present a Jewish opponent's position accurately enough. Given his rhetorical objective, which was to persuade his readers that he, not his opponents, was right, it is not surprising to see this. One gets the sense that a real opponent, or a more careful and less rhetorical Tertullian, would have written "the so-called Christ" or "the Christ whom you (Christians) believe to have come." To support my contention I refer to the next time Tertullian presented his opponent's position, which we discover shortly after, in 9.2: "iste, dicunt, qui uenit." Here "iste" has that sense of "so-called" or "as you claim." The same care was shown by Tertullian in using "iste" in *Adu. Marc.* 3.12.1 to represent what Marcion would have said. Thus, contrary to Skarsaune, the argument of the opponent in *Adu. Iud.* 9.1–2 and *Adu. Marc.* 3.12.1 could be at home equally on the lips of both Jews and Marcion (rather than being an argument of Marcion that was transferred by Tertullian to the Jews), provided we accept that Tertullian himself has represented what the Jews would have

114. Ibid., 201–2.   115. Ibid., 239–40.

116. Ibid., 380–81. See Jus., *Dial.* 67.1 (PTS 47.184–85).

117. Skarsaune, *Proof from Prophecy,* 239: "In adv. Jud. the Jews are made to argue that Is 7:14/8:4 do not fit *Christo qui iam uenit*—the Messiah who has already come. The implication must be that the Messiah spoken of in Isaiah has not yet come. But this is the position of Marcion—not of the Jews."

said inaccurately in 9.1.[118] Even granted that Jews would not have argued that the prophecy in Isaiah actually referred to a messiah, the fact that Tertullian indicated that opponents agreed that it did does not lead necessarily to the conclusion that he simply transferred Marcion's position to the Jews. It might well have been that Tertullian, however inaccurately, actually believed that the Jews and Marcion both held the same views on this matter.[119]

Having considered the introductory comments in 9.1a, we can examine the first argument, that from name, a *topos* or *locus* associated with arguments about person.[120] The case about the name Emmanuel appears at 9.1b–3. According to the Jewish claim, Jesus could not be the messiah because he had never been known as Emmanuel, the name the messiah would bear. Tertullian's response was to comment about the interpretation of Scripture as a document.[121] He stated that a passage was to be read in context, as opposed, one presumes, to some kind of literal or fundamentalist reading.[122] As I have pointed out elsewhere, Tertullian's approach to the interpretation of Scripture was highly rhetorical in that his approach was often determined by engagement with an opponent. Thus, he could argue for a literal reading of Scripture on one occasion, which he often did, and yet, on another, he could argue for an allegorical or contextual reading.[123]

Here he could admit that Jesus had never been called Emmanuel, but he had been described as "God is with us," which is what Emmanuel means, and hence the prophecy had been fulfilled in him (9.2–3). The name had been ap-

118. Here we may note that Skarsaune, *Proof from Prophecy,* 240, tends to support the views expressed by Quispel that *Adu. Marc.* predates *Adu. Iud.* He is prepared to accept Tränkle's reverse position so long as it is accepted that *Adu. Iud.* was merely a preparation for *Adu. Marc.* and, presumably, the opponent in *Adu. Iud.* was always understood by Tertullian to refer to Marcion, a position I cannot support.

119. I realize that what I am claiming is that Tertullian, presuming he had read Justin, did not pick up on Justin's point that the Jews rejected Is 7:14; 8:4 as referring to a messiah in the first place.

120. Cic., *Inu. rhet.* 1.24.34 (LCL 386.68–70); Quint., *Inst.* 5.10.30–31 (LCL 125.216–18).

121. *Rhet. Her.* 1.11.19 (LCL 403.34–36); 2.9.13–2.10.15 (LCL 403.80–84); Cic., *Inu. rhet.* 2.42.121–2.48.143 (LCL 386.288–312); Cic., *Part. or.* 38.133–39.138 (LCL 349.414–418); Quint., *Inst.* 7.6.1–12 (LCL 126.134–42).

122. Tert., *Adu. Iud.* 9.2 (CCSL 2.1365): "cohaerentia quoque huius capituli recognoscant."

123. See Dunn, "Tertullian's Exegesis," 141–55. See also Hanson, "Notes on Tertullian's Interpretation of Scripture," 273–79; T. P. O'Malley, *Tertullian and the Bible: Language-Imagery-Exegesis,* Latinitas Christianorum Primaeva 21 (Nijmegen and Utrecht: Dekker and van de Vegt, 1967); and J. H. Waszink, "Tertullian's Principles and Methods of Exegesis," in *Early Christian Literature and the Classical Intellectual Tradition: In Honorem Robert M. Grant,* ed. W. R. Schoedel and R. L. Wilken (Paris: Beauchesne, 1979), 17–31.

plied to him by those who believed in him. The observant opponent ought to have been able to spot a circular argument here: Jesus was the fulfillment of the prophecy because those who believed him to be that fulfillment gave him the name by which he would be recognized as the fulfillment. Among those who believed were Jews who had become Christian.[124] They are the subject of what remains to be said in 9.3 and equally they appear to be the same subject at the beginning of 9.4 ("[a]eque sono nominis inducuntur"), yet Tertullian was negatively critical of those people in 9.4 while he was positive about those mentioned in 9.3. One has to conclude that in 9.4 he has reverted to discussing the opinions of those Jews who do not believe that Jesus is the Christ: the Jews mentioned in 9.1b. Perhaps this could be used by some to suggest that this passage has been taken from the earlier section in *Adu. Marc.* 3.12.3 and reused here. I think not, because even in that passage we notice some anomaly. There Tertullian began by addressing Marcion, who supposedly rejected calling Jesus Emmanuel (*Adu. Marc.* 3.12.1), yet was prepared to call him "God is with us" (*Adu. Marc.* 3.12.2). Even the Jews who had become Christians, as well as the Marcionites, accepted that he was called Emmanuel.[125] It would seem to me that this contradiction in *Aduersus Marcionem* can best be explained as Tertullian's attempt to use a source without having ironed out first all the difficulties. Hence, I maintain the priority of *Aduersus Iudaeos* over *Aduersus Marcionem*. The problems found in *Aduersus Iudaeos* with the confusion over the change of subject from 9.3 to 9.4 have to be Tertullian's sloppiness, which should have been spotted in a revision of the initial draft.

Tertullian was only briefly interested in the *topos* of the nature of Jesus' birth being from a virgin, something that was truly of sign value (9.7–9 [= *Adu. Marc.* 3.13.4–6]).[126] Fredouille notes that Tertullian's emphasis, in contrast with Justin's, was on the novelty of the virgin birth, for only something unusual could serve as a sign. Justin had been more interested in connecting it with other prophecies.[127]

124. Tert., *Adu. Iud.* 9.3 (CCSL 2.1365): "qui ex Iudaismo credunt in Christum." If one accepts that Tertullian was doing more than simply repeating someone else's earlier arguments, then this clause can be taken as late-second-century evidence of some continuing source of Christian conversion from Judaism.

125. Tert., *Adu. Marc.* 3.12.3 (CCSL 1.523): "inuenies apud Hebraeos Christianos, immo et Marcionitas, Emmanuhelem nominare."

126. Thus, Tertullian wanted this part of Isaiah interpreted literally (given the text that he had, which used the term "virgin"), even though he did not want the other parts of the Isaiah prophecy that he had cited in 9.1 taken quite so literally.

127. Fredouille, *Tertullien et la conversion*, 265: "L'exégèse de Tertullien est identique [with

Tertullian was much more interested in the *topos* of Jesus' achievement as an infant. It was the young age at which he possessed the wealth of Damascus and the plunder of Samaria that made them remarkable in Jesus' life (9.4–6 [= *Adu. Marc.* 3.13.1–3]; 9.10–16 [= *Adu. Marc.* 3.13.6–10]). While we can see a number of close parallels with Justin,[128] we simply do not find Tertullian interested in refuting a view that Isaiah could only have referred to Hezekiah. In 9.6 we see a rare example in this pamphlet of a more emotive or sarcastic Tertullian who dismissed the idea that infants literally could be warriors.

We see here many examples of Tertullian first offering his opponent's view before refuting it (9.1, 2, 4, 7). We may observe also something of his approach to Scripture. In *Aduersus Iudaeos* as well he favored an allegorical interpretation when the literal seemed to support a Jewish understanding. Thus, while in 9.4–6 he was quite happy with the literal reading of Isaiah 8:4 as referring to an infant not a warrior, in 9.10–16, Damascus, Samaria, and Assyria[129] were interpreted allegorically,[130] as was the reference to gold, Egypt, Babylon, and the magi (much of 9.11–15 being a justification for this exegetical practice rather than particularly relevant to the topic of the chapter).[131]

Moving away from considering the warlike achievements of the infant Jesus, Tertullian also considered other warrior attributes of the Christ, taking Psalm 44(45):2–3, 5–6 as his starting point, and applied what he read there to Jesus (9.17–20a [= *Adu. Marc.* 3.14.1–2, 5–7]). Once again, warlike attributes could only be applied to the Christ figuratively. The sword of the Christ would be the word of God, arrows would be God's precepts. Justin too had

---

Justin's] quant au fond: mais l'accent y est mis, une fois de plus, sur la 'nouveauté' que constitue la naissance virginale du Christ."

128. We find this even in the use of Ez 16:3 as an explanation that sometimes Scripture needs to be interpreted figuratively: Jus., *Dial.* 77.4 (PTS 47.203–4); Tert., *Adu. Iud.* 9.14 (CCSL 2.1368) (= Tert., *Adu. Marc.* 3.13.9 [CCSL 1.525]).

129. Tertullian has translated "ἔναντι βασιλέως Ἀσσυρίων" (in LXX and Justin) as "aduersus regem Assyiorum" (9.4 [CCSL 2.1365]), giving his version of Is 8:4 a more intense meaning. Whereas in Jus., *Dial.* 77.4 (PTS 47.203–4), Herod was identified with the king of Assyria and, from the context of ch. 78, "ἔναντι" almost means "under his nose," in Tertullian the use of the preposition gives the impression that the magi's action was in direct opposition to the Assyrian king.

130. Tert., *Adu. Iud.* 9.6 (CCSL 2.1366]): "sequitur ut figurate pronuntiatum uideatur."

131. Peter Iver Kaufman, "Tertullian on Heresy, History and the Reappropriation of Revelation," *CH* 60 (1991): 175, states that Tertullian "seems to hug the coastline of sacred literature, seldom experimenting with allegory, save the relatively tame typological readings, which permitted him to strike at Marcion's disrespect for the Old Testament." See also Wiles, "The Old Testament in Controversy," 119.

cited this psalm as being of christological significance, although without offering much comment on it (*Dial.* 38).[132]

Tertullian returned to the rhetorical *topos* of name (9.20b–25 [= *Adu. Marc.* 3.16.3–6]). He wished to demonstrate that the Christ was prophesied in the Hebrew Scriptures to bear the name Jesus, for when the Son of God spoke to Joshua, son of Nun and assistant to Moses (for God could not be seen or heard directly), what is recorded is the fact that the Son's name was upon Joshua (Ex 23:20–21), hence the Son's name must be Jesus (although Tertullian allowed his readers to draw this conclusion for themselves) (9.22–23a). Hence, Joshua "figuram futuri fuisse."[133] This same argument may be found in Justin (*Dial.* 75). Skarsaune has pointed out the ways in which Justin's interpretation differs from earlier Christian and from Philo's interpretations.[134] He suggests that Justin's view that Joshua was the guardian angel might have been prompted by Deuteronomy 31:2–3 (*Dial.* 126.6). It is worth pointing out that in *Aduersus Iudaeos* Tertullian turned to this sentence in Deuteronomy immediately after the Exodus material (9.23b), although he offered the more usual Christian interpretation (Mt 11:10; Mk 1:2; Lk 7:27) of seeing John the Baptizer as the messenger who went before to prepare the way (9.23b–24). The material on John seems somewhat digressive.

Having examined his name, Tertullian proceeded to investigate Jesus' family, another standard rhetorical *topos* associated with person (9.26–27 [= *Adu. Marc.* 3.17.3b–4a]).[135] The scriptural prophecy that there would arise a twig from the root of Jesse (Is 11:1–2) was claimed to be fulfilled in Mary, who was from the house of David.[136] Even when Justin referred to the prophecy of Isaiah 11 (*Dial.* 87.2; *1 Apol.* 32.12), he did not mention Mary being of David's lineage.[137] There is only one reference in Justin to Mary's Davidic ancestry (*Dial.* 45.4).

---

132. Kaufman, "Tertullian on Heresy," 175.   133. Tert., *Adu. Iud.* 9.21 (CCSL 2.1370).

134. Skarsaune, *Proof from Prophecy,* 176, believes that Justin employed this psalm to refer to the universal reign of Christ. Justin cited the entire psalm while Tertullian went only as far as verse 5, omitting most of the universal reference.

135. Cic., *Inu. rhet.* 1.24.35 (LCL 386.70); Quint., *Inst.* 5.10.24 (LCL 125.214).

136. Tert., *Adu. Iud.* 9.26 (CCSL 2.1372): "et quoniam ex semine Dauid genus trahere deberet uirgo." On the evidence from Tertullian about Mary being a descendant of David see Geoffrey D. Dunn, "The Ancestry of Jesus According to Tertullian: *ex David per Mariam,*" in *Studia Patristica* 36, ed. M. F. Wiles and E. J. Yarnold, papers presented to the thirteenth International Conference on Patristic Studies, Oxford 1999 (Leuven: Peeters, 2001): 349–55.

137. Skarsaune, *Proof from Prophecy,* 446, states that Tert., *Adu. Iud.* 9.26, employed Is 11:1 in a different context than did Justin, though Tert., *Adu. Marc.* 3.17.4, might depend on Jus., *Dial.*

The next *topos* or *locus* of person considered was that of Jesus' character or nature (9.28 [= *Adu. Marc.* 3.17.4b]). Tertullian drew from Scripture (Is 53:3, 7; 42:2–3) to show that the Christ would be humble, patient, and tranquil.[138] The next *topos* was that of occupation (9.29–31 [= *Adu. Marc.* 3.17.5]).[139] Although he was aware that what was needed was to outline the preaching and healing ministry of Jesus in relation to the prophecies from the rule of Scripture (9.29),[140] which he exemplified with Isaiah 58:1–2 and 35:4–6, the only proof Tertullian offered that Jesus did fulfill those prophecies was a brief, compound extract from John 5:18 and 10:33.[141] Perhaps a clearer insight into Tertullian's attitude concerning the probative nature of Jesus' works is provided in *Aduersus Marcionem,* where he cited New Testament passages to show how Jesus himself did not place much emphasis upon them (*Adu. Marc.* 3.3.1–2). Given that it parallels what appears in *Aduersus Marcionem* and that references to humility, patience, and tranquility make more sense if found in a section on Jesus' character than in a section on his name, I agree with Tränkle against Kroymann that the sentence beginning "exploratio etiam" belongs in 9.27 rather than at the beginning of 9.26.

In 10.1–19a Tertullian continued his examination of the non-temporal, prophetic themes about the coming of the Christ (7.1) or of the signs and operations performed by the Christ (8.2), by examining the death of the Christ. In a forensic case the interest was nearly always with who did or did not kill the person who died. This was not Tertullian's interest. His concern was with establishing that the events surrounding the death of Jesus had been predicted in the Hebrew Scriptures, thus proving that he was the one who fulfilled the prophecies and thus was the new law-giver.

87.4f. Skarsaune does not allude to the close relationship/dependence between the two passages in Tertullian, and I would support seeing a downplaying in the idea of similarity at this point. Tert., *Adu Marc.* 3.17.4 (CCSL 1.530–31), contains only the briefest of mentions of the ancestry of Jesus. The focus of the chapter, particularly because of the insertion of 3.17.1–3a, was on the suffering of Jesus.

138. Säflund, *De pallio,* 125–28, used Is 53:3, 7 as one of the passages to demonstrate that in the latter half of *Adu. Iud.* the scriptural texts were not taken from a proto-Vulgate. That they were so taken is the position of those who wish to prove the latter half not to be by Tertullian because in the first half and in *Adu. Marc.* the scriptural texts seem to depend on the LXX. Säflund was able to show how both this and other instances of passages from Isaiah (13:21; 14:1) show closer resemblance to the LXX than to the Vulgate.

139. Is 58:1–2 is not referred to in Tert., *Adu. Marc.,* and Is 35:4–6 appears in *Adu. Marc.* 4.24.12 (CCSL 1.610).

140. On Tertullian's use of "regula" see L. Wm. Countryman, "Tertullian and the Regula Fidei," *The Second Century* 2 (1982): 208–27.

141. Nowhere else in Tertullian's writings are these two verses blended together.

He began by responding to a Jewish argument against the Christian belief that it was prophesied that the Christ would be crucified. The Jews had countered by referring to Deuteronomy 21:23 to support their own belief that, because Jesus was crucified, he could not be the Christ (10.1). By establishing that the Hebrew Scriptures prophesied that the Christ would suffer and die, and would die by crucifixion, this would be further proof that Jesus, who was crucified, was indeed the promised new law-giver, which was the rhetorical aim of the *confirmatio*. So while the overall rhetorical *topos* was that of a person's death, it was handled in such a way as to be a response to claims about what the Hebrew Scriptures did and did not mean.

Justin had made use of this text of Deuteronomy 21:23 and interpreted it in much the same way as Paul had (Gal 3:13), viz., that Jesus did indeed become accursed as was predicted and therefore, rather than being an embarrassment for Christians, this text was further confirmation of his being the fulfillment of the Hebrew Scriptures. Justin clarified Paul, stating that the one crucified was not cursed by God but by the people, and added some more recent information that the Jews in their synagogues cursed Christians (*Dial.* 96.1–2).[142] Irenaeus also cited Deuteronomy 21:23 to the same effect (*Adu. haer.* 3.18.3). Whereas Paul, Justin, and Irenaeus had used Deuteronomy 27:26 together with 21:23 to highlight the impossibility of fulfilling the law and that therefore the curse under which humanity lived could only be lifted by someone taking that curse on themselves, Tertullian did not use the notion that Jesus suffered vicariously. He offered a contextual, almost sophistic interpretation of Deuteronomy 21:23, without making use of Deuteronomy 27:26, such that the one hung upon the tree in Deuteronomy is cursed by God because of personal fault. So Jesus, who was hung upon the tree without having personal fault, would not be cursed by God (10.3).[143] The non-accursed

---

142. Skarsaune, *Proof from Prophecy*, 216–19, notes that from *Dial.* 89.2 on, Justin seems to have incorporated the Pauline insight into a tradition that rejected the notion that Jesus could be cursed, giving an overall yes and no balance. Theodore Stylianopolous, *Justin Martyr and the Mosaic Law*, Dissertation Series 20 (Missoula, Mont.: Society of Biblical Literature, 1975), 103–8, does not see the combination of two traditions, but only that Justin felt the need to modify the Pauline interpretation. He suggests (105, n. 68) that, unlike Paul, Justin did not apply Dt 21:23 to Christ, although he qualifies this by acknowledging that Justin saw, in the curse by the Jews, that it did apply. Willis A. Shotwell, *The Biblical Exegesis of Justin Martyr* (London: S.P.C.K., 1965), 99, calls Justin's interpretation far-fetched.

143. Skarsaune, *Proof from Prophecy*, 218, points out that when Justin relied upon the non-Pauline tradition, e.g., in *Dial.* 90.3 (PTS 47.226) and 94.5 (PTS 47.233), he accepted that Jesus had not been accursed by God.

Jesus suffered and died not vicariously but simply to fulfill what had been prophesied in such passages as Psalms 34(35):12; 68(69):4; 21(22):16; 68(69):22; and 21(22):18 (10.4–5).[144]

Certainly in other passages Tertullian accepted that Jesus died under the curse of the law and that his interpretation was aligned with that of Paul.[145] In *Adu. Marc.* 3.18.1 we have another example of Tertullian's acceptance of Jesus being cursed by God when he died. There is reference there to an earlier passage in his writings. Could this be proof of the priority of *Aduersus Iudaeos* over *Aduersus Marcionem?* Tränkle, however, understands the reference in *Adu. Marc.* 3.18.1[146] to be to *Adu. Marc.* 5.3.9–10.[147] Tränkle's main interest in this passage in *Aduersus Iudaeos,* though, was to disprove Corssen, who believed he could detect the influence of the unknown compiler, by showing that the same hand was responsible for the thoughts of both *Aduersus Iudaeos* and *Aduersus Marcionem* with regard to Deuteronomy 21:23.[148] Given that the explanation offered in *Adu. Marc.* 5.3.9–10 is thoroughly Pauline in accepting that Jesus was accursed and therefore so different from the explanation of Deuteronomy 21:23 offered in *Aduersus Iudaeos,*[149] I agree with Tränkle that the reference in *Adu. Marc.* 3.18.1 must be to *Adu. Marc.* 5.3.9–10 rather than *Adu. Iud.* 10.1. In other words, *Adu. Iud.* 10.1 is a unique interpretation of Deuteronomy 21:23 in Tertullian's writings. Of course, this need not suggest that we have evidence of another hand at work. I am suggesting that it suited Tertullian's purposes better in this pamphlet to write of Jesus' complete innocence and the thoroughly undeserved nature of his death to make the point about how he endured all that in order to fulfill what the Scriptures had prophesied about the Christ.

Having responded to that objection, Tertullian turned to scriptural texts

144. The question of why it even had been prophesied that the Christ would suffer and die this way was not asked. All Tertullian offered in 10.5 (CCSL 2.1375–1376) was a comment that the prophecies were obscure in order not to have been a stumbling block to belief.

145. Tert., *De pat.* 8.3 (CCSL 1.308); Tert., *Adu. Prax.* 29.3 (CCSL 2.1202); Tert., *De fug.* 12.2 (CCSL 2.1150).

146. Tert., *Adu. Marc.* 3.18.1 (CCSL 1.531): "Sed huius maledictionis sensum differo digne a sola praedicatione crucis, de qua nunc maxime quaeritur, quia et alias antecedit rerum probatio rationem."

147. Tränkle, *Tertullian, "Adversus Iudaeos,"* xli: "In Marc. 3, 18, 1 ist zwar der Ausgangspunkt der Überlegung der gleiche Einwand, die Antwort wird jedoch auf Marc. 5, 3, 9f. verschoben, wo diese Frage in Zusammenhang mit Gal. 3,13 . . . ebenfalls behandelt werden muß."

148. Tränkle, *Tertullian, "Adversus Iudaeos,"* xli–xlii.

149. Stylianopoulos, *Justin Martyr and the Mosaic Law,* 107, n. 75, recognized that the interpretations in *Adu. Marc.* and *Adu. Iud.* differed.

that predicted the "sacramentum passionis"[150] and to the figures from the Hebrew Scriptures, like Isaac, Joseph, Jacob, Simeon and Levi, and Moses (10.6–10 [= *Adu. Marc.* 3.18.2–7]), who became typological indicators of the manner in which Jesus died. We may notice how Tertullian claimed the blessing of Deuteronomy 33:17 to have been pronounced by Jacob rather than Moses.[151] Justin, who quoted this text, correctly attributed the blessing to Moses (*Dial.* 91.1–3). The fact that the interpretation of the text about the bull's horns representing the cross is so similar indicates that there must be some connection between the two. Genesis 49:5–7, with its reference to the hamstringing of a bull, which Tertullian applied to the Christ, had not been used in *Barnabas*, Justin, or Irenaeus. Mention of Moses praying with outstretched arms and the erecting of the bronze serpent as being figures for the cross, however, was common in early Christian literature.[152] Tertullian seems to have been reliant neither upon *Barnabas* nor Justin at this point.[153]

Other passages from the Hebrew Scriptures served, although non-typologically, to indicate the manner in which the Christ would die: Psalm 95(96):10; Isaiah 9:5; Jeremiah 11:19; Psalm 21(22): 17, 22; Isaiah 53:8–10; 57:2; Amos 8:9–10; and Exodus 12:2–10 (*Adu. Iud.* 10.11–19 [= *Adu. Marc.* 3.19.1–9]).[154] These prophecies could be fulfilled, according to Tertullian, by no one other than Jesus. Justin had been interested in pointing out that in passages like Jeremiah 11:19 and Psalm 95(96):10 the Jewish versions of the text had cut out words and phrases that the Christians would employ christologically (*Dial.* 72–73).[155] Skarsaune suggests that Tertullian derived his selection of texts here from different passages in Justin's *Apologia* and *Dialogus*.[156] Even though this may

150. Tert., *Adu. Iud.* 10.5 (CCSL 2.1375).

151. Ibid., 10.7 (CCSL 2.1376) (= Tert., *Adu. Marc.* 3.18.3 [CCSL 1.532]).

152. Jus., *Dial.* 90.4–5 (PTS 47.226); 91.3 (PTS 47.228); 111.1 (PTS 260); 112.2 (PTS 262); 131.4–5 (PTS 47.297)—(battle against Amalek); 91.4 (PTS 47.228); 94.1–2, 4–5 (PTS 47.232–33); 112.1–2 (PTS 47.261–62); 131.4 (PTS 47.297)—(the bronze serpent); and *Barn.* 12.2–7. See Skarsaune, *Proof from Prophecy*, 216–18.

153. James Carleton Paget, *The Epistle of Barnabas: Outlook and Background*, Wissenschaftliche Untersuchungen zum Neuen Testament 2, series 64 (Tübingen: J. C. B. Mohr [Paul Siebeck], 1994), 159–60, notes how, in the interpretation of Num 21:6–9, the author of *Barn.* focused on the life-giving properties of the serpent while Justin focused on the destruction of the power of the serpent. My reading of Tertullian suggests that he was highlighting more the typological relationship between the tree upon which the serpent was hung and the cross of Jesus.

154. Tert., *Adu. Iud.* 10.17–19 (CCSL 2.1380) is not paralleled in book 3 of *Adu. Marc.* In the latter treatise, Amos 8:9–10 is cited in 4.42.5 (CCSL 1.660). Indeed, the parallels between the two works do not recommence until *Adu. Iud.* 11.11.

155. Skarsaune, *Proof from Prophecy*, 35–42.

156. Ibid., 441–43.

be true, Tertullian did not use the texts for the same purpose. If Justin turned to Isaiah 53 to highlight the innocence of Jesus,[157] Tertullian was more concerned to point out simply the fact that this prophet indicated that the suffering servant would actually die, something Jesus did (10.15). Fredouille draws attention to Tertullian's interest in Isaiah 9:5 in arguing that the novelty or unusualness of something had significance.[158]

In this entire chapter Tertullian felt no need to explain or prove the details of the death of Jesus, presuming that his readers were familiar with the fact that Jesus went to his death silently and innocently (10.4, 5), that he was persecuted by the Pharisees and held to the cross by nails (10.9), that he was crucified (10.11, 14), that he called his body "bread" (10.12), that he rose from the dead (10.16), that he died in the middle of the day (10.17), and that he died at the time of Passover (10.18).

Having spent much of the chapter indicating that the Christ would suffer crucifixion (10.6–14a), Tertullian turned his attention to the fact that the Christ was predicted to die (10.14b–19a). The arguments here seem particularly weak. For one thing, it could be argued against Tertullian that the passages of Scripture he presented did not refer necessarily to the Christ and that the simple facts concerning the time and place of death, burial, and resurrection (itself a disputed fact) were insufficient to make him the only one who fulfilled Scripture.

Following this, Tertullian turned his attention to the events that were prophesied to be subsequent to the coming of the Christ (10.19b–14.10). He had examined this matter already with regard to the issue of the timing of the subsequent events in chapter 8. Here he would look at the nature of those subsequent events. This can be classified as still belonging to the third topic announced in 7.1, but as moving from the second to the third topic of the revised structure of the *confirmatio* announced in 8.2.

The lengthiest of Tertullian's extracts from the Hebrew Scriptures in this pamphlet (Ez 8:12–9:6) occurs in 11.2–8. This was the only occasion Tertullian ever used this passage from this prophet, except in *Adu. Marc.* 3.22.5 where he cited Ezekiel 9:4. In *Aduersus Iudaeos* this passage was able to indicate several things at once: the twofold negative judgment against the Jews (in the present age accomplished in the destruction of Jerusalem, and the univer-

---

157. D. Jeffrey Bingham, "Justin and Isaiah 53," *VChr* 54 (2000): 248–61.
158. Fredouille, *Tertullien et la conversion*, 266.

sal judgment to be accomplished in the age to come) and the favorable judgment that would be given to those marked with the sign of the cross. In 11.9 Tertullian added Deuteronomy 28:64–66 as yet another prophecy about the cross.[159]

Elsewhere I have commented on the arguments found in chapter 12 and its relationship with the material in 7.2–8.1a and in *Adu. Marc.* 3.20.1–4.[160] Using Psalm 2:7–8 and Isaiah 42:6–7, Tertullian applied the rhetorical *topos* of comparison to prove that the reference to the son begotten this day was to the Christ and not to David, because David never received the Gentiles as his inheritance. I have noted already, in the opening of the *confirmatio*, how Tertullian applied this prophecy to the Christian experience.[161]

In 13.1b it appears at first as though Tertullian were introducing a rhetorical *topos* of place with regard to the birth of the Christ, which would seem to belong to chapter 9, by citing Micah 5:1 as found in Matthew 2:6. This is what we find in Justin (*Dial.* 78.1 and 1 *Apol.* 34.1) and Irenaeus (*Dem.* 63). Tertullian did not develop such an argument. He used Micah as an argument about events subsequent to the death of Jesus. Here Tertullian was able to take recent historical events, like the expelling of the Jews from Bethlehem, to argue that it was now impossible for the Christ to be born in Bethlehem. Jesus, who was born in Bethlehem, must be the Christ (13.1b–3, 5). This information and argument are original to Tertullian. They make use of the forensic argument of comparison in conjunction with time and place.[162]

Tertullian produced other texts to illustrate that Scripture predicted the displacement of the Jews from their land (Is 1:7; 33:17), which would happen after the coming of the Christ (13.4). We have noticed already that Tertullian had cited a longer version of the first text (Is 1:7–8) in the context of the *refutatio*: that circumcision was the sign by which the Romans could keep the Jews out of Jerusalem (3.4). It was to be used again later in this chapter (13.26 [= *Adu. Marc.* 3.23.3 and even intimated at 3.23.7b, which has no parallel with

159. Tertullian mistakenly stated that the passage was from Exodus. Iren., *Dem.* 79 (SC 62.146), was the only other early Christian author who employed part of this prophecy in his writings.

160. Dunn, "The Universal Spread of Christianity," 12–15.

161. It is to be noted that in *Adu. Marc.* 3.20.5 (CCSL 1.535) Tertullian utilized yet another piece of Scripture (Is 55:4–5) to reinforce the idea that the Hebrew Scriptures foretold the universal spread of Christianity because the text referred not to David but to the Christ. The argument about the universal spread of Christianity continues in *Adu. Marc.* 3.21, with particular attention to the controversy with the Marcionites.

162. *Rhet. Her.* 2.4.6 (LCL 403.66); Cic., *Inu. rhet.* 2.13.43 (LCL 386.202–4).

Aduersus Iudaeos]). Whereas in *Adu. Iud.* 3.4, 6 and in Justin (*1 Apol.* 47; *Dial.* 16.2; 92.3)[163] it was clearly stated that they were excluded from Jerusalem, here the reference is a more general one.[164]

Coupled with the fact that the Christ would be born in Bethlehem was that he was to be anointed. Since the destruction of the temple anointing was no longer possible (13.5b–7). The conclusion was that the Christ must have come already. While this may be so, it is to be noted that nothing was put forward that would identify Jesus as the one who had been anointed as required. Reference was made to Daniel 9:26, where Tertullian has "unctio," referring to the end of anointing, rather than "unctus," referring to the death of the anointed one. This is another example of an argument from comparison used in conjunction with time and place. Tertullian had presented it already in 8.17.

I observed in the previous chapter how much of the material from 13.11–23 does not at first seem to fit in the context of this part of the pamphlet because Tertullian spent too much time writing about the cross rather than about events that were to take place after the death of the Christ. Indeed, from his version of Daniel 9:26b about the death of the Christ being at the same time as the destruction of Jerusalem (with Tertullian simply ignoring the problem of the forty-year time difference), Tertullian added (8.10) Isaiah 65:2 (the only time he ever used this piece of Scripture) and Psalms 21(22):17–18 and 68(69):22 (the first part of which had appeared already at 8.17 and 10.4, 13). While these passages may point to the death of the Christ (something Tertullian felt the need to cover once again in 13.11–23), they do not relate in any way to the destruction of Jerusalem. The whole argument "that the city was due to be destroyed at the same time as when its leader was having to suffer in it"[165] is not supported by what is found in 13.11–23 at all.[166] The failure to make a connection means that the material in this section ought to be found in chapter 10. It is interesting that none of chapter 13 is paralleled in *Aduersus Marcionem* until 13.24. Tränkle notes that the author's

163. Dunn, *"Pro Temporum Condicione,"* 328.
164. Tert., *Adu. Iud.* 13.4 (CCSL 2.1385): "quod uobis, pro meritis uestris post expugnationem Hierusalem prohibitis ingredi in terram uestram, de longinquo eam oculis tantum uidere permissum est."
165. Tert., *Adu. Iud.* 13.10 (CCSL 2.1386): "quod ciuitas simul eo tempore exterminari deberet, cum ducatus eius in ea pati haberet."
166. The only exception being 13.14b–16 about how the Spirit had deserted the Jewish synagogues.

reference in 13.8 that this argument was being discussed a second time cannot be accurate because nowhere earlier had the ascension and second coming of Jesus been mentioned.[167]

We can consider some of Tertullian's treatment of scriptural passages in this section from 13.10–23. The use of Isaiah 65:2 and Psalm 21(22):17–18 together is also found in Justin (*Dial.* 97 and *1 Apol.* 35.2–5). The coupling of Psalm 68(69):22 with Psalm 21(22), though, is not found in Justin. Indeed, Psalm 68(69):22 is not referred to in Justin's writings at all. In Tertullian, this coupling occurs also in *Adu. Iud.* 10.4 and *De res.* 20.5. The difference between these two instances and the one in *Adu. Iud.* 13.10 is that in the former there is some indication that he has not blended the two into one, which appears to be the case in the latter instance. Skarsaune notes how Tertullian's interpretation of Psalm 21(22) in *Adu. Iud.* 13.10, in referring it not to David but to the Christ, is identical to Justin's (*1 Apol.* 35.6), and how *Adu. Iud.* 10.14 seems to be a condensing of Justin's own commentary on Psalm 21(22) in *Dial.* 105 and seems to parallel *Dial.* 97.4.[168] While I can agree with Skarsaune that *Adu. Iud.* 10.11–14 depends directly upon Justin, I am not convinced that the same thing can be said about *Adu. Iud.* 13.10–11 because of the coupling of Psalm 68(69) with Psalm 21(22). Here it would seem that Tertullian has gone back to his *testimonia* source, even though keeping Justin's interpretation in mind (unless it can be argued that Justin derived the interpretation from his source, to which Tertullian had access and that, therefore, in this instance, Tertullian did not rely upon Justin). This view is reinforced when we consider Irenaeus, *Adu. haer.* 4.33.12, where we find Psalm 68(69):22, Isaiah 65:2, and Psalm 21(22):19, among other pieces of Scripture, cited together. In the midst of all this there is another reference to Psalm 95(96):10, which had appeared in *Adu. Iud.* 10.11.

Some of the other scriptural texts in chapter 13 do not have a parallel in Justin (Ps 66[67]:7; Joel 2:22; Jer 2:10–12;[169] and Amos 8:9).[170] While Justin had used Jeremiah 2:13 to refer to circumcision (*Dial.* 19.2; 114), Tertullian

---

167. Tränkle, *Tertullian, "Adversus Iudaeos,"* xlv.

168. Skarsaune, *Proof from Prophecy,* 441.

169. However, Jer 2:12–13 does appear in *Barn.* 11.2 (SC 172.160) and Jer 2:13 in Jus., *Dial.* 114.5 (PTS 47.267), as it does in Tert., *Adu. Iud.* 13.14 (CCSL 2.1387).

170. Perhaps there is even an allusion to Is 16:3, which is noteworthy in that both *Barn.* 11.3 (SC 172.160) and Jus., *Dial.* 114.5 (PTS 47.267), used Is 16:1–2 (which Tertullian did not). Skarsaune, *Proof from Prophecy,* 183, notes that in combining Jer 2:13 and Is 16:1 with Jer 3:8, Justin was referring to the Hadrianic ban on Jews entering Jerusalem.

used it to refer to the abandonment of Jewish synagogues by the Holy Spirit (13.15),[171] as he could find prophesied in Isaiah 65:13–14 (a passage he used in a similar fashion in *Adu. Marc.* 4.14.10–11 and 4.15.13).

Tertullian could find more predictions of the cross in 2 Kings 6:1–7 (13.17–20a) and Genesis 22:1–14, which was joined with Isaiah 53:7–8 and Hosea 6:1–3 (13.20b–23). All of this, though, was merely preparatory for a conclusion about how the destruction of Jerusalem was to occur after the death of the Christ, but it is a conclusion that is easily lost among so much detail on the death of the Christ.

From 13.24 to the end of the chapter the parallel with *Aduersus Marcionem* (3.23.1–7) is resumed. Tränkle sees this as the beginning of "ein neuer Gedankengang" and that, even though the fate of the Jews would follow on naturally from a discussion of the death of Jesus, 13.24–29 and that finishing at 13.23 "gehören nicht ursprünglich zusammen und wir mussen hier ähnlich wie zwischen den Kap. VIII und IX, XII und XIII einen Trennungsstrich ziehen."[172] He offers an alternative: "denn ihr Schicksal war im Vorausgehenden stets als bekannt vorausgesetzt worden."[173] It is that alternative I wish to adopt. Tränkle argues that the words "recognoscant . . . exitum suum" of 13.24 were "sinnlos" if they had to refer to the section ending in 13.23, because he believed that earlier section only to be about "Christi Geburt, Tod und Auferstehung."[174] I have argued that 13.8–23 is only the main part of the major premise of a syllogism (stated most clearly in 13.9 and 24), whose conclusion was that the Christ had come and suffered already (13.1, 8, and 24), and whose minor premise was that the destruction had taken place.[175] However, what is lacking is any real consideration of the vital part of the major premise: establishing that the death of the Christ had to be connected with the destruction of Jerusalem. While he had made this connection with regard to Daniel 9:26, all the argument in 13.11–23 failed to do the same. Here I think we can say that Tertullian was carried away with some scriptural interpretations about the suffering of the Christ. Only from 13.24 does he return to consider the fate of the Jews after the destruction of Jerusalem.

The argument in the last section of chapter 13 is that the conversion of the

---

171. Skarsaune, *Proof from Prophecy*, 450, argues that Tert., *Adu. Iud.* 13.13–14, does not derive from Justin or Barnabas.

172. Tränkle, *Tertullian*, "*Adversus Iudaeos*," xlviii.

173. Ibid.   174. Ibid.

175. Tert., *Adu. Iud.* 13.9 (CCSL 2.1386): "et ita factum recognoscimus."

Gentiles (an event that could take place, Tertullian presumed, only with the giving of the new law) must take place before the destruction of Jerusalem. Isaiah 2:20 and 3:1 were joined together (13.24–25 [= *Adu. Marc.* 3.23.1–2]) to demonstrate that the Jews were taken away from Jerusalem after the Gentiles had turned away from idols, which, for Tertullian, meant not simply their conversion but their conversion through Jesus who, by implication, must have come before the Jews were taken from Jerusalem. This text does not seem to have been used in Christian literature prior to Tertullian. This taking away of the Jews from Jerusalem was an indication that God had now rejected them (Is 5:6–7): the blessing of God, seen as rain, stopped because the Jews had brought forth thorns, understood as the suffering of Jesus (13.25–26 [= *Adu. Marc.* 3.23.2–3]). Again, we may notice how the subsequent event proves the earlier's occurrence.

Here we notice how Tertullian remained conscious of the work's overall aim expressed in 1.8: the Christian people "superauit" the Jews.[176] This exclusion of the Jews from God's grace is certainly not highlighted in the pamphlet, for when there is discussion about who God's people are Tertullian was interested in arguing for Christian inclusion rather than Jewish exclusion.[177] He cited several scriptural passages that indicated that God would turn away from the Jews (Is 52:5; Ez 36:20, 23; Is 1:7–8, 20; Ps 58[59]:12; and Is 50:11),[178] but he was content not to comment further. Here he was just slightly more forthcoming, stating that "from then on the grace of God has ceased among them"[179] and that "the showers of spiritual gifts were withdrawn . . . and the pool of Bethsaida stopped curing the illnesses within Israel."[180]

At the end of the chapter we find a repetition of the syllogism that had been at the center of the argument derived from the *topos* of subsequent events: calamities were predicted to befall the Jews after the coming of the Christ, such calamities have befallen, and therefore the Christ must have come.[181] In what amounts to a rather barbed and condescending piece of

176. In one of his rare instances of employing the New Testament, we find Mt 11:13/Lk 16:16 cited by Tertullian in *Adu. Iud.* 13.26 (CCSL 2.1390).

177. Perhaps this is an example of the subtlety of Tertullian. See Osborn, "The Subtlety of Tertullian," 361–62.

178. Tert., *Adu. Iud.* 13.26–27 (CCSL 2.1390–91) (= Tert., *Adu. Marc.* 3.23.3–4 [CCSL 1.540–41]).

179. Ibid., 13.25 (CCSL 2.1390): "exinde destitit apud illos dei gratia."

180. Ibid., 13.26 (CCSL 2.1390): "Et ita subtractis charismatum roribus . . . et piscina Bethsaida usque ad aduentum Christi ualetudines apud Israhel curare non desiit."

181. Ibid., 13.28 (CCSL 2.1391): "Haec igitur cum pati praedicarentur Iudaei propter Christum et passos eos inueniamus et in dispersionem demorari cernamus, manifestum est prop-

wit, Tertullian asked a series of rhetorical questions about where the Jewish cities were that would be destroyed in some imaginary future if he were
wrong about the Christ having come (13.29 [= *Adu. Marc.* 3.26.6–7]).

The last of Tertullian's examples from the *topos* of subsequent events concerns the second coming (14.1–10 [= *Adu. Marc.* 3.7.1–8]). This has received detailed treatment by me elsewhere,[182] so it is only necessary to offer a summary
here. The central part of the argument about the second coming is based on
a typological interpretation of Leviticus 16:5–28. Whereas in *Barn.* 7.6–11 the
first goat, offered in sacrifice, represented Jesus offered in sacrifice (and possibly had eucharistic implications) and the second goat, the scapegoat, represented Jesus as one who was rejected and tormented (and who would come
again), in Justin and Tertullian the two goats were interpreted with the two
comings of Jesus more clearly and explicitly in mind. Unlike *Barnabas,* in Justin
and Tertullian the second goat was identified with the first coming of Jesus because of the treatment it received. They both identified the first goat with the
second coming (incongruous as it may appear given that the first goat is sacrificed) because, for Justin, the goat was sacrificed in Jerusalem where the re-
turning Christ would be recognized and, for Tertullian, the goat sacrificed represented the eucharist, which would be celebrated until the return of Jesus.

Like Justin's, Tertullian's main purpose in referring to the two comings of
the Christ was to counter the Jewish argument that the Christ would come
only once, in glory. While these Christian authors accepted that the Christ
would come in glory, they stated that this would only be after he had come
first in humility. The suffering of Jesus, as predicted in the scriptural texts cited in 14.1–2, made him the Christ whose first coming was in humility. It has
to be admitted that in adopting this argument from his source (whether Justin or a common one), Tertullian has not quite integrated it into his rhetorical argument, for the subsequent event has not taken place. What he wanted
to argue was that this subsequent event would only take place given a certain prerequisite event (the first coming in humility). Tertullian did next to
nothing in this chapter to prove that, even if the Christ were first to come
in humility before coming in glory, that he had, in fact, come the first time.
Of course, for him, this had been established already in previous chapters. I

---

ter Christum Iudaeis ista accidisse, conspirante sensu scripturarum cum exitu rerum et ordine
temporum."

182. Geoffrey D. Dunn, "Two Goats, Two Advents and Tertullian's *Adversus Iudaeos*," *Augustinianum* 39 (1999): 245–64.

do not doubt the place of this part of the chapter in the work. It fits into the chronological sequence Tertullian had been following in the *confirmatio* and it is plausible that Tertullian liked the argument he found in his source and wanted to include it in this work even though it did not quite fit.

Peroratio (14.11–14)

I have indicated already my strong suspicion that 14.11–14 does not really belong here and that Tertullian never wrote a conclusion to this work. The conclusion that is offered here really only deals with the argument from the *topos* of subsequent events, the third of the topics announced in 8.2. Then it mentions only one of the examples of the events that, having occurred after the Christ was to come, were meant to prove that the Christ had indeed come already, viz., the coming of the Gentiles to faith. My belief that this passage is an interpolation is strengthened by the unique interpretation of Psalm 2:7 in 14.12, where, in contrast with what is found in *Adu. Iud.* 12.2 and *Adu. Marc.* 3.20.3, "Dauid filium" is understood to be Solomon.[183] No mention is made of the other topics of the *confirmatio*—the *topos* of time or the *topos* from person (the birth and death of the Christ)—nor of the *refutatio* or of the overall argument set out in the *partitio*. We find no attempt at the end of the *confirmatio* to draw the conclusion that had been outlined at the beginning of the *confirmatio*, viz., proving that the new law-giver had come would be proof that the new law had come, which, in turn, would complement and conclude the argument of the *refutatio* that the old law had ceased.

Conclusion

A thorough examination of the rhetorical arguments to be found in Tertullian's *Aduersus Iudaeos* reveals a number of things. First, it demonstrates that he was familiar with the details of the rhetorical theory of argumentation. He relied mainly upon Scripture as a source of evidence, yet was able to incorporate historical events (particularly the chronological time frame in Daniel 9, which culminated in the capture of Jerusalem) as needed. On the whole Tertullian treated Scripture not as a written text that needed to be interpreted (although, when necessary, he did engage in such an activity to remove ambiguity and clarify what for him was the authentic—which, for him,

183. For further details see Dunn, "The Universal Spread of Christianity," 15–18.

meant appropriate in its particular context—meaning). Instead, it was the source for *inuentio*. Arguments from the *topoi* of time, place, person, and subsequent events abound throughout the *confirmatio* of *Aduersus Iudaeos*.

There is very little presence of the invective and sarcasm that characterize some of Tertullian's other works.[184] Here the author was no less convinced of the absolute truth of his own position and of the falsity of his opponent's, but he was, for the most part, a model of restraint in *Aduersus Iudaeos*. After the earlier heated exchange, it would certainly have worked in his favor if he could present his arguments in a dispassionate manner. The real issue—the place of the Hebrew Scriptures in Christian theology—was never out of his mind. For him they were important and of ongoing relevance, but in the sense that they contained promises that had been fulfilled in Jesus and proved him to be the new law-giver, not that they contained promises awaiting realization.

The arguments of the *confirmatio* hold together to form a sustained whole, and we see how most of the arguments developed in the second half of the work had been announced already in the first half as needing to be presented. This undermines the belief of those who reject the second half of the pamphlet as spurious. This is so despite the undeniable fact that not only is the structure of the second half of the work in need of editing, but so too are some of the arguments. As one reads this text more carefully there are signs that the author sometimes includes information and develops a line of debate that is only partially relevant to the main issue. The use of Cain and Abel in chapter 5 and the treatment of the second coming of the Christ in chapter 14 may be given as examples. The inclusion of the material in chapter 7, about the universal spread of Christianity, is certainly out of place and would have been more effective if joined with similar material in chapter 12, where it best fits into the chronological way in which this work unfolds. That material itself would have been better if it did not divide chapters 11 and 13. The early *peroratio* in 11.10–12 is premature. Some of the points made in chapter 13, particularly 13.8–23, appear to be off the topic. Either they should have been incorporated into chapter 10 or Tertullian should have concentrated more in chapter 13 on sticking with the point at issue about the destruction of Jerusalem taking place after the death of the Christ, rather than dealing too extensively with

---

184. Eric Osborn, "Tertullian as Philosopher and Roman," in *Die Weltlichkeit des Glaubens in der Alten Kirche. Festschrift für Ulrich Wickert zum siebzigsten Geburtstag,* Beihefte zur Zeitschrift für die neutestamentliche Wissenschaft und die Kunde der älteren Kirche 85 (Berlin: Walter de Gruyter, 1997), 231, notes that much of Tertullian's aggression and passion must be seen in the light of his intellectual environment.

only the death. If this work were submitted for publication, no doubt a refer-ee's comments would indicate that there was some interesting material here but that it was in much need of revision before it could be accepted.

In a comparison with the passages that are paralleled in *Aduersus Marcio-nem,* I would contend, against Neander,[185] that even though there is much improvement in the work against Marcion in terms of the presentation of the argument, what we find in *Aduersus Iudaeos,* with its chronological devel-opment of the argument from the birth of the Christ through to the second coming of the Christ, is that the passages in that work are connected with one another in a logical way (even if that is sometimes obscured by extrane-ous material, which might have been the point Neander was making). This suggests the priority of *Aduersus Iudaeos* over *Aduersus Marcionem.*

There is a cleverness in Tertullian's oratory. Sometimes he offers argu-ments that are flawed, incomplete, circular, or not convincing. It would seem that in stating them boldly or in connection with a series of others he hoped that his readers and opponents would not notice his inconsistencies, which they ought to notice if they were competent in the art of oratory themselves. One could mention the way Tertullian gave more weight to some pieces of Scripture than others (1.2–3) or the fact that, just because he might have been able to prove that the Jewish law was temporary, this did not automatical-ly prove that the law given to Christians necessarily was eternal. Only the most attentive would notice the way Tertullian inverted the time periods in Daniel 9 to suit himself and tinkered with rulers and their reigns to produce just the right number of years in chapter 8.

Finally, I would agree with Skarsaune that Tertullian used Justin's works. When one pays attention to the pieces of Scripture they both used, it would seem to suggest something more than that they used the same *testimonia.* Yet Tertullian was doing more than re-editing Justin and translating him into Latin for his Carthaginian readers. Close attention to the pamphlet discloses a number of instances where Tertullian drew a different understanding of what a passage meant than had Justin, making it appropriate for a rhetorical *topos.* For example, Justin related Jeremiah 2:13 to circumcision, while Tertul-lian used it to refer to the abandonment of the Jewish synagogues (13.15), part of the *topos* of subsequent events. At the level of detail Tertullian displayed great originality.

185. Neander, *History of the Planting and Training of the Christian Church,* 2:530.

CHAPTER FIVE

ひひ

Style

Matters of style in Tertullian are not the focus of Sider's monograph. He notes that those who have recognized rhetorical elements in Tertullian's writing generally have limited their observations to matters of style.[1] He does not deny that close attention to issues of style can indeed be very helpful regarding questions such as dating and editions, yet he intended to look deeper and more broadly into the rhetorical influences on Tertullian rather than consider mere stylistic ornamentation.[2] In this chapter I intend to see how patterns of rhetorical style can assist in our questions about the integrity and authorship of *Aduersus Iudaeos* and its place within the history of the engagement between Jews and Christians in late antiquity. In the course of the pages of this chapter I shall argue that the author of the pamphlet achieved the style that is evident in this work not through raw natural talent but through familiarity with rhetorical precepts; that the rhetorical style reveals the unfinished nature of the pamphlet, particularly in chapters 9 and 13; that the author wrote in the plain style in order to remain focused on the issue of the correct interpretation of Scripture rather than engage in personal polemic; and that the style is consistent with what we find elsewhere in Tertullian, particularly early in his literary career. We begin with some comments about

---

1. Sider, *Ancient Rhetoric*, 3–4. He referred to E. Norden, *Die antike Kunstprosa vom VI. Jahrhundert v. Chr. bis in die Zeit der Renaissance*, vol. 2 (Leipzig: G. B. Teubner, 1909), 606–15; H. Hoppe, *Syntax und Stildes Tertullian* (Leipzig: G. B. Teubner, 1903), 9–10, 146–93; Quacquarelli, *Tertulliani: "Ad Scapulam,"* 31–42; Quacquarelli, ed., *Q. S. F. Tertulliani: "Ad martyras." Prolegomeni, testo critico, traduzione e commento*, Opuscula patrum 2 (Rome: Desclée, 1963), 45–59; Säflund, *De pallio;* and C. Becker, *Tertullians Apologeticum. Werden und Leistung* (Munich: Kösel-Verlag, 1954).

2. Sider, *Ancient Rhetoric*, 2–3. See F. H. Colson, "Two Examples of Literary and Rhetorical Criticism in the Fathers," *JTS* 25 (1924): 364–77.

the classical theories of rhetorical style, as always to provide the background for the later analysis.

Classical Rhetoric on Style

Quintilian noted that all orators agreed that the theory of style *(elocutio)*[3] presented the greatest difficulty and that its rules often required the greatest effort both to articulate and follow.[4] It was in matters of style that orators could make themselves most noticed and by which they were most often judged, for it involved the words one chose to present the content of one's argument and to create the right effect on one's audience. It is impossible here to present the full complexity of the rhetorical theories of style but some broad outline is necessary in order to provide us with criteria to examine Tertullian's style in *Aduersus Iudaeos* and in comparison with that of his other writings.

Ad Herennium divided *elocutio* into two subjects: styles *(genera)* and qualities or virtues *(res)*.[5] The three *genera* were the grand *(graue* or *plenum)*, middle *(mediocre)*, and plain *(attenuatum* or *tenue)*. The first involved ornate words and impressive thoughts, the second involved not nearly so ornate a language, and the last involved everyday speech.[6] Each style also had an oppo-

---

3. S. E. Sprott, "Cicero's Theory of Prose Style," *PhQ* 34 (1955): 2–3, argued, with regard to Cicero at least, that *elocutio* is best translated into English as "expression" and *genus dicendi* as "style" in the sense of a particular kind of speech, and that *ornatus* is best translated as "stylishness" (rather than "style," "ornament," or "embellishment") in the sense of the more abstract quality.

4. Quint., *Inst.* 8.pr.13–16 (LCL 126.184).

5. Kennedy, *A New History of Classical Rhetoric*, 125, notes that Greek and later Roman rhetoricians would have used a more technical term than *res*.

6. *Rhet. Her.* 4.8.11–4.10.15 (LCL 403.252–64); Cic. *De or.* 3.52.199 (LCL 349.158); Cic., *Orat.* 23.76–31.112 (LCL 342.360–88). Cf. Cic., *Brut.* 82.284–95.327 (LCL 342.246–84) where, as G. L. Hendrickson, "The Origin and Meaning of the Ancient Characters of Style," *AJPh* 26 (1905): 264–65, noted, there is no evidence of a theory of three styles of oratory, only the twofold scheme of Attic, a less ornate, less emotional style, and Asiatic, either a balanced and symmetrical or a free-flowing and ornate style. Unlike Calvus, Cicero defined Attic in a broader sense than just applicable to the plain style. See also Cic., *Opt. gen.* 3.7–7.23 (LCL 386.358–72). On all this see G. L. Hendrickson, "Cicero's Correspondence with Brutus and Calvus on Oratorical Style," *AJPh* 47 (1926): 234–58; Harry M. Hubbell, "Cicero on Styles of Oratory," *YCS* 19 (1960): 173–86; G. M. A. Grube, "Educational, Rhetorical, and Literary Theory in Cicero," *Phoenix* 16 (1962): 234–57; Leeman, "*Orationis Ratio*," 1:143–44; and Erich S. Gruen, "Cicero and Licinius Calvus," *HSCPh* 71 (1967): 215–33. Kennedy, *A New History of Classical Rhetoric*, 154, concludes that "[a] result of Cicero's tactics is that 'Attic' was often used by later writers in a rather general sense to describe any admired, disciplined prose style, while 'Asian' often means any style perceived as inflated and faulty."

site: swollen *(sufflata)*—characterized by turgid and inflated language; slack *(dissolutum)* or drifting *(fluctuans)*—characterized by loose construction that does not engage the listener; and meager *(exile)*—characterized by mean and trifling language.[7] Late in his career, Cicero linked each of the three *genera* with one of the three *officia* or tasks of the orator: the plain style for proof, the middle for pleasure, and the grand for persuasion.[8] Douglas believed this linking of the three functions with the three styles was a Ciceronian contribution to rhetorical theory.[9]

The four *res* were correct language *(Latinitas)*, clarity *(explanatio* or *planum)*,[10] appropriateness *(decorum)*, and distinction *(dignitas* or *ornatus)*.[11] Most attention was given to the last of these elements. The author of the textbook *Ad Herennium* and Cicero divided this last element into two: figures of speech *(in uerborum exornationes)* and figures of thought *(in sententiarum exornationes)*.[12] They needed to be used sparingly and with variety for the best effect.[13]

Quintilian did not divide his material on *elocutio* into the three *genera* and the four *res*. Instead, he wrote about single words and groups of words, arguing that the former could be characterized by correct language *(Latinitas)*, clarity *(perspicuitas)*, elegance *(ornatus)*, and appropriateness *(accomodatus)*, and the latter by correctness *(emendata)*, proper placement *(coniunctis)*, and

7. *Rhet. Her.* 4.10.15–4.11.16 (LCL 403.262–68). See Leeman, "*Orationis Ratio,*" 1:29–31, for examples.

8. Cic., *Orat.* 21.69 (LCL 342.356): "Sed quot officia oratoris tot sunt genera dicendi: subtile in probando, modicum in delectando, uehemens in flectendo; in quo uno uis omnis oratoris est." Cf. Quint., *Inst.* 8.pr.7 (LCL 126.180), who linked the three *officia* with something akin to the three Aristotelian proofs (in this case: argument, emotions, and charm [*delectatio*]). The latter was associated with style. See G. L. Hendrickson, "The Peripatetic Mean of Style and the Three Stylistic Characters," *AJPh* 25 (1904): 125–46.

9. Alan Edward Douglas, "A Ciceronian Contribution to Rhetorical Theory," *Eranos* 55 (1957): 18–26.

10. *Rhet. Her.* 4.12.17 (LCL 403.268) combined these two as taste *(elegantia)*, thus having only three *res*.

11. *Rhet. Her.* 4.12.18–4.55.69 (LCL 403.270–410) omitted *decorum* from his scheme and substituted it with composition *(conpositio)*, which in the Theophrastean scheme was part of *dignitas*. See Cic., *De or.* 3.10.37 (LCL 349.30). Solmsen, "The Aristotelian Tradition," 181; and William W. Fortenbaugh, "Cicero's Knowledge of the Rhetorical Treatises of Aristotle and Theophrastus," in *Cicero's Knowledge of the Peripatos,* ed. William W. Fortenbaugh and Peter Steinmetz, Rutgers University Studies in Classical Humanities 4 (New Brunswick, N.J.: Transaction, 1989), 46–54, argue that this is evidence of Cicero's Theophrastean source.

12. *Rhet. Her.* 4.13.18 (LCL 403.274). The former are considered in 4.13.19–4.34.46 (LCL 403.274–346) and the latter in 4.35.47–4.55.69 (LCL 403.346–410). Cic., *De or.* 3.25.96 (LCL 349.76), called them *uerborum sententiarumque floribus*. They are listed here in 3.52.200–3.54.208 (LCL 349.158–66).

13. See Elaine Fantham, "*Varietas* and *Satietas: De oratore* 3.96–103 and the limits of *ornatus,*" *Rhetorica* 6 (1988): 276–80.

adornment *(figurata).*[14] In *De oratore* and *De partitione oratoria* Cicero considered single words and groups of words as sections of *ornatus.*[15] It was in his section on adornment that Quintilian presented the *figurae.*[16] It is to these *figurae* or *exornationes* that we now turn our attention. It would be tedious and pointless to list and describe them all, but several may be chosen and outlined as illustrations of the type, with further detail to be mentioned when appropriate as they occur in *Aduersus Iudaeos.*[17]

While *Ad Herennium* combined consideration of the figures of speech and thought with tropes, Cicero and Quintilian kept them separate.[18] Tropes involved changes in the meaning of a word, as with metaphor and synecdoche (where a part stands for the whole or vice versa). Figures of thought *(figurae sententiae* or *in sententiarum exornationes)* involved alterations to concepts and ideas, while figures of speech *(figurae uerborum* or *in uerborum exornationes)* consisted of changes in the expressions used. Among the figures of thought were questions designed to emphasize a point or embarrass an opponent rather than elicit information, replies that answered questions not asked, anticipation, hesitation or understatement, simulation, impersonation, animation, irony, concession, imitation, and hidden meaning. Among the figures of speech were those that involved the addition of words (doubling, beginning or ending clauses with the same word or words, comparisons and contrasts established by repetition, various arrangements and repetitions of clauses, beginning or ending clauses with different words that have similar meaning, etc.), the omission of words (asyndeton of connecting particles, the use of one verb for several clauses, etc.), and the use of similar or contrasting words (one word repeated with different meanings, contrasts between words that sound similar, words repeated in different tenses, moods, or cases, etc.).

14. Quint., *Inst.* 8.1.1 (LCL 126.194). In the section on *accomodatus* (*Inst.* 11.1.3 [LCL 127.154]) Quintilian made passing reference to the different *genera dicendi.*

15. Cic., *De or.* 3.37.149–3.43.170 (LCL 349.118–34) and 3.43.171–3.51.198 (LCL 349.134–58). He considered single words contributing to *elocutio* as proper (even rare), metaphorical, and newly coined. Words in combination were examined in terms of structure and rhythm and balance. Cic., *Part. Or.* 5.16–7.24 (LCL 349.322–30), presented the same divisions.

16. Quint., *Inst.* 9.1.1–9.3.102 (LCL 126.348–506).

17. See Murphy, "The Codification of Roman Rhetoric," 120–27; and Galen O. Rowe, "Style," in *Handbook of Classical Rhetoric in the Hellenistic Period, 330 B.C.–A.D. 400,* ed. Stanley E. Porter (Leiden: E. J. Brill, 1997), 124–50, for useful summaries.

18. Cic., *De or.* 3.38.155–3.43.170 (LCL 349.120–34); Quint., *Inst.* 8.6.1–76 (LCL 126.300–344). See Doreen Innes, "Cicero on Tropes," *Rhetorica* 6 (1988): 307–25.

Style in Tertullian

Satterthwaite has drawn attention recently to passages in Tertullian's writings in which he gave us clues about his attitude to matters of rhetorical style: the orator must convey truth and do so briefly.[19] Earlier, Fredouille considered these passages from Tertullian's writings in comments on his rhetorical style and objectives. He saw Tertullian's interest in the truth over matters of eloquence as being firmly in the Platonic tradition.[20] He noted as well Tertullian's desire to be brief,[21] his portrait sketches of opponents as a means of *delectans*,[22] and his caution in going overboard in *mouens*.[23] Fredouille concluded that Tertullian was thoroughly familiar with the rhetorical theory of Cicero with regard to matters of style and yet could, at the same time, be thoroughly contemporary, even original in a bizarre and baroque fashion.[24] He examined some of the work by Mohrmann, Norden, and Marache about whether Tertullian's style was Asiatic or whether it had true brevity, simplicity, and precision without affectation.[25]

Quasten too has made general comment about Tertullian's style, noting that he knew the literary tradition and was inspired by the Asiatic style in that he wrote short sentences, often piled up questions with staccato answers, was fond of antithesis and balance, was terse, and coined new and exotic words and expressions, all of which leads to an obscurity in his writings.[26]

Barnes draws attention to the ways in which Tertullian's style was influenced by or in reaction to oratory, particularly that of the Second Sophistic: his eloquence with set theme, his restraint with defamation and slander, his use of *exempla,* his use of satire, ridicule, and penetrating insight, his ability to summarize in pithy epigram, his love of apparent paradox, and his ability

---

19. Satterthwaite, "The Latin Church Fathers," 688. See Tert., *Apol.* 46.1 (CCSL 1.160); Tert., *Adu. Val.* 1.4 (CCSL 2.753–54) (where Tertullian was aware of the Ciceronian distinction between *probare* and *flectere*); Tert., *Adu. Marc.* 2.28.3 (CCSL 1.508); Tert., *De an.* 2.7 (CCSL 2.785); and Tert., *De uirg.* 4.4 (CCSL 2.1213).

20. Fredouille, *Tertullien et la conversion,* 31.

21. Ibid., 32–34.　　　　　　　　　　22. Ibid., 37–65.

23. Ibid., 143–70.　　　　　　　　　24. Ibid., 172.

25. Ibid., 172–73. See Christine Mohrmann, "Observations sur la langue et le style de Tertullien," in *Études sur le latin des chrétiens,* vol. 2: *Latin chrétien et médiéval* (Rome: Edizioni di Storia e Letteratura, 1961), 235–46; Norden, *Die antike Kunstprosa;* and René Marache, *La critique littéraire de langue latine et le développement du goût archaïsant au IIe siècle de notre ère* (Rennes: Presses universitaires de Rennes, 1952).

26. Quasten, *Patrology,* 2:249.

to transcend the limits of genre.[27] Anderson agrees with Barnes, in particular with reference to *De pallio*.[28]

To this we must add Osborn's observation that Tertullian's general style changed depending upon the intended readership: in *Aduersus Hermogenem,* Tertullian met logic with argument, while in *Aduersus Valentinanos,* he met fable with ridicule.[29] It is hard to date a work or decide on its authenticity simply on the basis of its overall style. Despite this warning, Barnes elsewhere turns his attention to the comments of Säflund about details of Tertullian's style in order to confirm theories about dating his treatises. He notes that in the later works there is a slight increase in the use of epanaphora (*repetitio*—the figure of speech where successive clauses begin with the same word or group of words), a marked increase in the use of *et* in syndeton, and a degree of asyndeton (*solutum*—the omission of conjunctions). This makes his later works more mannered and artistic.[30] Yet Barnes warns that too much can be made of this.[31]

Others have examined particular aspects of Tertullian's style in some detail. One is reminded of the painstaking work dedicated to analyzing Tertullian's use of clausulae.[32] Such a detailed examination is not possible within this volume without distorting its overall aim.

Those who translate Tertullian into English often feel the need to apologize for their results. In his translation of *Aduersus Hermogenem,* Waszink was aware that his efforts had produced "laborious and, in some cases, immoderately long sentences" because Tertullian's style was "even for his standard—particularly intricate."[33] Le Saint pointed to the fact that ambiguity of thought and distortions of style turned translating Tertullian into something similar to translating St. Paul, for Tertullian had a "vigorous and imaginative but highly irregular prose," which the modern reader finds foreign.[34] He said that Tertullian's style was often incoherent:

---

27. Barnes, *Tertullian,* 214–26.

28. Anderson, *The Second Sophistic,* 207–8.   29. Osborn, *Tertullian,* 183.

30. Barnes, "Tertullian's *Scorpiace*," 121; Barnes, *Tertullian,* 49; and Säflund, *De pallio,* 60–74.

31. Barnes, "Tertullian's *Scorpiace*," 122.

32. Waszink, "The Technique of Clausula," 212–45; and Valerio Ugenti, "Norme Prosodiche nelle Clausole Metriche del *De Idololatria* di Tertulliano," *Augustinianum* 35 (1995): 241–58.

33. J. H. Waszink, trans., *Tertullian: The Treatise against Hermogenes,* Ancient Christian Writers 24 (New York: Newman Press, 1956), 25.

34. William P. Le Saint, trans., *Tertullian: Treatises on Penance,* Ancient Christian Writers 28 (New York: Newman Press, 1959), 7.

His sentences are quite often poorly constructed, a jumble of ideas which pour out in unnatural combinations of words and phrases, strange metaphors, neologisms, cryptic allusions, paradoxes and paralogisms, antithesis, multiple parentheses—a rich but disordered miscellany complicated by asyndeton, ellipsis and the use of every form of brachylogy known to grammarians.[35]

Style in *Aduersus Iudaeos*

With the previous two sections of this chapter by way of background, we are now in a position to consider the rhetorical style of *Aduersus Iudaeos*. This is a useful, if tedious and complicated, exercise that can help us appreciate the pamphlet as a piece of literature. What makes it even more useful is that it helps us address the broader questions of the place of this work in Tertullian's corpus and in early Christian anti-Judaic literature. Rather than analyze the rhetorical style of *Aduersus Iudaeos* and then compare it with the rest of Tertullian's works, it will suffice, and may be more appropriate, simply to compare the first half with the second. This may reveal something further about the unity and integrity of the pamphlet. This was the method employed by Säflund in his examination of the text.[36] We may begin by presenting the insights of other scholars with regard to the rhetorical style of this pamphlet in order to provide a point of comparison with what I have discovered.

One of the things that an analysis of Tertullian's language and style would contribute to is an understanding of his dependence upon or relationship with early Latin translations of Scripture. This is an immense task in itself and one that could easily be the focus of its own detailed treatment. Such an analysis is not undertaken in this study in order that the focus remain on the rhetorical influences, rather than the scriptural, on Tertullian's style. Säflund gave some attention to this matter when he took issue with Åkermann's proposal that, in the second half of *Aduersus Iudaeos,* the biblical extracts followed the wording of the Old Latin closely, while in Tertullian on the whole biblical extracts followed the Septuagint. Säflund could point to examples like Psalm 44(45):5 in 9.17 and Isaiah 53:7 in 9.28 (he considered eleven examples in all), where the version found in the corresponding section of *Aduersus Marcio-*

---

35. Ibid., 8.

36. Säflund, *De pallio,* 152: "Ich verwiese ferner auf die charakteristische Abundanz in einem 'echten' Teil wie Adv. Iud. 8."

nem is closer to the Old Latin than the version in *Aduersus Iudaeos*.[37] Indeed, Tertullian often obviously engaged in his own loose translating of Scripture in both sections of *Aduersus Iudaeos* and in other writings.[38]

With regard to this particular pamphlet, Fredouille has noted that it has a certain rhythm, is full of figures, and has a vigorous and didactic tone, all of which adds to its persuasiveness.[39] Interestingly enough, Fredouille divides his monograph into three parts: the first concerned with rhetorical aspects of Tertullian's works (further divided into consideration of the three *genera dicendi: delectare, docere,* and *mouere*), the second with polemic, and the third with spiritual matters.[40] It is in the second that he treats *Aduersus Iudaeos,* unfortunately separating polemic from rhetoric.[41]

Tränkle noted certain stylistic points that he used to compare *Aduersus Iudaeos* with *Aduersus Marcionem* in order to determine priority in dating. He observed, with regard to the former, that its author was at pains to make all possible explanation and to leave nothing unsaid. This means that the work tends to drag and that it is possible to become lost in the detail and lose track of the argument.[42] One does not need here to repeat all that evidence, but the conclusions may be drawn from it that, in parts, *Aduersus Iudaeos,* where it tends to be "Träges und Zähes," or where the sentences are "verschlungene,"[43] could be described as drifting, the opposite of the middle style, and lacking in brevity and clarity. The argument advanced here is that this is not the sign of a foreign and inferior hand, for, as Tränkle has noted, such char-

37. Ibid., 124–44.
38. Ibid., 129, with reference to Is 11:1 in *Adu. Iud.* 9.26 (CCSL 2.1373). See G. J. D. Aalders, "Tertullian's Quotations from St Luke," *Mnemosyne* series 3, 5 (1937): 241–82; A. J. B. Higgins, "The Latin Text of Luke in Marcion and Tertullian," *VChr* 2 (1951): 1–42; O'Malley, *Tertullian and the Bible;* J. K. Elliott, "The Translation of the New Testament into Latin: The Old Latin and the Vulgate," in *Aufstieg und Niedergang der Römischen Welt,* part II: *Principat,* vol. 26.1: *Religion (vorkonstantinisches Christentum: Neues Testament [Sachthemen]),* ed. Wolfgang Haase (Berlin and New York: Walter de Gruyter, 1992), 201; and Dunn, *Tertullian,* 19–23.
39. Fredouille, *Tertullien et la conversion,* 262.
40. Ibid., 27–178 (37–65, 67–142, 143–70), 179–358, and 359–478.
41. Ibid., 23–24: "Mais la rhétorique ne constitue pas à elle seule toute la culture. Celle-ci véhicule un système de valeurs hiérarchisées, des traditions intellectuelles, morales, religieuses, des instruments conceptuels, bref une 'mentalité', que Tertullien devenu chrétien devait, selon les cas, soit conserver, soit adapter, soit rejeter, mais dont il gardait néanmoins l'empreinte. C'est à ce niveau que nous avons tâché de comprendre la polémique de Tertullien contre les païens. Mais ceux-ci ne furent pas ses seuls adversaires: il eut à combattre les juifs, les hérétiques, les 'psychiques.'"
42. Tränkle, *Tertullian, "Adversus Iudaeos,"* liii–lvii.
43. Ibid., lvi–lvii, lix.

acteristics are found throughout the whole work, but of an early draft, where the author was more concerned with gathering arguments than with how they were expressed, and of something from early in Tertullian's career when he tended to be more verbose.

One may note here the instances of words that occur in *Aduersus Iudaeos* but not elsewhere in Tertullian's writings[44] or that are hapax legomena in all of Latin literature. Many of these are proper names and technical terms that we would not expect necessarily to find Tertullian using on other occasions. Tertullian has the reputation of being able to create new words and there is nothing in *Aduersus Iudaeos* inconsistent with that.[45] Quite a number of words, not listed here, are late Latin, used in early Christian writers in particular, sometimes for the first time with Tertullian. This occurs in both halves of the pamphlet and is what we would expect of Tertullian.

Exordium (1.1–3a)

The rhetorical style of the *exordium* is further evidence in support of my position that Tertullian intended to write in the plain style in order to remain focused on the issues rather than get caught up in personal polemic, as had

---

44. Tert., *Adu. Iud.* 1.3b (CCSL 2.1339): "pollicitatorem"; 1.6 (CCSL 2.1340): "abrelicta"; 1.7 (CCSL 2.1340): "Bahal"; 2.1–2 (CCSL 2.1341): "plasmator"; 2.7 (CCSL 2.1342): "Leuiticae"; 3.1 (CCSL 2.1344): "praefocatus fuisset"; 3.10 (CCSL 2.1346): "praedemonstro"; 4.5 (CCSL 2.1348—twice), 5.1 (CCSL 2.1349), 5.3 (CCSL 2.1350), and 6.1 (CCSL 2.1352): "praeostendo"; 6.1 (CCSL 2.1352): "pollicitatio"; 6.2–3 (CCSL 2.1352–53): "lator"; 7.4, 8 (CCSL 2.1354–55): "Getuli"; 7.5 (CCSL 2.1355): "abante"; "ualuae"; 7.7 (CCSL 2.1355): "Dan"; "India"; 8.10 (CCSL 2.1359–60): "Artaxerxes"; "Ochus"; "Argus"; "Melas"; "Euergetes"; "Philopator"; "Epiphanes"; 8.14 (CCSL 2.1362): "baptistam" (from Mt 11:31); 8.16 (CCSL 2.1362): "Caius"; "Caligula"; "Otho"; 8.18 (CCSL 2.1363): "Rubellius Geminus"; "Fufius Geminus"; "Martio"; 9.5 (CCSL 2.1366): "crepitaculo"; "mammis" (in *Adu. Marc.* 3.13.2 [CCSL 1.524] both these words appear as diminutives); (CCSL 2.1366): "lanciare" (in *Adu. Marc.* 3.13.3 [CCSL 1.524] the word appears as "lanceare"); 9.22 (CCSL 2.1370); 13.12 (CCSL 2.1387); 13.15 (CCSL 2.1388): "commoror"; 10.10 (CCSL 2.1377): "peccantia" (found in the manuscripts and editions PNFR [and "pecantia" in T]. Kroymann, "[Tertulliani]: *Aduersus Iudaeos*," 1377, emended the text to read "petulantia." Säflund, *De pallio*, 145, noted a number of hapax legomena in other treatises of Tertullian in a form similar to "peccantia." He concluded: "Die Form 'peccantia' ist in eine symmetrische Satzpartie mit Homoioteleuton eingefügt: 'a delictorum peccantia / ad crucis istius sacramenta'—eine weitere Stütze für ihre Echtheit."); 10.17 (CCSL 2.1380): "tenebresceret" (from Amos 8:9–10); 13.6 (CCSL 2.1385): "chrismatus"; 13.10 (CCSL 2.1386): "ducator" (found in the manuscripts and editions PNFR. Kroymann, "[Tertulliani]: *Aduersus Iudaoes*," 1386, followed T, which has "ducatus." Säflund, *De pallio*, 146–47, noted that although the word is not found in the rest of Tertullian it is to be found in Old Latin versions of Mt 2:6 in which the passage from Mic 5:2 is quoted); 13.12 (CCSL 2.1387): "indulcauit"; 13.21 (CCSL 2.1389): "uepre" (from Gen 22:13); "spinea" (from Mt 27:29; Mk 15:17; Jn 19:2); 13.24 (CCSL 2.1390): "abominamenta" (from Is 2:20); 14.8 (CCSL 2.1393): "Iosedech."

45. Säflund, *De pallio*, 145.

happened apparently at the earlier encounter. Thus, we see the opponent at the earlier exchange described simply by the familiar technical term of "proselytus." While not a common term in Tertullian it does occur seven times in *Adu. Marc.* 3.21.2–4, besides it appearances in *Adu. Iud.* 1.1; 2.2; 4.4 (quoting an unidentifiable passage from Isaiah). Tertullian used the word in its accepted technical sense to refer to a non-Jew by birth who had converted to Judaism.[46] That encounter is described as a *disputatio.* While the word could have shades of meaning, Tertullian tended to use the word with its fuller flavor, in contexts where it was clear that he was referring to adversarial, even conflictual, encounters between opposing groups.[47] The use of the word was probably in order to draw a distinction between the debate and the pamphlet, suggesting that the earlier heated exchange would be contrasted with this calm, rational, and therefore persuasive piece of writing.

Although the *exordium* reads as a brief series of factual statements in a fairly direct presentation, one should not imagine that Tertullian's words are not carefully chosen and well crafted. Further, the repetition of the pamphlet's thesis provided Tertullian with some opportunity for refining through restatement in similar words *(interpretatio)*—one of the figures of thought[48]—and through offering the example *(exemplum)* of the proselyte himself in order to make his point both clearer and more believable.[49] In the *exordium* we notice the briefest of alliteration[50] and assonance.[51] *Ad Herennium* advised against the excessive use of such techniques for artistic composition.[52] The activity of the debaters is described through the metaphors *(translationes)* of a tug-of-war[53] and of the day being dragged into evening.[54] The activity of the supporters is described using a simile *(imago):* the truth is obscured by

46. Cohen, *The Beginnings of Jewishness*, 140–62, reminds us that what converts believed about how Jewish they had become might be quite different from the extent to which Jews believed the Gentile convert had become Jewish. In Tertullian's eyes, at least, being a proselyte meant becoming completely Jewish

47. Tert., *De praescr.* 15.3 (CCSL 1.199); Tert., *De pat.* 5.1 (CCSL 1.303); Tert., *De idol.* 17.2 (CCSL 2.1118); and Tert., *Ad nat.* 2.12.34 (CCSL 1.64). Cf. Tert., *De uirg.* 11.1 (CCSL 2.1220).

48. *Rhet. Her.* 4.28.38 (LCL 403.324).

49. Ibid., 4.49.62 (LCL 403.382–84).

50. Tert., *Adu. Iud.* 1.1 (CCSL 2.1339): "retractatas terminare."

51. Ibid., 1.3a (CCSL 2.1339): "stillicidium situlae." There is an element of alliteration with this as well.

52. *Rhet. Her.* 4.12.18 (LCL 403.270).

53. Tert., *Adu. Iud.* 1.1 (CCSL 2.1339): "Alternis uibibus contentioso fune uterque."

54. Ibid.: "diem in uesperam traxerunt." On metaphor see *Rhet. Her.* 4.34.45 (LCL 403.342–344) and Quint., *Inst.* 8.6.8 (LCL 126.304).

their clamoring as if by a cloud.[55] Isaiah 40:15 itself offers the simile of comparing the Gentiles with a drop in the bucket or the dust from the threshing floor.[56] All of this suggests that, although the section is brief and has not too many *figurae*, Tertullian had spent time polishing the opening lines of his pamphlet to achieve a pleasing yet restrained effect.

We find several instances of Tertullian's use of the word "gens" in these opening lines. In a study of Tertullian's use of "natio," "gens," "ethnicus," and "gentilis," Balfour notes that in contrasting Jew and non-Jew, Tertullian used a variety of words, "natio" being the most frequent for the non-Jew.[57] In *Aduersus Iudaeos*, though, the word "gens" was used for the same purpose (and such a meaning for "gens" is limited almost exclusively to *Aduersus Iudaeos*). He concludes that Tertullian never used "gens" to refer to a pagan as opposed to a Christian, that when he wanted to contrast Gentile with Jew his preferred term was "natio," that almost never outside of *Aduersus Iudaeos* did he use "gens" as a term to contrast Gentile with Jew, and that "gens" was a word Tertullian employed in his early literary career in particular.[58] Balfour believes that on twenty-four occasions in *Aduersus Iudaeos* "gens" referred to pagans or heathens (mostly in contrast with Jews) and on twenty occasions it referred to some meaning other than heathen, although he does not specify what those other meanings are.[59]

It is obvious in the *exordium* that "gens" means non-Jew, for the proselyte was described as "ex gentibus." Indeed, in many instances where he used the word, Tertullian was quoting from the Hebrew Scriptures, where Gentile or foreigner is the obviously intended meaning.[60] Only in several instances

55. Tert., *Adu. Iud.* 1.1 (CCSL 2.1339): "nubilo quodam ueritas obumbrabatur." On simile see *Rhet. Her.* 4.49.62 (LCL 403.384–86); Quint., *Inst.* 8.6.9 (LCL 126.304).

56. Tert., *Adu. Iud.* 1.3a (CCSL 2.1339).

57. I. L. S. Balfour, "Tertullian's Description of the Heathen," in *Studia Patristica* 17, part 2, ed. Elizabeth A. Livingstone, papers presented to the eighth International Conference on Patristic Studies, Oxford 1979 (Oxford: Pergamon, 1982), 788–89. In his chart at the end, Balfour lists *Adu. Iud.* as an apologetic work addressed to heathens.

58. Ibid., 786–88.

59. Ibid., 789. I point out, Dunn, *Tertullian*, 166, n. 4, that in my translation I render "gens" as "Gentile" or "foreigner" rather than "heathen" when the contrast is with Jews, and simply as "clan" when the context is unclear. I prefer "clan" to ethnic, racial, or political terms like "race" or "nation."

60. Tert., *Adu. Iud.* 1.3 (CCSL 2.1339): Is 40:15; 3.8 (CCSL 2.1346): Is 2:2–3; 3.9 (CCSL 2.1346): Is 2:3 (the first instance is a quotation, the second instance is Tertullian's explanation, and in the third instance, from Is 2:4, the word means "clan"); 5.4 (CCSL 2.1351): Mal 1:10–11; Ps 95(96):7; 5.7 (CCSL 2.1352): Mal 1:10–11; 7.2 (CCSL 2.1354): Is 45:1; 12.1 (CCSL 2.1384): Ps 2:7–8 (= 14.12 [CCSL 2.1395] = Tert., *Adu. Marc.* 3.20.3 [CCSL 1.535]); 12.2 (CCSL 2.1384): Is 42:6–7 (cf. Tert.,

in the pamphlet is it clear that "gens" does not mean "Gentile": 1.4 (CCSL 2.1339–1340)—where the two instances include Jews as one of the "gens"; 1.5 (CCSL 2.1340)—"gens Iudaeorum"; 3.5 (CCSL 2.1345)—where "gens peccatrix" from Isaiah 1:4 refers to the Jews;[61] 7.4 (CCSL 2.1354)—"multarum gentium"; 7.8 (CCSL 2.1356)—"gentes Maurorum et Getulorum" and "istas gentes"; 7.9 (CCSL 2.1356)—"ab omnibus gentibus supra enumeratis"; and 13.29 (CCSL 2.1391)—where "dispersio gentis" refers to the Jews. Beyond these few, I would argue, all the other instances of Tertullian's use of "gens" in this pamphlet may be determined, from the context of the overall argument, to refer to the Gentiles or foreigners (i.e. non-Jews), whether they were pagans or Christians. The nearly unique use of this word in this way in this pamphlet, a word that might have been used more frequently than "natio" by Jews themselves, suggests that Tertullian wanted to use the language of the Hebrew Scriptures in order to respond to Jewish argument in a way they would have understood. The use of "gens" rather than "natio" in this pamphlet suggests that Tertullian was influenced by real encounters and wanted his arguments to be used in future real encounters.

Partitio (1.3b–2.1a)

Tertullian's supersessionist argument was presented by way of contrast (contentio) between Christian and Jew. This was one of the figurae.[62] Given that the contrast between Rebekah's children and between the Jews and Christians is designed to prove the whole pamphlet's point at issue, one would expect the words here to be the result of careful drafting and polishing. Thus we find in this section frequent use of synonymy (interpretatio), a figura in which a statement is repeated not in the same but in similar words.[63] Here it occurs as doubling: God is both "idoneus pollicitator" and "fidelis sponsor,"[64] Rebekah's offspring will be both "duo populi" and "duae gentes,"[65] the Jewish people are

Adu. Marc. 3.20.4 [CCSL 1.535], where "in lucem gentium" has become "in lucem nationem"); 13.13 (CCSL 2.1387): Jer 2:10–12; and 13.26 (CCSL 2.1390): Is 52:5 (cf. Tert., Adu. Marc. 3.23.3 [CCSL 1.540], where "inter gentes" has become "in nationibus").

61. I note that in Dunn, Tertullian, 73, I have violated my own principles and mistakenly translated this as "sinful nation."

62. Rhet. Her. 4.45.58 (LCL 403.376); Quint., Inst. 9.3.81 (LCL 126.494).

63. Rhet. Her. 4.28.38 (LCL 403.324); Quint., Inst. 9.3.45 (LCL 126.470). In 9.3.98 (LCL 126.502) Quintilian denied that this was a figura.

64. Tert., Adu. Iud. 1.3b (CCSL 2.1339).

65. Ibid. This is repeated three times in 1.4 (CCSL 2.1339–1340), one of them being Gen 25:23. Even though Tertullian did not invent this synonymy he certainly exploited it in the partitio

both "anterior tempore" and "maior,"[66] they both "derelicto deo idolis dese-
ruiuit" and "diuinitate abrelicta simulacris fuit deditus."[67] This also provided
Tertullian with the opportunity for homoeoptoton, where several words appear together with the same case ending: "ipsum deum idoneum pollicitatorem et fidelem sponsorem."[68] Again, to make the contrast, Tertullian offered
brief definitions of the two peoples: "utique Iudaeorum, id est Israëlitum, et
gentium, id est noster."[69] There is alliteration with "secundum diuinarum
scripturarum memorias populus Iudaeorum," and "derelicto deo idolis dese-
ruiuit et diuinitate abrelicta simulacris fuit deditus, dicente."[70] A striking *figurae* is antimetabole or reciprocal change *(commutatio),* where a chiastic pattern of contraries is presented, often involving the same words.[71] Tertullian
offered an obvious example: "[prior] maior populus, id est Iduaicus, seruiat
necesse est minori, et minor populus, id est Christianus, superet maiorem."[72]

I have highlighted quite a number of examples of rhetorical style to demonstrate that, given the importance of *partitio* to forensic rhetoric, the author of this pamphlet has quite consciously used more than just natural flair
to construct this crucial section of the text in a charming and polished style
that would contribute to making the reader more responsive to the argument it contains.

Refutatio (2.1b–6.1)

The *refutatio* is conducted through a series of enthymemic syllogisms, arguments in which one of the propositions or the conclusion is unexpressed
and based upon probability rather than necessity. Tertullian used them to
disguise leaps of logic. In the first section, on the law (2.1b–10a), Tertullian

---

through repetition, which is itself another *figura*, that of reduplication or *conduplicatio (Rhet. Her.* 4.28.38 [LCL 403.324]; Quint., *Inst.* 9.3.28–29 [LCL 126.460–62]), where the same word or words are repeated to heighten the emotional impact.

66. Tert., *Adu. Iud.* 1.5 (CCSL 2.1340).

67. Ibid., 1.6 (CCSL 2.1340).

68. Ibid., 1.3b (CCSL 2.1339): "the sufficient promiser and faithful guarantor, God actually." See *Rhet. Her.* 4.20.28 (LCL 403.298); Quint., *Inst.* 9.3.78 (LCL 126.490–92).

69. Tert., *Adu. Iud.* 1.3b (CCSL 2.1339): "They are, of course, the Jews—that is, Israel—and the Gentiles—that is, us." This also occurs in 1.5.

70. Ibid., 1.6 (CCSL 2.1340): "according to the records of the divine Scriptures, the Jewish people . . ." and "were devoted to idols, as they had deserted God, and were addicted to images, as they had abandoned the divinity. [The people] were saying . . ." Some of the alliteration is captured in my English translation of the second.

71. *Rhet. Her.* 4.28.39 (LCL 403.324–26); Quint., *Inst.* 9.3.85–86 (LCL 126.496).

72. Tert., *Adu. Iud.* 1.5 (CCSL 2.1340): "the first, the elder people, namely the Jewish, inevitably will serve the younger. The younger people, namely the Christian, will rise above the elder."

showed, by arguing that a proselyte had access to God's law, that the Jewish position that the law was given only to one people was wrong and that God had given the law to all peoples. Even if Tertullian had proved that God gave the law to more than the Jews it did not prove that God had given it to all peoples. The same is found in the next section, on circumcision (2.10b–3.6), except in reverse. Circumcision was given only to one people in order to identify them for the punishment they deserved in failing to keep God's commands. The third section, on the Sabbath (4.1–11), contains all parts of the argument: the observance of the Sabbath had been broken legitimately by the Maccabees, therefore it could only be a temporary injunction. So too the last section, on sacrifice (5.1–7), is more developed but equally sweeping. Physical sacrifice has come to an end with the destruction of Jerusalem so the spiritual sacrifices offered by Christians now operate. Throughout these chapters characters from the Hebrew Scriptures—Adam, Eve, Cain, Abel, Noah, Enoch, Abraham, and Melchizedek—are used to indicate all people instead of just the Jewish people, an example of rhetorical synecdoche.

We can see that the *refutatio* is a series of little declamatory elaborations on set themes or set questions. Like a good orator, Tertullian was able to employ the standard means of developing his theme, but instead of using maxims and anecdotes he used the Hebrew Scriptures. Such a pattern in the *refutatio* reveals Tertullian's rhetorical perceptiveness. As is to be expected in such a work, the whole argument is based upon antithesis: old is contrasted with new, physical with spiritual, and temporary with permanent. The whole *refutatio* remains focused on interpreting Hebrew Scriptures to show that the Jewish position was contrary to God's intentions. Other than saying that the Jews were justly kept out of Jerusalem (3.4), by keeping his attention on God Tertullian avoids personal invective against Jews.

When we consider stylistic patterns of repetition it can be noted that there are several examples of alliteration but only in moderation: "morte morerentur" in 2.2 (CCSL 2.1341); "praemiserat praeceptum" in 2.6 (CCSL 2.1342); "circumcisio carnalis cessatura" in 3.11 (CCSL 2.1346); "auditu auris obaudiuit" in 3.12 (CCSL 2.1347—which we may also take as an example of periphrasis [*circumitio*], saying something in a more expanded fashion than was actually required;[73] this *figura* derives from Psalm 17[18]:44–45, which Tertullian had just cited in 3.11); "circumferrent in circuitu ciuitatis" in 4.8 (CCSL 2.1349); "domi-

---

73. *Rhet. Her.* 4.32.43 (LCL 403.336); Quint., *Inst.* 8.6.61 (LCL 126.336).

nus deus daturus" in 5.3 (CCSL 2.1350); and "postea per prophetas praedicat" in 5.4 (CCSL 2.1350).

In 2.6 we find an example of synonymy: Tertullian repeats in similar words that God's right to add to or change the law is upheld.[74] Not only that, Tertullian engaged in a little refinement of the topic *(expolitio)*,[75] a figure of thought that was somewhat more extensive than synonymy in the way it extended a point, by repeating his statements as questions.[76] Indeed, rhetorical questions are scattered throughout the *refutatio*.[77]

A specific example of synonymy is found at the very start of the *refutatio* with the series of titles attributed to God: "deus, uniuersitatis conditor, mundi totius gubernator, hominis plasmator, uniuersarum gentium sator."[78]

There is a series of synonyms in 3.10. The first, that of "gladia et lanceae," is derived from Isaiah 2:3–4, as is the third, that of "actus arandae et colendae terrae" to some degree. The second, that of referring to both "aemuli et hostes," seems to have been created by Tertullian to preserve the sense of balance. On a slightly broader basis, there is the synonymy between "pristinam ferocitatem gladiorum et lancearum ad tranquillitatem conuertebat" and "belli pristinam in aemulos et hostes executionem in pacificos actus arandae et colendae terrae reformabat."[79] Not only is there synonymy in 4.10 with "sabbatis pugnando fortiter fecerunt" and "hostes allophylos expugnauerunt," but there is reduplication *(conduplicatio)*, the repetition of words (rather than the use of different words to express the same thing as in synonymy), in this case "sabbatis pugnando."[80] We also find synonymy in 5.3 ("sacrificia et holocausta" and "pro peccatis quam pro animabus")[81] and in 5.4 ("in omni loco et in omni terra").

74. Tert., *Adu. Iud.* 2.6 (CCSL 2.1342): "Eiusdem est enim postea superducere legem, qui ante praemiserat praeceptum, quoniam et ipsius est erudire postea, qui antea iustos formare instituerat."
75. *Rhet. Her.* 4.42.54 (LCL 403.364). See Quint., *Inst.* 9.2.8–16 (LCL 126.378–82), for discussion about rhetorical questions.
76. Tert., *Adu. Iud.* 2.7 (CCSL 2.1342): "Quid enim mirum, si is auget disciplinam qui instituit, si is perficit qui coepit?" We have already noted the epanaphora in these questions.
77. Ibid., 2.1b (CCSL 2.1341); 2.7 (CCSL 2.1342) (five times); 2.11 (CCSL 2.1343); 3.5 (CCSL 2.1345); 3.10 (CCSL 2.1346); 3.12 (CCSL 2.1347); 4.2 (CCSL 2.1348); 5.4 (CCSL 2.1350).
78. Ibid., 2.1b (CCSL 2.1341): "God, the founder of the universe, the governor of the whole world, the creator of humankind, the instigator of every clan."
79. Ibid., 3.10 (CCSL 2.1346): "was changing the previous savagery of sword and lance into stillness" and "was reforming the previous conduct of war against rivals and enemies into the peaceful actions of ploughing and cultivating the land."
80. Ibid., 4.10 (CCSL 2.1349).
81. Ibid., 5.3 (CCSL 2.1250): "por (sic!) peccatis."

We find metaphor in Tertullian's description of Enoch who "necdum mortem gustauit."[82] There is simile in the depiction of God's fashioning Adam and Eve from the mud of the earth as though from a mother's womb.[83]

There are several examples of epanaphora *(repetitio)*, a *figura* where successive phrases or clauses open with the same word or group of words. In 2.4b–5 we find the repeated use of "si." In 2.7 there is the repeated use of "si is" and "unde" in a series of questions. The first example, that of the love of God, sets up the pattern.[84] The second example seems to follow it.[85] The third example, about killing, however, does not begin with its protasis but joins the apodosis to the apodosis of the previous example.[86] There is no mention of adultery. The example about stealing is expressed in a reverse pattern, with one part of the apodosis (concerning robbery) mentioned before the protasis and the other part (about hiding from God) mentioned after it.[87] The example on lying, like that of killing, is attached to the apodosis of the previous example without its own conditional statement.[88] There is no mention of parental respect, not surprising given that Tertullian was writing about Adam and Eve. The last example, about coveting, also follows the reverse pattern.[89] One of four things must be concluded about this example of epanaphora: either Tertullian did not want to follow the epanaphoric pattern slavishly, or he was not thinking to create the epanaphoric effect and what we have here is rather accidental, or this section lacks polish and is in need of revision to bring out the full effect, or the parallels he thought he could establish between the law given to Moses and the law given to Adam could not be established as neatly as he had first imagined. The presence of the other elements of style, like alliteration and synonymy, would lead me to conclude

---

82. Ibid., 2.13 (CCSL 2.1344): "had not yet tasted death."

83. Ibid., 2.5 (CCSL 2.1342).

84. Ibid., 2.4 (CCSL 2.1341–1342): "si dominum deum suum dilexissent, contra praeceptum eius non fecissent."

85. Ibid., 2.4 (CCSL 2.1342): "si proximum diligerent, id est semetipsos, persuasioni serpentis non credidissent." One may note again how Tertullian liked to offer definition frequently.

86. Ibid.: "atque ita in semetipsos homicidium non commisissent."

87. Ibid., 2.5 (CCSL 2.1342): "A furto quoque abstinuissent, [si de fructu arboris non clam degustassent] nec a conspectu domini dei sui sub arbore delitescere gestissent." I would maintain, against Kroymann, that the protasis should not be excluded from the text.

88. Ibid.: "nec falsum adseueranti diabolo mendacii participes efficerentur credendo ei, quod similes dei essent futuri"

89. Ibid.: "atque ita nec dominum deum offendissent ut patrem, qui eos de limo terrae quasi ex utero matris figurauerat, si alienum non concupiscentes de fructu inlicito non degustassent."

that this section of the pamphlet has been revised and polished and that he did not want to follow the epanaphoric pattern slavishly.

At the end of the *refutatio,* in a summary that forms a transition to the *confirmatio,* we find the antitheses that gave structure to the section presented in a series of parallel isocola, phrases of nearly equal syllable value that create a pleasing rhythm:[90] the temporal and eternal Sabbath, the physical and spiritual circumcision, the temporal and eternal law, and the physical and spiritual sacrifices.[91] This conclusion too shows how the author has put time and effort into making the *refutatio* stylistically euphonious and elegant, although not excessively. The pleasing prose provides more punch for his position.

Tränkle has pointed to the presence of asyndeton, the suppression of conjunctions,[92] in 2.2 with the use of "certis statutis temporibus."[93] There is ellipsis, the omission of words, in 2.9 with something like "data est" missing. Quintilian points out that rather than being a *figura* this could simply be a blemish in a writer's style,[94] but it is characteristic of Tertullian, particularly later in life. The infrequency of its appearance in this pamphlet is a reason to date it early in Tertullian's literary career.

Confirmatio (6.2–14.10)

In this section of my chapter my intention is to comment on the rhetorical style to show that there are parts of the pamphlet that have the appearance of being a first draft waiting for revision, but given that those parts are announced earlier in the pamphlet I do not think that they are the result of someone other than Tertullian finishing the work. There are still sections of the *confirmatio* that have received sufficient editorial attention to support further the notion that a skilled exponent of classical rhetoric like Tertullian wrote the whole work as a contribution to interactions that took place between Jews and Christians in Carthage.

Throughout the *confirmatio* there are a number of examples of the use of *figurae* based on patterns of repetition. Often such *figurae* would be used to produce emotional impact, so perhaps their moderate occurrence in this pamphlet is another indication that its author wished to avoid the same kind of emotional uproar that ostensibly was responsible for the premature end-

90. *Rhet. Her.* 4.20.27–28 (LCL 403.298); Quint., *Inst.* 9.3.80 (LCL 126.492–94).
91. Tert., *Adu. Iud.* 6.1 (CCSL 2.1352).
92. *Rhet. Her.* 4.30.41 (LCL 403.330); Quint., *Inst.* 9.3.50 (LCL 126.474).
93. Tränkle, *Tertullian, "Adversus Iudaeos,"* 45.
94. Quint., *Inst.* 9.3.18 (LCL 126.454).

ing of the earlier encounter. On the other hand, the scarcity of such *figurae* perhaps indicates parts of the work that still lacked polish. We can illustrate this by considering alliteration, epanaphora, antistrophe, synonymy, transplacement, polyptoton, antimetabole, polysyndeton, interlacement, epanelepsis, climax, indecision, and correction.

There are few obvious examples of alliteration.[95] With the exception of the instance in 13.18, they all occur in parts of the pamphlet I have identified as belonging more obviously with the unfolding argument. Examples of epanaphora occur throughout the *confirmatio*. The first is at the very beginning: "nouae legis lator et noui testamenti heres et nouorum sacrificiorum sacerdos et nouae circumcisionis purgator et aeterni sabbati cultor."[96] We also find disjunction *(disiunctum)*, where differing though related verbs end a series of phrases,[97] and polysyndeton with the repeated "et." One should note that this whole construction does not become tedious, given that Tertullian combined his comments about circumcision and the Sabbath and presented comments on sacrifice out of the sequence in which it appears in the *refutatio*. Here one may notice the synonymy between "sacerdos" of the previous sentence and "antistes" here in 6.3.

There is another example of epanaphora in the next chapter, where Tertullian engaged in elimination *(expeditio)*[98] to establish that there was no one else but Christ whose reign was universal. Yet Tertullian did not allow this to become boring. Toward the end of his list, the Britons, Moors, Gaetulians, and even the Romans themselves are introduced not as conditional statements introduced by "si," as were the others, but as indicative statements.[99] To stress the universality of Christ's reign we find a series of different epana-

95. Tert., *Adu. Iud.* 9.21 (CCSL 2.2370): "figuram futuri fuisse"; 9.23 (CCSL 2.1371–1372): "angelum appellat per prophetam spiritus sanctus dicens ex persona patri . . . nec nouam est spiritui sancto angelos appellare eos"; 10.6 (CCSL 2.1376): "itaque inprimis Isaac"; 10.7 (CCSL 2.1376): "cuius cornua essent crucis"; 10.14 (CCSL 2.1379): "alterius alicuius prophetari passionem"; 13.7 (CCSL 2.1385): "Unctio, unde unguetur"; 13.16 (CCSL 2.1388): "passuros praedicat propheta"; 13.18 (CCSL 2.1388): "fuerat ferrum, <et ferrum> statim supernatauit"; 14.9 (CCSL 2.1394): "et consputatus et conuulsus et compunctus and qui coccinea circumdatus ueste et consputatus et omnibus contumeliis adflictus extra ciuitatem crucifixus est."

96. Ibid., 6.2 (CCSL 2.1353): "a proposer of the new law, an heir to the new covenant, a priest of the new sacrifice, a purifier of the new circumcision, and an establisher of the eternal sabbath." One notes that the reference to the Sabbath breaks this pattern. One can note also that this is a fine example of isocolon.

97. *Rhet. Her.* 4.27.37 (LCL 403.322). Cf. Quint., *Inst.* 9.3.64 (LCL 126.482).

98. *Rhet. Her.* 4.29.40 (LCL 403.328). Quintilian did not include this as a *figura* but as part of the main body of a speech.

99. Tert., *Adu. Iud.* 7.7–8 (CCSL 2.1355–56).

·

phora at the end of this digression. The use is obviously deliberate here in order to emphasize that Christ is far superior to any other ruler:

Christi autem nomen ubique porrigitur, ubique creditur, ab omnibus gentibus supra enumeratis colitur, ubique regnat, ubique adoratur. Omnibus ubique tribuitur aequaliter; non regis apud illum maior gratia, non barbari, alicuius inferior laetitia; non dignitatum uel natalium cuiusquam discreta merita; omnibus, aequalis, omnibus rex, omnibus iudex, omnibus dominus et deus est.[100]

The repeated use of "ubique," "omnibus," and "non" allows for the possibility of synonymy, as well as a contrast between the phrases introduced by the first two words and those introduced by the third. One may also note the antithesis *(contentio)* in "non regis apud illum maior gratia, non barbari alicuius inferior laetitia," and the ellipsis in the next sentence. This whole digression[101] shows signs of greater finish than other sections of the *confirmatio.* So, even though it appears out of place in terms of the announced structure, it is a passage that is no mere first draft. It seems that Tertullian, since the passage reads like the early and more expansive Tertullian, had thought carefully about what he wanted to say but not enough about when he should say it. Other minor examples of epanaphora occur in 6.3 (CCSL 2.1353); 9.6 (CCSL 2.1366); 9.15 (CCSL 2.1368); 10.5 (CCSL 2.1375–1376);[102] 10.7 (CCSL 2.1376); and 13.20 (CCSL 2.1388).

There are a couple of examples of antistrophe *(conuersio),*[103] the opposite *figura* to epanaphora, where successive phrases end in the same word: "in ipso et per ipsum" (7.1 [CCSL 2.1353]); "suspensus in ligno . . . suspenderetur in ligno" (10.3 [CCSL 2.1375]); "iam uenisse Christum . . . iam uenisse Christum" (13.1 [CCSL 2.1384);[104] "in Bethleem? . . . in Bethleem?" (13.7 [CCSL 2.1385–1386]); and "simul cum duce. Quo duce?" (13.9 [CCSL 2.1386).[105]

Synonymy is present throughout the *confirmatio,* mostly involving the join-

---

100. Ibid., 7.9 (CCSL 2.1356): "On the other hand, the name of Christ is extended everywhere, believed everywhere, honoured by all the above-named clans. It reigns everywhere. It is cultivated in worship everywhere. It is assigned on an equal basis to everyone everywhere. No king has greater grace in his presence and no barbarian less joy. No dignity or birthright [is given] to anyone by the distinction of merit. He is fair to all, king to all, judge to all, lord and God to all."

101. See Dunn, "The Universal Spread of Christianity," 6–9.

102. This is also an example of synonymy.

103. *Rhet. Her.* 4.13.19 (LCL 403.276–78); Quint., *Inst.* 9.3.30 (LCL 126.462).

104. Säflund, *De pallio,* 165, noted that Tertullian had a preference for "einprägende Wiederholungen," but did not see it in terms of rhetorical technique.

105. One may also note the use of the rhetorical question.

ing of two similar words rather than phrases. In its very opening Tertullian announced that he intended "ostendere et probare."[106] In 7.3 (CCSL 2.1354) to hear and to believe are equated. Open gates are referred to four times in 7.5.[107] From chapter 9 we may mention "superstitionis [et maledictionis]";[108] "compungentes et transfigentes";[109] and "bellipotens et armiger."[110] In 10.5 Tertullian wrote that the prophecies of the suffering of the Christ are difficult to grasp in the Scriptures and he repeated this in a negative synonymy.[111] There is the replacement of "serpens" with "colubris" in 10.10 (CCSL 2.1377) and of "inriserit" with "respuerit" in 10.14 (CCSL 2.1379). A more extensive example is found in chapter 13.[112] The church is described as the temple of God, the holy city, and the home of the Lord.[113] The final examples are at the end of the *confirmatio*: "non lapsis offensionis nec petra scandali" and "comminuet et conteret" in 14.3 (CCSL 2.1392).

There are several examples of transplacement *(traductio)*, where a word is used several times in a phrase or sentence, sometimes in different cases or with different meanings.[114] At 6.2 we find "praedicatam nouam legem a prophetis praediximus."[115] In 7.1–2 (CCSL 2.1353) Tertullian employed "uenire" in a variety of forms in the space of a few lines: "uenturus" (thrice); "uene-

---

106. Tert., *Adu. Iud.* 6.2 (CCSL 2.1352): "to show and prove."

107. Ibid., 7.5 (CCSL 2.1355): "utpote ante quem omnium ciuitatium portae sunt apertae et cui nullae sunt clausae, abante quem ferreae serae sunt comminutae et ualuae aereae sunt apertae." The second instance is expressed negatively for variation.

108. Ibid., 9.15 (CCSL 2.1368): "superstition and abomination."

109. Ibid., 9.19 (CCSL 2.1370): "pierce and transfix."

110. Ibid., 9.20 (CCSL 2.1370): "a warrior and an armed man."

111. Ibid., 10.5 (CCSL 2.1375–1376): "quanto incredibile, tanto magis scandalum futurum, si nude praedicaretur, quantoque magnificium, tanto magis obumbrandum."

112. Ibid., 13.11 (CCSL 1387): "nondum pluuiis rigata nec imbribus fecundata."

113. Ibid., 13.25 (CCSL 2.1390): "ecclesiam, dei templum et ciuitatem sanctam et domum domini." One can note the homoeoptoton present in this example of synonymy. In addition, it must be pointed out that reference to the holy city has disappeared from my translation (Dunn, *Tertullian*, 100).

114. *Rhet. Her.* 4.14.20–21 (LCL 403.278–80); Quint., *Inst.* 9.3.42 (LCL 126.468). This is distinguished from *conduplicatio*, which is a repetition of a word or words, rather than the use of the same word several times. There seems to be a subtle difference. Part of *traductio*, according to *Rhet. Her.*, was the use of a word with changed cases. This seems indistinguishable from polyptoton, the third form of paronomasia, where the same noun is used repeatedly with case changes (4.22.31 [LCL 403.306]). Quintilian mentioned polyptoton (*Inst.* 9.3.36–37 [LCL 126.464–66]) separately from paronomasia (*Inst.* 9.3.66–74 [LCL 126.484–88]). Under paronomasia is what Cornificius described as *traductio* (9.3.71 [LCL 126.486]). Keeping these two *figurae* distinct was not always possible even among classical rhetoricians.

115. Tert., *Adu. Iud.* 6.2 (CCSL 2.1352). One may note the typographical mistake in the word "paediximus" in Kroymann's text.

rit"; "uenturum" (twice); and "uenisse" (twice). In 7.6–7, part of which has
been considered already in terms of epanaphora and elimination, there is the
frequent use of "regnare" in various persons and the noun "regnum":

Quis enim omnibus gentibus regnare potuisset, nisi Christus, dei filius, qui omnibus
regnaturus in aeternum nuntiabatur? Nam si Solomon regnauit, sed in finibus Iudae-
ae tantum; a Bersabee usque Dan termini regni eius signantur. Si uero Babyloniis et
Parthis regnauit Darius, ulterius [ultra fines regni sui] non habuit potestatem [in omnibus gentibus]; si Aegyptiis Pharao uel quisque ei in hereditario regno successit, illic
tantum potitus est regni sui dominium; si Nabuccodonosor, cum suis regulis ab India
usque Aethiopiam habuit regni sui terminos.[116]

Other examples of polyptoton occur in 8.1, where Tertullian cited Daniel 9:26: "et ciuitatem sanctam et sanctum exterminari";[117] in 8.9–10 (CCSL
2.1359): "quando hanc uidit uisionem Daniel. Videamus igitur"; in 8.17 (CCSL
2.1363) with the variants of "exterminare"; in 9.12 (CCSL 2.1368) with "cuius tunc 'uirtutem' Christus accepit, accipiendo insignia eius"; in 9.24 (CCSL
2.1372) with "lucerna lucens"; and in 10.3 (CCSL 2.1375) with "ut qui in aliquo
delicto iudicium mortis habuisset et moreretur suspensus in ligno . . . delictorum suorum suspenderetur in ligno." There is also the use of "dimicare" in
10.10 (CCSL 2.1377); "procedere" in 13.2–3 (CCSL 2.1384–1385);[118] "unctio" and
"ungo" in 13.6–7 (CCSL 2.1385); and "lignum" in 13.19 (CCSL 2.1388).

I can detect one clear case of reduplication, where a word or phrase is repeated for the emotional impact. In 13.14 (CCSL 2.1387), Tertullian cites Jeremiah 2:13 on the earth shuddering, and then these words are repeated in a
rhetorical question to establish that only with the crucifixion did the words
of the prophet come true.

There are a couple of examples of antimetabole, the chiastic pattern of

116. Ibid., 7.6–7 (CCSL 2.1355): "In fact, who could have reigned over all clans if not Christ,
the son of God, whose eternal reign over all was announced? For if Solomon reigned, yet it was
only within the boundaries of Judaea. The limits of his kingdom are marked from Beersheba to
Dan. If Darius truly reigned over the Babylonians and Parthians, he did not have further power
beyond the boundaries of his kingdom, among every clan. If Pharaoh, or whoever succeeded
him in his hereditary rule over the Egyptians, [reigned] only there did he possess the authority
of his rule. If Nebuchadnezzar with his princes [reigned] from India to Ethiopia, there he had
the boundaries of his kingdom." One may note the omission of several examples of the verb in
Tertullian's text, the inclusion of which would have added to the total.

117. Ibid., 8.1 (CCSL 1356): "both the holy city and sanctuary are destroyed." In 8.6 and 8.8
(CCSL 2.1358), where this is repeated, Tertullian wrote "et ciuitatem et sanctum exterminari."

118. One may also note the presence of adjunction (adiunctio)—Rhet. Her. 4.27.38 (LCL
403.322).

reversing words: in 9.3 (CCSL 2.1365) with "credunt in Christum, ex quo in eum credunt" and "iam uenisse illum, qui praedicabatur Emmanuel, quia quod significat Emmanuel uenit." There is another in 9.20.[119]

An example of polysyndeton (the frequent use of connecting particles) occurs in 8.2 with the list of the proofs by which it could be known that the Christ had come.[120] Another example is in 13.14, where the reduplication of the conjunction emphasizes the number of events that took place after the death of Jesus.[121] Another occurs when the torments of the scapegoat are listed.[122]

We find no examples of interlacement (conplexio), the figura that combines epanaphora and antistrophe by repeating both the first and last words in successive phrases;[123] epanelepsis, where the same word is at the beginning and end of the one phrase;[124] climax (gradatio), where the last word of one phrase becomes the first one of the next in a series of phrases;[125] indecision (dubitatio), where one says that one does not know what to say;[126] or correction (correctio), where a word is emphasized by being retracted and replaced.[127] While we should not expect to find many examples of these figurae, because their overuse would give one's style the appearance of being contrived and not natural, to find none is a surprise. The efficient use of some of these figurae distinguished a polished speaker from an ordinary one, for they required the most craft and skill. Rather than being evidence of an inferior composing hand, it is just as possible that such figurae, which required the highest degree of ability, would be attended to last in composition, after the draft completion of a work.

Attention may be turned now to that group of figurae that produces a sense of balance in one's work. There is much evidence of parallelism in

119. Tert., *Adu. Iud.* 9.20 (CCSL 2.1370): "Sic bellipotens et armiger Christus et sic accipiet spolia non solius Samariae uerum et omnium gentium. Agnosce et spolia figurata, cuius et arma allegorica didicisti."

120. Ibid., 8.2 (CCSL 2.1357): "et ex temporibus praescriptis et ex signis competentibus et ex operationibus eius, quae proba<bi>mus et ex consequentibus."

121. Ibid., 13.14 (CCSL 2.1387): "cum terra quoque contremuit et sol in media die tenebricauit et uelem templi scissum est et monumenta dirupta sunt?"

122. Ibid., 14.9 (CCSL 2.1394): "unus autem eorum circumdatus coccino, maledictus et conspetatus et conuulsus et compunctus."

123. *Rhet. Her.* 4.14.20 (LCL 403.278); Quint., *Inst.* 9.3.31 (LCL 126.462).

124. Quint., *Inst.* 9.3.34 (LCL 126.464).

125. *Rhet. Her.* 4.25.34–35 (LCL 403.314); Quint., *Inst.* 9.3.54–57 (LCL 126.476–78).

126. *Rhet. Her.* 4.29.40 (LCL 403.328); Quint., *Inst.* 9.2.19–20 (LCL 126.384).

127. *Rhet. Her.* 4.26.36 (LCL 403.318–20); Quint., *Inst.* 9.3.89 (LCL 126.498).

this pamphlet.[128] A few pages earlier I noted that in 6.2 there is epanaphora and isocolon where Tertullian discussed whether there was one promised to bring the new law. Immediately after that, he expanded that observation by stating that such a one would abolish the old law and establish the new.[129] There is the antithesis between old and new (repeated as new and ancient, and old and new) expressed in a series of cola of equal word length (except the last has a relative clause attached to it).

As I have mentioned earlier, in a work such as *Aduersus Iudaeos* reasoning by contraries and antithesis can be expected to lie at the very heart of the writing, and indeed it does. When discussing and interpreting Deuteronomy 33:17 in 10.7 (CCSL 2.1376), Tertullian comments on the two characteristics of the Christ: a fierce judge to some and a gentle savior to others. In the next section (10.8) the contrast is between Jesus lifting people up to heaven through the resurrection and casting them down from heaven to earth in the final judgment. The Christian belief in the death and resurrection of Jesus provided a moment of antithesis between Jesus going into the tomb dead and coming out of the tomb resurrected (10.16). There is the metaphorical contrast presented in 13.12 between the thirsting heathens and the revived Christians who have drunk the faith that comes from the cross of Jesus. The two advents of the Christ, which is the topic of chapter 14, also allows for antithesis, this time between the first coming in ignobility and the second in sublimity (14.3), between the sordid garments of the first coming and the festal garments of the second coming (14.7), and between the two goats of Leviticus 16 (14.9).

There are many examples of parenthesis in the *confirmatio*, particularly with regard to the interpretation and identification of metaphors and allegories in Scripture.[130] Säflund has drawn attention to this as being characteristic

128. Säflund, *De pallio*, 165–66, indicated a number of instances in chapter 13 where he detected parallels arising out of rhyming cola, viz., 13.1 with "praedicabatur" and "nuntiabatur"; 13.9 with "legimus" and "recognoscimus"; 13.10 with "deberet" and "haberet"; 13.11 with "exterminantur" and "suspenditur," with "irrigata" and "fundata," and with "plasmatus est" and "natus est"; 13.15 with "immoratur" and "commorabatur"; 13.17 with "sacramentum" and "celebratum"; 13.20 with "lapidauerunt," "fugauerunt," "tradiderunt," and "possunt"; and 13.22 with "locutus est" and "sublatum est."

129. Tert., *Adu. Iud.* 6.2 (CCSL 2.1353): "qui legem ueterem compescat et nouum testamentum statuat et noua sacrificia offerat et ceremonias antiquas reprimat et circumcisionem ueterem cum suo sabbato compescat et nouum regnum, quod non corrumpatur, adnuntiet."

130. Ibid., 8.12 (CCSL 2.1361): anointing of the holy of holies; 8.14 (CCSL 2.1361–1362): the sealing of prophecy and vision, and the baptism of Christ; 8.15 (CCSL 2.1362): the coming of the Christ; 10.6 (CCSL 2.1376): Joseph; 10.9 (CCSL 2.1377): the killing of men and the hamstrung

of both halves of the work.[131] We need only consider chapter 9 in detail to il-lustrate. When dealing with prophecies about the birth of the Christ, partic-ularly Isaiah 8:4 about the wealth of Damascus and the plunder of Samaria, Tertullian made a number of parenthetical comments. The wealth of the East is its strength.[132] Samaria was identified with idolatry.[133] The metaphorical in-terpretation of Christ as warrior concludes with the aside that the sword of Psalm 44(45):3 is the divine word of God.[134] In the argument from family, the root of Jesse is explained as being Mary.[135] The bruised reed of Isaiah 42:2–3 was the faith of Israel, and the burning flax was the faith of the converted Gentiles.[136] All in all, it must be said that 9.5–20 is loose in its construction, pe-dantic in its explanations, repetitious in its examples, torturous in its clarity, and complex in its arguments. Other than the flash of wit and sarcasm in 9.6, where Tertullian decried the literal interpretation of Isaiah 8:4, this section is dull and verbose, unlike Tertullian's usual style. Yet it is the style of one who seems to have compiled a list of scriptural passages relevant to the topic and made preliminary observations about their content, but has not yet eliminat-ed unnecessary duplication or polished and crafted his statements to be scin-tillating and charming. Like Tränkle, I still believe that what was written here provided the basis for the revision that we find in *Aduersus Marcionem* rather than that someone took a perfectly sensible piece of writing in *Aduersus Mar-cionem* and inflated it with tedious repetition.[137]

When Tertullian felt the need to make a parenthetical explanation that the solemn feast celebrated before the departure of the people of Israel from Egypt was the Passover, one may wonder whether such a thing would re-ally be necessary if this work were intended for Jews.[138] The explanation is

---

bull; 10.10 (CCSL 2.1378): the serpents in the desert; 10.12 (CCSL 2.1378): what is on the shoul-der of the child; 10.13 (CCSL 2.1379): the mouth of the lion; 12.2 (CCSL 2.1384): the blind, the bonds, prison, and darkness; 13.4 (CCSL 2.1385): alien people and the bright king; 13.15 (CCSL 2.1388): worn-out troughs; 13.19 (CCSL 2.1388): the wood of Christ; 14.9 (CCSL 2.1394): the spiri-tual temple.

131. Säflund, *De pallio*, 164: "Das wiederholte Abbrechen der Bibelzitate durch eingescho-bene Erläuterungen, eingeleitet durch 'id est', 'scilicet', 'videlicet', 'utique', 'indubitate', ist für Tertullians exegetischen Stil bezeichnend. So finden sich auf einer Seite im ersten Kapitel von Adv. Iud. (Oe. II 702) nicht weniger als sechs 'id est', nebst einem 'utique'. Im Verhältnis zu 'id est' hat 'utique' bei Tertullian eine deutlich polemische Spitze."

132. *Adu. Iud.* 9.11 (CCSL 2.1367).   133. Ibid., 9.12 (CCSL 2.1368).
134. Ibid., 9.17 (CCSL 2.1369).   135. Ibid., 9.26 (CCSL 2.1373).
136. Ibid., 9.28 (CCSL 2.1373).
137. Tränkle, *Tertullian, "Adversus Iudaeos,"* liii–liv.
138. Tert., *Adu. Iud.* 10.18 (CCSL 2.1380).

redundant particularly because in the next sentence Tertullian referred to the statement in Exodus 12:11 that the celebration was called the Passover of the Lord. To this he added the comment that this referred to the sufferings of the Christ. Another redundant parenthetical comment occurs in the next sentence, about the day turning into evening in the middle of the day, when Tertullian felt the need to add that evening meant darkness.[139]

This stylistic technique of adding brief comments of explanation was part of Tertullian's method of arguing, for the content of those passages was understood as types, or as being fulfilled in Jesus or his followers. Arguing about the meaning of scriptural words and statements is precisely the kind of thing that one would expect in a debate about whether Jewish Midrash on particular verses was correct or not. It would be a style of argument familiar to Jews.

Rhetorical questions are a common feature in Tertullian's writings and we find them frequently enough in the *confirmatio*: 7.3; 7.4 (twice); 7.6; 7.8; 8.9; 8.12; 9.5; 9.17 (twice); 10.10 (twice); 10.11; 10.12; 10.16; 13.2; 13.5 (twice); 13.7 (twice); 13.9; 13.13; 13.14; 13.19; 13.22; 13.23; 13.29 (three times); and 14.9. I have drawn attention to several of them already. Sometimes an answer is provided and sometimes not. They are an effective way of advancing an argument along the ways intended by the speaker or writer.

Again, I have pointed to one or two examples of elimination in the *confirmatio*, where Tertullian guided the argument by setting out choices and removing all but the one he advocated. In the introduction to the *confirmatio* we find such an example. Tertullian set out the alternatives: either the giver of the new law had come (in which case service was to be given to him) or he had not (in which case he was to be awaited), but, given that the old law could not cease until the new law-giver had come, he had to demonstrate only that Jesus was the promised one in order to show that the Jewish law had ceased.[140] Throughout the last three chapters we find instances where an alternative is offered but, upon examination, it is argued by Tertullian that it is an impossible one.[141]

We find two examples where the author used paralipsis *(occultatio)*, where one says that one will not say something but in such a way as to say it anyway.[142] In 7.2 (CCSL 2.1353–1354) we find the statement that nothing further

---

139. Ibid., 10.19 (CCSL 2.1380).   140. Ibid., 6.3–4 (CCSL 2.1353).
141. Ibid., 12.2 (CCSL 2.1384); 13.3–5 (CCSL 2.1385).
142. *Rhet. Her.* 4.27.37 (LCL 403.320); Quint., *Inst.* 9.2.47–48 (LCL 126.400–402).

need be said about the Jewish expectation of the coming of a messiah, and yet the author continued with an extract from Isaiah 45:1. In 10.6 (CCSL 2.1376) Tertullian wrote that Joseph is the only type of Jesus that need be discussed, and yet went on to discuss Jacob and Moses.

Hypophora occurs when an opponent is asked what they could say in support of their own position or against one's own stance, which is then addressed.[143] We find some near examples of this in *Aduersus Iudaeos*. In 8.13 (CCSL 2.1361) Tertullian asked the Jews to put forward something positive of their own to prove that there still was prophecy after Jesus, having said already that this was impossible. The Jews were also invited to offer their understanding of what God reigning from a tree meant. Tertullian did not even entertain the notion that the reference could be to some woodcutter (10.11 [CCSL 2.1378]).

Of the tropes, we find hyperbole[144] in 7.3 (CCSL 2.1354) with the claim that "omnes gentes" had heard and believed in God's Son. This is continued in 7.5 (CCSL 2.1355) with the assertion that no city in the world had been able to keep Christianity out. The statement that "Britannorum inaccessa Romanis loca"[145] may show Tertullian's limited knowledge of events away from North Africa, and his exaggeration. The boast that the name of Christ is "ubique adoratur" is obviously hyperbole. The use of "constat" in 9.23 (CCSL 2.1371), with regard to the belief that it was the Son of God who addressed Moses through the burning bush, does not state by whom it was agreed; the use of such a claim in a pamphlet designed to be used in future debates with Jews deliberately suppresses the fact that they certainly would not have agreed with this. There is a touch of irony in the statement that the Germans were shut in by the Romans, and paradox in the observation that the Romans' fortifications had brought a halt to their expansionist policies.[146]

Perhaps one could describe some of the passages of the *confirmatio* like 7.3–8.1a; 9.10–16a; 10.8b–10a; and 13.10–23 as dwelling on the point *(commoratio)*, the technique whereby an orator would return frequently to his strongest point to reinforce it and impress it upon his hearers' memory.[147] How-

---

143. *Rhet. Her.* 4.23.33 (LCL 403.310); Quint., *Inst.* 9.3.98 (LCL 126.502).

144. *Rhet. Her.* 4.33.44 (LCL 403.338–40); Quint., *Inst.* 8.6.67–76 (LCL 126.338–44).

145. Tert., *Adu. Iud.* 7.4 (CCSL 2.1354): "the region of the Britons that is inaccessible to the Romans."

146. Ibid., 7.8 (CCSL 2.1355–1356).

147. *Rhet. Her.* 4.45.58 (LCL 403.374); Quint., *Inst.* 9.2.4 (LCL 126.376).

ever, these passages are really digressions. Perhaps this says something about the modern reader, but after having Tertullian make his point about the wealth of Damascus and the plunder of Samaria in 9.4–9, it seems tedious, overblown, and long-winded of him to spend 9.10–16a discussing it further. The trouble with discussing things at great length and offering example after example is that the main point can be overlooked and lost.

Taking my own advice, it is appropriate to end this discussion about the *confirmatio* with the general observation that it is littered with many other examples of rhetorical *figurae,* some of which any speaker or writer could have produced even without rhetorical training. Some, however, are polished and positioned in such a way as to render unmistakable the fact that its author was skilled in the rhetorical art. Yet the whole *confirmatio* is not a fine example of rhetorical *elocutio.* It would seem that the author of *Aduersus Iudaeos* had such a vast number of illustrations to prove that Jesus was the Christ promised in the Hebrew Scriptures that matters of style took a back seat, so to speak. There is a verbosity in this pamphlet that is not characteristic of the mature Tertullian, but that does not mean that we must rule him out as its author. I am quite happy to accept *Aduersus Iudaeos* as one of his earliest works, written before his terse and often cryptic style matured fully. There certainly are pointers to that here. Even though he tends toward being verbose, there are numerous instances where the style is underdeveloped, particularly where he lists numerous examples. One imagines that, had this work been revised, some examples would have been removed and those that were left would have been reworked more carefully.

Peroratio (14.11–14)

The unsatisfactory nature of this desultory and desiccated appendage has been mentioned already in previous chapters. There is nothing with regard to its style that would redeem it from this judgment. Quintilian had advised that in a *peroratio* one ought either to summarize the facts or appeal to the emotions of the listener/reader. If one chose to summarize then one needed to avoid dry and tiresome repetition of points made already by appropriate insights and a good use of *figurae.*[148]

We see a metaphorical description of the gospel as rays illuminating the world in 14.12 (CCSL 2.1395). There is a sense of *eliminatio* in 14.14 with the

---

148. Quint., *Inst.* 6.pr.2 (LCL 125.372).

choice either of denying that there was prophecy about the coming of the Christ and the events that were to take place after his coming or of accepting that the prophecies had been fulfilled.[149] These choices are presented in an isocolon characteristic of Tertullian.[150] Yet I remain convinced that the material in this last section of *Aduersus Iudaeos* was taken from *Aduersus Marcionem* by someone other than Tertullian and was added to Tertullian's *Aduersus Iudaeos* on the basis of the interpretation of Psalm 2:7–8, as argued in the previous chapters. Questions of style offer no further insight into questions of authorship and integrity.

Conclusion

A chapter detailing the presence of various rhetorical *figurae* in the work of an early Christian author does not make for entertaining or easy reading. Indeed, to some extent the precise claims I have made throughout the chapter have to be somewhat tentative given that a rhetorician like Quintilian disagreed with so many other theoreticians, and indicated that they disagreed among themselves, about just what should and should not be considered a *figura*. What I have wanted to demonstrate is not so much the specific detail but the overall impression, which is, I believe, that the author of the whole work demonstrated a facility with his language that went beyond what someone untrained in rhetoric would have been able to produce, and that the argument was advanced through the employment of these rhetorical techniques of style.

There are a number of words in *Aduersus Iudaeos* that do not appear elsewhere in the corpus of Tertullian's writings. For several reasons this does not suggest that another person was responsible for writing it. The phenomenon occurs in both parts of the pamphlet and so, if one wants to dismiss the second half of the work as someone else's piece on this basis one would have to say the same for the first half as well, which is not claimed by many scholars. Further, some of these words may derive from Old Latin versions of Scripture and, given that some of those passages were not the subject of consideration anywhere else in Tertullian's writings, it is not surprising to find them

---

149. The third choice, the Jewish position, of believing that there were prophecies but that they were still to be fulfilled was not presented as an option.

150. Tert., *Adu. Iud.* 14.14 (CCSL 2.1396): "Haec aut prophetata nega, cum coram uidentur, aut adimpleta, cum leguntur."

used only here. Also, it is to be expected that one would find some almost specialized words here, like the proper nouns of chapter 8, that he did not use elsewhere.

The most typical characteristic of the style of this pamphlet is with the antithetical presentation of scriptural interpretation. The exegetical understanding of the Jews was contrasted with that of the Christians in order to show Jewish misunderstanding and Christian accuracy with regard to the question of whether or not the Christ had come in Jesus. In this we find some examples of Tertullian engaging in allegorical interpretation (in the sense of examining a text for a deeper, even hidden, meaning that goes beyond the literal), but even more typically we find him engaging in typological interpretation (in the sense of seeing the future announced in the present).[151] On this basis we may conclude that Tertullian's interest lay in refuting Jewish interpretation of Scripture rather than in attacking Jews themselves. Except for the sarcasm in 9.6, this pamphlet cannot be characterized as vitriolic or abusive. The impression created in the opening lines of the pamphlet, that this would be a work of substance rather than of slander, seems to have been carried through to the end. Appeals to the emotions play almost no part in these pages. The plain style suits the forensic nature of this pamphlet. As I have stated earlier, rather than seeing this approach as a sign that the issue of Christians and Jews was not relevant to Christians in Carthage in the late second century, I believe that Tertullian's care in not succumbing to satire (which, as we know from his other treatises, he could do so easily) may be taken as an indication of the importance and intensity of the debate between Jews and Christians and of the fact that he expected his writings to be perused by Jews or heard by them from the lips of other Christians who made use of his writing.

Some passages in *Aduersus Iudaeos* seem more finished or more fashioned than others. Attention has been drawn already to passages such as 1.5; 3.10; 6.1–2; 7.6–9; and 9.23 in particular. Other passages (9.10–16a; 10.14b–19a; and 13.8–23 being the most glaring) seem labored, long-winded, lethargic, and in need of pruning and polish. Quintilian had warned orators against long sentences that become obscure through too much hyperbaton and parenthesis, and against superfluous words.[152] Cicero claimed that the plain style

---

151. See O'Malley, *Tertullian and the Bible*, 148, for comment about this distinction.

152. Quint., *Inst.* 8.2.14–17 (LCL 126.204–206). In the last section we find this insightful comment: "dum communem loquendi morem reformidant, ducti specie nitoris circumeunt omnia copiosa loquacitate, eo quod dicere nolunt ipsa."

ought to have some vigor about it, to have no deliberate rhythm, to be loose but not rambling, not to be too smooth, not to have obvious ornament except some metaphor, and to have clear, simple, and everyday language.[153] It would seem to me that these passages in chapters 9, 10, and 13 are not just characteristic of Tertullian's early, loquacious style. They are more than just wordy, they are unrefined. Here the lack of *figurae* indicates not the plain style but the lack of much rhetorical style at all. What we have in these chapters appear to be the sketches and raw material that still need attention before being ready to read.

My conclusion is that there is enough in *Aduersus Iudaeos* that is consistent with Tertullian's style to decide that it was his. Because it was a work written early in his literary career when, one must presume, the influence of his rhetorical training would have been strongest, one must conclude further not that its author lacked experience or ability with regard to style but that its author did not spend enough time and effort on drafting. *Aduersus Iudaeos* reads like many student essays: desperately in need of major overhaul in order to salvage the few decent insights that seem likely to drown in a sea of indifferent prose.

153. Cic., *Orat.* 23.75–25.86 (LCL 342.360–68).

Conclusion

The purpose of these final pages is simple. I would like to summarize my findings from the rhetorical analysis of *Aduersus Iudaeos* and draw some conclusions about the work and about Christians and Jews in Carthage in the late second century.

This is the first time *Aduersus Iudaeos,* which I prefer to describe as a pamphlet rather than a treatise because of its more occasional and less systematic and comprehensive nature, has been examined from a rhetorical perspective. The present study is the first full-length treatment of the text in English and one of the very few in any language, particularly in the last century. The evidence that has been extracted from the analysis supports the arguments advanced by scholars like Tränkle, Säflund, Aziza, and Fredouille that the whole *Aduersus Iudaeos* is an authentic work of Tertullian.

Maintaining a rhetorical perspective enables the modern reader to keep in mind that the author of this piece of literature was putting forward a point of view and wanted to do so in a persuasive and convincing manner. As with all debate and argument, those engaged in rhetoric do not try to be objective. They try to win their case. Supposition and conjecture can be given the appearance of fact. Facts that are helpful are included, those that are not are explained away or excluded. Facts are arranged in a particular order to be at their most compelling and are presented in the best possible light. This is true not only of *Aduersus Iudaeos* but of scholarly literature in general. Anyone who presents a thesis, as I am doing in this volume, is engaged in the art of persuasion.

Robert Sider has shown that Tertullian was well versed in this art. It is not surprising that he was. Anyone in his age who had a good education had spent many an hour mastering the discipline. Rhetorical theory and oratorical practice must be considered a major influence on the composition of all Christian literature in antiquity that was written by those who had any formal Graeco-Roman education. An appreciation of rhetoric helps put the quest for objectivity into a more realistic perspective. In reading, one never has access to undiluted facts but only to someone's interpretation, presentation, or even obfuscation of the facts. Rhetoric is a crucial hermeneutical tool for the scholar of early Christianity.

The oratory of Tertullian's age was predominantly sophistic: concerned with matters of style and entertainment where historical themes and fictitious settings were all the rage. Yet the Christian literature of that century that shows the influence of rhetoric does not have this sense about it. Christians needed all their skills to survive, not to entertain. Even though persecution was sporadic, hostility toward Christians on social and intellectual grounds was always in fashion in local communities. There is a certain rawness and immediacy about Christian oratory. Tertullian is a fine example of the way in which rhetoric was used for very practical purposes by early Christians. I think it unjust to characterize Tertullian's rhetoric as sophistic.

Whom did Tertullian seek to persuade by writing this work? The first thing to notice is that, unlike Justin's *Dialogus,* which purports to be the record of a conversation with a Jew and was therefore, ostensibly at least, designed for or directed at or intended for Jews, *Aduersus Iudaeos* is not a record of a conversation. This is a point that is sometimes overlooked by modern scholars. It claims to be a record of what should have been said during that earlier encounter but was not, owing to the breakdown in communication that resulted from some heated exchanges. More accurately even than that, it claims to be a record of what should be said at future such encounters, given that Tertullian, having been privy to the kinds of arguments that the proselyte Jew put forward to support his case in the earlier encounter, had taken the opportunity to refine the Christian position.

This becomes the first question that may be raised: did this precipitative exchange actually take place? I am inclined to believe that it did, despite the fact that it was something of a standard rhetorical technique of declaimers to create a fictitious setting or an imagined audience. The important point is that, whether or not that earlier encounter was a literary fiction, it does not mean that we can conclude that Tertullian never met Jews in debate or that there was no contact between Christians and Jews in Carthage at the end of the second century. Therefore, the question of whether this earlier encounter took place is a different one from the question of whether any encounters occurred at all. A negative answer to the first (something I am not suggesting) does not necessarily imply the same for the other.

An analysis of the persons addressed throughout the work reveals, I believe, evidence not of an incompetent imitator who attempted to complete what Tertullian had started but could not maintain consistency of person, or of someone who was only partially successful in transforming references to Marcion in *Aduersus Marcionem* into references to the Jews in *Aduersus Iudaeos*. It is evidence instead of the orator in Tertullian coming to the fore. My conclusion is that Tertullian wrote the work imagining he was before the gathering he described in its opening sentences, which had reassembled in order this time to hear a more polished Christian performance. Instead of degenerating into a cacophony of verbal abuse, his idealized future encounter was one in which he imagined that he would be able to present all his arguments and that they would be persuasive. That imagined future gathering was the same as the previous gathering (leaving aside, as I said, the issue of whether it was in any way a real gathering), consisting of Jews, Christians, and possibly curious onlookers. Most of the time the Jews in that audience were to be addressed in the third person, which leads to the conclusion that Tertullian was imagining himself talking about them to the Christians rather than talking to them, for only the Christians would be permitted by Tertullian to vote on his performance. To preserve an atmosphere of learned disputation rather than personal acrimony, he addressed his opponents in the third person, but sometimes, perhaps to heighten the emotional intensity, he addressed them directly.

While this deals with questions of the imagined readership, we still need to ask about the intended readership. As I suggested in the second chapter, I believe this work was intended for Christians in order to supply them with debating ammunition in their own encounters with Jews in Carthage, for I am convinced that contact between Jews and Christians continued in Carthage in Tertullian's time. The fact that much of the evidence from Scripture used by Tertullian was also used by Irenaeus and Justin (even though there are considerable differences in some of the arguments constructed from that evidence, if one pays close enough attention to detail) could well mean that the same issues kept arising in different localities at different times and that the Christian response needed to be repeated constantly, for their interpretation was rejected constantly by Jews. The point was not necessarily to persuade Jews to convert to Christianity but to convince Christians themselves that they were in the right. At its heart the pamphlet is about offering the correct interpretation of passages from the Hebrew Scriptures and so, either directly or, more likely, indirectly (with other Christians using what Tertullian had written to conduct their own debates with Jews), Tertullian wanted Jews to realize where they were going wrong in their understanding. This work was written to accomplish several tasks at the same time; it was written both for matters of internal self-definition within Christianity and for encounters between Christians and Jews.

The second question that this analysis sought to answer through its rhetorical investigation concerned authorship. The most solid information with regard to this matter came from a consideration of whether this work contains a rhetorical structure or not. One can discern such a structure in *Aduersus Iudaeos,* and a fairly standard one at that. The work begins with an *exordium* (1.1–3a), concerning the history of events that led to the writing of the text, and a *partitio* (1.3b–2.1a), in which Tertullian stated his position that the Christians had indeed replaced the Jews as God's people and his intention to examine all the relevant matters methodically. I repeat here the modification, first expressed in my 2004 English translation of the text, of my earlier views that *Aduersus Iudaeos* contained a *narratio* in 1.3b–7.

The major body of the pamphlet follows: *refutatio* (2.1b–6.1) first and then *confirmatio* (6.2–14.10). The inversion of the standard order was not altogether unusual and it enabled Tertullian to present his two main rhetorical elements in chronological order. The *refutatio* argued that God had made promises to replace the Jews and these promises could be found in the Hebrew Scriptures. He argued also that the Jewish position, that God had made no such promises, was false, and he did this by offering his own interpretation of what those scriptural passages really meant. The *confirmatio* argued that those promises had been fulfilled in Jesus. The *refutatio* was divided into consideration of the law (2.1b–10a), circumcision (2.10b–3.6), the Sabbath (4.1–11), and sacrifices (5.1–7). There is a small passage (3.7–13) on the promises of a new law and new circumcision that would make more sense if it were integrated with its relevant sections. At the beginning of the *confirmatio* Tertullian announced that there were two questions to be considered: whether there was any prophecy about the coming of a new law-giver and whether that promised new law-giver had arrived. Only the second question was addressed because, he argued, no one disagreed about the first. In 7.1 we find a statement about what four areas Tertullian intended to cover in order to answer the second question in the affirmative. This was revised in 8.2 into three areas: the time when the Christ would come (8.3–18), the signs and operations of the Christ (9.1–10.19), and subsequent events since the Christ's coming (11.1–14.10). In between 7.1 and 8.1a is a passage about the universal spread of Christianity, which makes more sense, in terms of its position in the argument, when it reappears under the area of subsequent events.

There is no real *peroratio* to the pamphlet: 14.11–14 is a repetition of 11.10–11a, where Tertullian had begun to draw his arguments to a conclusion before realizing that there was still further evidence to present. Not only is 14.11–14 a repetition but, on the basis of a misreading of Tertullian's interpretation of Psalm 2:7, I would conclude that it is an interpolation (the only one in the text) by a foreign hand.

Determining a rhetorical structure for the entire pamphlet leads to several conclusions. The first is that finding a *partitio* enables one to discover the work's focus. The second is that whoever wrote the first half (up to the end of chapter 8), the authenticity of which is not usually in dispute, intended to write what is found in the second half, because the author's comments in that first half about what would be discussed in the second are matched by what is found there. The third conclusion is that this work remains in an incomplete state. More time spent on it would perhaps have seen (or should have seen) a number of revisions: the incorporation of 3.7–13 into 2.1–3.6 more effectively, the elimination of the *digressio* in 7.2–8.1a, the elimination of the premature *peroratio* in 11.10–11a, the relocation of 12.1–2 to before 11.1 (enabling 11.1–9 and 13.1–29 to flow together smoothly), the elimination of some meandering in chapter 13 that obscures the argument, and the addition of a proper *peroratio*.

Of course, it could be argued that even though Tertullian had announced what would occur in the second half of the work, he never got around to writing that half and that someone else, taking material from *Aduersus Marcionem*, completed that plan. Rather than accusing that anonymous completer of plagiarism I would respond, as have Tränkle, Säflund, and Barnes, that there is every reason to think that Tertullian himself found it convenient to reuse material from one piece of writing in another. Given that Tertullian's characteristic terseness was a development in his writing, and given that the pattern of the material used in both works makes rational and logical sense in the order in which it appears in *Aduersus Iudaeos,* I would accept its priority over *Aduersus Marcionem*.

This enables me to comment on the date of the pamphlet. The rhetorical analysis supports the conclusion that we ought to date *Aduersus Iudaeos* prior to *Aduersus Marcionem*. The third edition of the latter work began appearing in 207 and the second edition, which appears to have included book 3,[1] must have been some time before that. We can repeat Noeldechen's observation more than a century ago that *Adu. Iud.* 9.12 indicates that the work was written after 194, when Syria was split into two provinces. The style of writing would indicate that it ought to be included among Tertullian's earliest works, written even before *Apologeticum*, so a date of about 195 or 196 seems likely.

Concerning the work's rhetorical arguments, I have suggested that *Aduersus Iudaeos* should be considered a *controuersia*, not because it dealt with a fantastic theme but because of the way Tertullian idealized its setting (again, without implying that such a setting was unlikely to ever occur) and because of the way he expressed the *partitio* of the work. God is the defendant, and the argument between Tertullian and his Jewish opponents was over whether or not God had changed the covenant with Moses by abandoning the Jews and reaching out to Gentiles. Remembering that prosecutors accused people of wrongdoing, it is clear that Tertullian was not prosecuting God. However, and this is what gives the pamphlet its novelty and reveals its author's talents, in defending God Tertullian did not argue that God was innocent because God had done nothing. Instead, God was "guilty" of doing something (and therefore innocent of the Jewish charge of having done nothing to change the covenant). Such a twist is more characteristic of the approach that would be taken in a *controuersia* than in a formal forensic setting. In saying that *Aduersus Iudaeos* has characteristics of a *controuersia*, though, I am not saying that, like contemporary declaimers, Tertullian chose a theme that was fictitious or bizarre, but one that was real and relevant to Christians of his time.

In this *controuersia* the chief witness to be plundered was Hebrew Scripture. Tertullian argued that a correct understanding of this documentary evidence would reveal that God had promised to do what Tertullian "accused" God of intending to do (or, more confusedly, God was innocent of the Jewish charge of not having done anything to change the covenant) and that, in Jesus, God had brought that promise to fulfillment. Throughout the chapter on rhetorical argumentation I highlighted those instances when Tertullian offered a literal interpretation of a scriptural passage and other instances when he offered a typological or even allegorical interpretation, usually to counter the opposite approach taken by his opponents. The point to be made is that

---

1. Tert., *Adu. Marc.* 3.1.1 (CCSL 1.509).

Tertullian adopted a particular method depending upon what was most helpful in winning his point.

Although many of the passages of the Scriptures about which Tertullian proffered comment had been used in earlier generations, by the author of *Barnabas,* Irenaeus, or Justin, reinforcing the belief that they all made use of *testimonia* or each other, it is to be noted that the way in which Tertullian used that piece of scriptural evidence to construct his argument was often original. When one pays close attention not just to the fact that a certain piece of Scripture was used frequently in early Christian literature but to the fact that authors made different arguments from the same pieces of evidence, statements that anti-Jewish literature was repetitive appear too sweeping and generalized. Attention to details reveals the originality of Tertullian's work.

In terms, then, of how this pamphlet fits into Tertullian's theology, a rhetorical perspective helps us realize, as Evans pointed out in his 1976 article to which I referred in the second chapter, that this is no simple matter. Tertullian wrote for different audiences and varied what he said on a particular topic depending upon that audience. His theology in this pamphlet is overtly supersessionist: Christians have replaced Jews as God's people. The Hebrew Scriptures themselves pointed to a time when God would reform the covenant and choose a new people. This theological position does not change in *Aduersus Marcionem.* As others have pointed out, Tertullian was able to rescue the Hebrew Scriptures from the oblivion into which Marcion had wanted to cast them without rehabilitating the Jews from the oblivion into which Tertullian himself had cast them.

I have been able to illustrate how Tertullian made use of the full range of rhetorical *topoi* or *loci communes* in the course of his writing: degree, priority, opposites, contraries, possibility, time, subsequent events, etc. As well, I have drawn attention to weaknesses in his argument where a competent opponent could have challenged the logic of the conclusions he was trying to draw. We can see the full force of rhetorical skill involved in the ways in which Tertullian tried to mask these weaknesses and draw attention away from them.

One of those weaknesses is the way in which, particularly in 9.1–16a and 13.8–23, Tertullian got carried away with himself. We can see why he included these arguments where they are and how they relate to the section in which they are found. By arguing them at great length, however, the balance and feel for what is essential in the pamphlet is somewhat lost.

In terms of style I have offered a tentative conclusion that *Aduersus Iu-*

daeos was written in the plain style, one that disguised its craft under the veil of simplicity. This would be in accord with his stated desire not to write in such a way as to inflame emotions. There is almost the complete absence of wit and satire, which is unusual for Tertullian, but perhaps not surprising in a work he intended for his opponent to know either directly or indirectly. Other than long-winded passages that are too unrefined even for this style, much of the time this pamphlet avoids excessive use of ornamental *figurae* and maintains a clear and direct language, even though with proper words that would rarely be used elsewhere. The whole purpose of the work was to contrast Jewish and Christian understandings of Scripture, and so it is not surprising to find an antithetical style in the presentation of ideas. Much of Tertullian's own style of expression was derived from the scriptural passages. Despite the plainness, there are enough examples of a subtle and careful use of rhetorical techniques of style to confirm that the author of *Aduersus Iudaeos* was thoroughly familiar with its precepts and that some parts appear in a more finished state than others.

This analysis and the conclusions I have reached about the integrity and authenticity of *Aduersus Iudaeos* stand in stark contrast with the position taken by several scholars and support that taken by others, all of which was outlined in some detail in the opening chapter. It was necessary to provide sufficient detail in order to demonstrate the unique contribution this volume makes to those controversies.

Further, in that opening chapter, I summarized the recent scholarship on ongoing contact between Christians and Jews in the years after the destruction of Jerusalem. In that debate Tertullian does not feature to any great extent and, when he does, *Aduersus Iudaeos* is rarely mentioned. If one can accept the conclusions of my analysis then Tertullian's pamphlet is a work that ought to be taken more into account in answering the question of ongoing interaction instead of being explained away when it appears not to suit one's predetermined position.

While it is fairly easy to determine Tertullian's attitude toward the Jews, which was negative, it is a much harder task to determine his contact with them. Even though Tertullian seems to have been well aware of what the Jews were doing in Carthage in his own time,[2] this was not the topic to de-

---

2. See, e.g., Tert., *De iei.* 16.6 (CCSL 2.1275) (not *Adu. Marc.* 2.18.2, as John Lund, "A Synagogue at Carthage? Menorah-lamps from the Danish Excavations," *JRA* 8 [1995]: 258, claims) for

bate with them. The argument was about the enduring meaning of past events as recorded in Scripture. Since it was so fundamental to the self-identity of both groups, I would argue that Christians and Jews never tired of arguing this point with each other. Even though the Christian anti-Judaic literature, on the whole, reconstructed Jewish opponents in such a way that they appeared only as straw figures,[3] we must realize that early Christian writers were not trying to present objective accounts but were employing rhetorical strategies in order to win arguments, achieved not necessarily through the capitulation or conversion of one's opponents. Winning in the eyes of one's supporters was what really mattered. It may well be under-handed, but stereotyping has always been a part of maximizing one's potential for victory. I believe that Tertullian provides us with evidence that there was both contact and conflict between Jews and Christians in Carthage in the years of the Severan dynasty. Perhaps one could say that Christian anti-Judaic literature was written primarily for fellow Christians, but written so that they would be better prepared for ongoing encounters with Jews where the meaning of Scripture could be debated yet again.

I hope that this rhetorical analysis of Tertullian's *Aduersus Iudaeos* helps rehabilitate this text as an authentic, unified, though unrevised work of the first Latin Christian theologian and makes a contribution to the academic investigation into ongoing contact between Jews and Christians in the post–New Testament world of the Roman empire. With my perspective added to those already offered by the few scholars who have chosen to treat this work, perhaps even more notice will be given to it in the literature on ancient anti-Judaism and to the rhetorical nature of theological literature in general. As I finish I wish to endorse the words of Lloyd Gaston, who indicated that he considered Tertullian a significant figure for Christian anti-Judaism:

In many respects Tertullian represents a turning point in the development of Christian doctrine, in which certain tentative second-century developments receive a clear formulation which will dominate all further doctrine, and that is also the case here. Anti-Judaism, then, can be defined as what Tertullian says about Jews.[4]

---

the Jews celebrating fast days on the beach. Aziza, *Tertullien et le judaïsme,* 29, identifies this as the celebration of Yom Kippur.

3. Moore, "Christian Writers on Judaism," 198; and Lee Martin McDonald, "Anti-Judaism in the Early Church Fathers," in *Anti-Semitism and Early Christianity: Issues of Polemic and Faith,* ed. Craig A. Evans and Donald A. Hagner (Minneapolis: Fortress Press, 1993), 227.

4. Gaston, "Retrospect," 163. I do not agreed with everything he writes with regard to Ter-

Aduersus Iudaeos is a significant text. Like this volume, it seeks to be persuasive and, like this volume, it has its shortcomings, limitations, and narrowness of perspective. As any good orator should, one must end stressing the importance of one's message and apologize for the lack of ability of the messenger, entrusting the final decision to one's reading audience.

---

tullian, for I believe Tertullian's anti-Judaism was expressed as an inner theological debate within Christianity that arose out of the ongoing rivalry between Christians and Jews.

Bibliography

Primary Sources

The Apostolic Fathers. *Clement, Ignatius, and Polycarp.* Edited by J. B. Lightfoot. 5 vols. 2nd ed. Peabody, Mass.: Hendrickson, 1889–1890.

Aristides. *Panathenaic Oration and In Defence of Oratory.* Translated by C. A. Behr. LCL 458. Cambridge, Mass.: Harvard University Press, 1973.

Aristotle. *The "Art" of Rhetoric.* Translated by John Henry Freese. LCL 193. Cambridge, Mass.: Harvard University Press, 1926.

Barnabas. *Épître.* Translated and edited by Pierre Prigent and Robert A. Kraft. SC 172. Paris: Les Éditions du Cerf, 1971.

[Cicero]. *Ad C. Herennium. De Ratione Dicendi (Rhetorica ad Herennium).* Translated by Harry Caplan. LCL 403. Cambridge, Mass.: Harvard University Press, 1954.

Cicero. *Brutus, Orator.* Translated by G. L. Hendrickson and H. M. Hubbell. 2nd ed. LCL 342. Cambridge, Mass.: Harvard University Press, 1962.

———. *De Inventione, De Optimo Genere Oratorum, Topica.* Translated by H. M. Hubbell. LCL 386. Cambridge, Mass.: Harvard University Press, 1949.

———. *De Oratore, De Fato, Paradoxa Stoicorum, De Partitione Oratoria.* Translated by E. W. Sutton and H. Rackham. 2 vols. LCL 348–349. Cambridge, Mass.: Harvard University Press, 1942.

Fronto. *The Correspondence of Marcus Cornelius Fronto.* Translated by C. R. Haines. 2 vols. LCL 112–113. Cambridge, Mass.: Harvard University Press, 1919–1920.

Irenaeus of Lyons. *Démonstration de la "predication" apostolique.* Translated by L. M. Froidevaux. SC 62. Paris: Les Éditions du Cerf, 1959.

———. *Epideixis, Adversus Haereses.* Translated by Norbert Brox. 5 vols. FC 8/1–5. Freiburg: Herder, 1993–2001.

Justin Martyr. *Dialogus cum Tryphone.* Edited by Miroslav Marcovich. PTS 47. Berlin and New York: Walter de Gruyter, 1997.

Juvenal. *Satires.* Translated by G. G. Ramsay. In *Juvenal and Persius.* Translated by G. G. Ramsay. LCL 91. Cambridge, Mass.: Harvard University Press, 1940.

Philostratus. *The Lives of the Sophists.* Translated by Wilmer C. Wright. In Philostratus and Eunapius, *The Lives of the Sophists.* Translated by Wilmer C. Wright. LCL 134. Cambridge, Mass.: Harvard University Press, 1921.

Pliny. *Letters and Panegyricus.* Translated by Betty Radice. 2 vols. LCL 55, 59. Cambridge, Mass.: Harvard University Press, 1969.

Quintilian. *The Institutio Oratoria.* Translated by H. E. Butler. 4 vols. LCL 124–127. Cambridge, Mass.: Harvard University Press, 1920–1922.

Seneca the Elder. *Controversiae and Suasoriae*. Translated by Michael Winterbottom. 2 vols. LCL 463–464. Cambridge, Mass.: Harvard University Press, 1974.

Suetonius. *Lives*. Translated by John C. Rolfe. 2 vols. 2nd ed. LCL 38. Cambridge, Mass.: Harvard University Press, 1997.

Tacitus. *Dialogus*. Translated by W. Peterson. Revised by M. Winterbottom. In Tacitus, *Agricola, Germania, and Dialogus*. Translated by M. Hutton and W. Peterson. Revised by R. M. Ogilvie, E. H. Warmington, and M. Winterbottom. 2nd ed. LCL 35. Cambridge, Mass.: Harvard University Press, 1970.

Tertullian. *Adversus Marcionem*, vol. 1: *Books 1 to 3*. Translated by Ernest Evans. Oxford Early Christian Texts. Oxford: Clarendon Press, 1972.

———. "Against the Jews." Translated by Geoffrey D. Dunn. In *Tertullian*, 68–104. The Early Church Fathers. London and New York: Routledge, 2004.

———. *Opera*. Edited by Eligius Dekkers et al. 2 vols. CCSL 1–2. Turnhout: Brepols, 1954.

———. *Opera, II, 2*. Edited by Emil Kroymann, *Tertulliani Opera*, II, 2. CSEL 70. Vienna: Verlag der Österreichischen, Akademie der Wissenschaften, 1942.

———. *Polemica con i Giudei*. Translated by Immacolata Aulisa. Testi Patristici 140. Rome: Città Nuova, 1998.

[Q. S. F. Tertulliani]. *Aduersus Iudaeos*. Edited by Emil Kroymann. In *Tertulliani Opera*, pars 2: *Opera Montanistica*. Edited by Eligius Dekkers et al., 1337–96. CCSL 2. Turnhout: Brepols, 1954.

Secondary Sources

Aalders, G. J. D. "Tertullian's Quotations from St. Luke." *Mnemosyne* series 3, 5 (1937): 241–82.

Åkerman, Malte. *Über die Echtheit der letzteren Hälfte von Tertullians Adversus Iudaeos*. Lund: Lindstroem, 1918.

Altaner, B. *Patrologie. Leben Schriften und Lehre der Kirchenväter*. 8th ed. Revised Alfred Stuiber. Freiburg: Herder, 1978.

Anderson, Graham. "The Second Sophistic: Some Problems of Perspective." In *Antonine Literature*, edited by D. A. Russell, 91–100. Oxford: Clarendon Press, 1990.

———. *The Second Sophistic: A Cultural Phenomenon in the Roman Empire*. London and New York: Routledge, 1993.

Aulisa, Immacolata, trans. *Tertulliano. Polemica con i Giudei*. Testi Patristici 140. Rome: Città Nuova, 1998.

Aziza, Claude. *Tertullien et le judaïsme*. Publications de le Faculté des Lettres et des Sciences Humaines de Nice 16. Nice: Les Belles Lettres, 1977.

Balfour, I. L. S. "Tertullian's Description of the Heathen." In *Studia Patristica* 17, part 2, edited by Elizabeth A. Livingstone, 785–89. Papers presented to the eighth International Conference on Patristic Studies, Oxford 1979. Oxford: Pergamon, 1982.

Barnes, Timothy D. "Tertullian's *Scorpiace*." *JTS* n.s. 20 (1969): 105–32.

———. "Tertullian the Antiquarian." In *Studia Patristica* 14, edited by Elizabeth A. Livingstone, 3–20. Papers presented to the sixth International Conference on Patristic Studies, part 3, Oxford 1971. Berlin: Akademie-Verlag, 1976.

———. *Tertullian: A Historical and Literary Study*. 2nd ed. Oxford: Clarendon Press, 1985.

Barwick, Karl. "Die Gliederung der Rhetorischen TEXNH und die Horazische Epistula ad Pisones." *Hermes* 57 (1922): 1–62.

Bauckham, R. "The Parting of the Ways: What Happened and Why." *STh* 47 (1993): 135–51.

Baumgarten, Albert I. "Marcel Simon's *Verus Israel* as a Contribution to Jewish History." *HTR* 92 (1999): 465–78.

Becker, Adam, and Annette Yoshiko Reed, eds. *The Ways That Never Parted: Jews and Christians in Late Antiquity and the Early Middle Ages.* Texts and Studies in Ancient Judaism 95. Tübingen: Paul Siebeck, 2003.

Becker, C. *Tertullians Apologeticum. Werden und Leistung.* Munich: Kösel-Verlag, 1954.

Bingham, D. Jeffrey. "Justin and Isaiah 53." *VChr* 54 (2000): 248–61.

Blair, Carole. "Contested Histories of Rhetoric: The Politics of Preservation, Progress, and Change." *QJS* 78 (1992): 403–28.

Bodenmann, Reinhard. *Naissance d'une Exégèse. Daniel dans l'Eglise ancienne des trois premiers siècles.* Beiträge zur Geschichte der biblischen Exegese 28. Tübingen: J. C. B. Mohr (Paul Siebeck), 1986.

Bonner, Stanley F. *Roman Declamation in the Late Republic and Early Empire.* Liverpool: University Press of Liverpool, 1949.

———. *Education in Ancient Rome: From the Elder Cato to the Younger Pliny.* Berkeley: University of California Press, 1977.

Bouchier, E. S. *Life and Letters in Roman Africa.* Oxford: Blackwell, 1913.

Boyarin, Daniel. "Martyrdom and the Making of Christianity and Judaism." *JECS* 6 (1998): 577–627.

———. *Dying for God: Martyrdom and the Making of Christianity and Judaism.* Stanford, Calif.: Stanford University Press, 1999.

———. *Border Lines: The Partition of Judaeo-Christianity.* Divinations: Rereading Late Ancient Religion. Philadelphia: University of Pennsylvania Press, 2004.

Braet, Antoine. "The Classical Doctrine of *status* and the Rhetorical Theory of Argumentation." *Ph&Rh* 20 (1987): 79–93.

Bratton, Fred Gladstone. *The Crime of Christendom: The Theological Sources of Christian Anti-Semitism.* Santa Barbara, Calif.: Fithian Press, 1969.

Braun, René. "Aux origines de le chrétienté d'Afrique: un homme de combat, Tertullien." *BAGB* 4th series (1965): 189–208.

Bray, Gerald. "The Legal Concept of Ratio in Tertullian." *VChr* 31 (1977): 94–116.

Brunschwig, Jacques. "Aristotle's Rhetoric as a 'Counterpart' to Dialectic." In *Essays on Aristotle's* Rhetoric, edited by Amélie Oksenberg Rorty, 34–55. Philosophical Traditions 6. Berkeley: University of California Press, 1996.

Bryant, Donald C. "Rhetoric: Its Function and Scope." *QJS* 39 (1953) (reproduced in *The Province of Rhetoric,* edited by Joseph Schwartz and John A. Rycenga, 3–36. New York: Ronald Press, 1965).

Buell, Denise Kimber. "Rethinking the Relevance of Race for Early Christian Self-Definition." *HTR* 94 (2001): 449–76.

———. "Race and Universalism in Early Christianity." *JECS* 10 (2002): 429–68.

———. *Why This New Race? Ethnic Reasoning in Early Christianity.* New York: Columbia University Press, 2005.

Burkitt, F. C. *The Old Latin and the Itala.* Cambridge: Cambridge University Press, 1896.

Burnyeat, M. F. "Enthymeme: Aristotle on the Logic of Persuasion." In *Aristotle's "Rhetoric": Philosophical Essays,* edited by David J. Furley and Alexander Nehamas, 3–55. Princeton, N.J.: Princeton University Press, 1994.

———. "Enthymeme: Aristotle on the Rationality of Rhetoric." In *Essays on Aristotle's "Rhetoric,"* edited by Amélie Oksenberg Rorty, 88–115. Philosophical Traditions 6. Berkeley: University of California Press, 1996.

Cameron, Averil. *Christianity and the Rhetoric of Empire: The Development of Christian Discourse.* Berkeley: University of California Press, 1991.

Caplan, Harry. "The History of the Jews in the Roman Province of Africa: A Collection of the Sources." Ph.D. diss., Cornell University, 1921.

Carey, Christopher. "Rhetorical Means of Persuasion." In *Persuasion: Greek Rhetoric in Action,* edited by Ian Worthington, 26–45. London and New York: Routledge, 1994.

Carleton Paget, James. *The Epistle of Barnabas: Outlook and Background.* Wissenschaftliche Untersuchungen zum Neuen Testament 2, series 64. Tübingen: J. C. B. Mohr (Paul Siebeck), 1994.

———. "Anti-Judaism and Early Christian Identity." *ZAC* 1 (1997): 195–225.

Champlin, Edward. *Fronto and Antonine Rome.* Cambridge, Mass.: Harvard University Press. 1980.

Claesson, Gösta. *Index Tertullianeus.* 3 vols. Collection des Études Augustiniennes Série Antiquité 62–64. Paris: Études Augustiniennes, 1975.

Clark, Donald Lemen. *Rhetoric in Greco-Roman Education.* New York: Columbia University Press, 1957.

Clarke, Martin Lowther. *Rhetoric at Rome: A Historical Survey.* 3rd ed. Revised with new introduction by D. H. Berry. London and New York: Routledge, 1996.

Cohen, Shaye J. D. *The Beginnings of Jewishness: Boundaries, Varieties, Uncertainties.* Hellenistic Culture and Society 31. Berkeley: University of California Press, 1999.

Colson, F. H. "Two Examples of Literary and Rhetorical Criticism in the Fathers." *JTS* 25 (1924): 364–77.

Conley, Thomas M. "The Enthymeme in Perspective." *QJS* 70 (1984): 168–87.

Consigny, Scott. "Dialectical, Rhetorical, and Aristotelian Rhetoric." *Ph&Rh* 22 (1989): 218–87.

Corssen, P. *Die Altercatio Simonis Judaei et Theophili Christiani auf ihre Quellen geprüft.* Berlin: Weidmann, 1890.

Countryman, L. Wm. "Tertullian and the Regula Fidei." *The Second Century* 2 (1982): 208–27.

Culpepper, R. Alan. *Anatomy of the Fourth Gospel: A Study in Literary Design.* Minneapolis: Fortress Press, 1983.

Dekkers, Eligius, ed. *Clavis Patrum Latinorum.* 3rd ed. CCSL. Steenbrugge: Brepols, 1995.

Dominik, William J. "The Style Is the Man: Seneca, Tactitus, and Quintilian's Canon." In *Roman Eloquence: Rhetoric in Society and Literature,* edited by William J. Dominik, 50–68. London and New York: Routledge, 1997.

Douglas, Alan Edward. "A Ciceronian Contribution to Rhetorical Theory." *Eranos* 55 (1957): 18–26.

Dunn, Geoffrey D. "Tertullian and Rebekah: A Re-Reading of an 'Anti-Jewish' Argument in Early Christian Literature." *VChr* 52 (1998): 119–45.

———. "*Pro Temporum Condicione:* Jews and Christians as God's People in Tertullian's *Adversus Iudaeos."* In *Prayer and Spirituality in the Early Church,* vol. 2, edited by Pauline Allen, Wendy Mayer, and Lawrence Cross, 315–41. Brisbane: Centre for Early Christian Studies, 1999.

———. "A Rhetorical Analysis of Tertullian's *adversus Iudaeos."* Ph.D. diss., Australian Catholic University, 1999.

———. "Two Goats, Two Advents and Tertullian's *Adversus Iudaeos." Augustinianum* 39 (1999): 245–64.

———. "The Universal Spread of Christianity as a Rhetorical Argument in Tertullian's *adversus Iudaeos." JECS* 8 (2000):1–19.

———. "The Ancestry of Jesus According to Tertullian: *ex David per Mariam."* In *Studia Patristica 36,* edited by M. F. Wiles and E. J. Yarnold, 349–55. Papers presented to the thirteenth International Conference on Patristic Studies, Oxford 1999. Leuven: Peeters, 2001.

———. "Rhetorical Structure in Tertullian's *Ad Scapulam." VChr* 56 (2002): 47–55.

———. "Tertullian and Daniel 9:24–27: A Patristic Interpretation of a Prophetic Time-Frame." *ZAC* 6 (2002): 330–44.

———. *"Probabimus venisse eum iam:* The Fulfilment of Daniel's Prophetic Time-Frame in Tertullian's *Adversus Iudaeos." ZAC* 7 (2003): 140–55.

———. *Tertullian.* The Early Church Fathers. London and New York: Routledge, 2004.

———. "Tertullian's Scriptural Exegesis in *de praescriptoine haereticorum." JECS* 14 (2006): 141–55.

Dunn, James D. G. *The Parting of the Ways between Christianity and Judaism and their Significance for the Character of Christianity.* Philadelphia: Trinity Press International, 1991.

———, ed. *Jews and Christians: The Parting of the Ways, A.D. 70–135.* Rev. Eng. ed. The Second Durham-Tübingen Research Symposium on Earliest Christianity and Judaism, Durham 1989. Grand Rapids, Mich.: Eerdmans, 1999.

Edwards, Mark, Martin Goodman, Simon Price, and Christopher Rowland. "Introduction: Apologetics in the Roman World." In *Apologetics in the Roman Empire: Pagans, Jews and Christians,* edited by Mark Edwards, Martin Goodman, Simon Price, and Christopher Rowland, 1–13. Oxford: Oxford University Press, 1999.

Efroymson, David. "Tertullian's Anti-Judaism and Its Role in His Theology." Ph.D. diss., Temple University, 1976.

———. "The Patristic Connection." In *Anti-Semitism and the Foundation of Christianity,* edited by Alan T. Davies, 98–117. New York: Paulist, 1979.

———. "Tertullian's Anti-Jewish Rhetoric: Guilt by Association." *Union Seminary Quarterly Review* 36 (1980): 25–37.

Elliott, J. K. "The Translation of the New Testament into Latin: The Old Latin and the Vulgate." In *Aufstieg und Niedergang der Römischen Welt,* part II: *Principat,* vol. 26.1: *Religion (vorkonstantinisches Christentum: Neues Testament [Sachthemen]),* edited by Wolfgang Haase, 198–245. Berlin and New York: Walter de Gruyter, 1992.

Evans, Craig A. "Faith and Polemic: The New Testament and First-century Judaism." In *Anti-Semitism and Early Christianity: Issues of Polemic and Faith,* edited by Craig A. Evans and Donald A. Hagner, 1–17. Minneapolis: Fortress Press, 1993.

Evans, Ernest. *Tertullian: "Adversus Marcionem,"* vol. 1: *Books 1 to 3.* Oxford Early Christian Texts. Oxford: Clarendon Press, 1972.

Evans, R. F. "On the Problem of Church and Empire in Tertullian's *Apologeticum*." In
Studia Patristica 14, edited by Elizabeth A. Livingstone, 21–36. Papers presented to
the sixth International Conference on Patristic Studies, part 3, Oxford 1971. Berlin:
Akademie-Verlag, 1976.

Fantham, Elaine. "Imitation and Evolution: The Discussion of Rhetorical Imitation
in Cicero *De Oratore* 2.87–97 and Some Related Problems of Ciceronian Theory."
CPh 73 (1978): 1–16.

———. "*Varietas* and *Satietas*: *De oratore* 3.96–103 and the Limits of *ornatus*." *Rhetorica*
6 (1988): 275–90.

———. "The Contexts and Occasions of Roman Public Oratory." In *Roman Eloquence: Rhetoric in Society and Literature*, edited by William J. Dominik, 111–28.
London and New York: Routledge, 1997.

Ford, J. Massingberd. "Was Montanism a Jewish-Christian Heresy?" *JEH* 17 (1966):
145–58.

Fortenbaugh, William W. "Cicero's Knowledge of the Rhetorical Treatises of Aristo-
tle and Theophrastus." In *Cicero's Knowledge of the Peripatos*, edited by William W.
Fortenbaugh and Peter Steinmetz, 39–60. Rutgers University Studies in Classical
Humanities 4. New Brunswick, N.J.: Transaction, 1989.

Fredouille, Jean-Claude. *Tertullien et la conversion de la culture antique*. Collection des
Études Augustiniennes Série Antiquité 47. Paris: Études Augustiniennes, 1972.

Frend, W. H. C. "The Persecutions: Some Links between Judaism and the Early
Church." *JEH* 9 (1958): 141–58.

———. "The *Seniores laici* and the Origins of the Church in North Africa." *JTS* n.s.
12 (1961): 280–84.

———. "Tertulliano e gli Ebrei." *RSLR* 4 (1968): 3–10.

———. "A Note on Jews and Christians in Third-Century North Africa." *JTS* n.s. 21
(1970): 92–96.

———. "A Note on Tertullian and the Jews." In *Studia Patristica* 10, part 1, edited by
F. L. Cross, 291–96. Papers presented to the fifth International Conference on Patristic Studies, Oxford 1967. Berlin: Akademie-Verlag, 1970.

———. "Jews and Christians in Third-Century Carthage." In *Paganisme, Judaïsme,
Christianisme. Influences et affrontements dans le monde antique*, edited by A. Benoit,
185–94. Paris: de Boccard, 1978.

Froelich, Karlfried. *Biblical Interpretation in the Early Church*. Sources of Early Christian Thought. Philadelphia: Fortress Press, 1984.

Gager, John G. *The Origins of Anti-Semitism: Attitudes toward Judaism in Pagan and
Christian Antiquity*. Oxford: Oxford University Press, 1983.

Gamble, Harry Y. *Books and Readers in the Early Church: A History of Early Christian
Texts*. New Haven, Conn.: Yale University Press, 1995.

Garver, Eugene. *Aristotle's "Rhetoric": An Art of Character*. Chicago and London: University of Chicago Press, 1994.

Gaston, Lloyd. "Judaism of the Uncircumcised in Ignatius and Related Writers." In
Anti-Judaism in Early Christianity, vol. 2: *Separation and Polemic*, edited by Stephen
G. Wilson, 33–44. Études sur le christianisme et le judaïsme 2. Waterloo, Ontario:
Wilfrid Laurier Press, 1986.

———. "Retrospect." In *Anti-Judaism in Early Christianity*, vol. 2: *Separation and Po-*

lemic, edited by Stephen G. Wilson, 163–74. Études sur le christianisme et le judaïsme 2. Waterloo, Ontario: Wilfrid Laurier Press, 1986.

Goldhill, Simon. "The Erotic Eye: Visual Stimulation and Cultural Conflict." In *Being Greek under Rome: Cultural Identity, the Second Sophistic and the Development
of Empire,* edited by Simon Goldhill, 154–94. Cambridge: Cambridge University
Press, 2001.

Groningen, B. A. van. "General Literary Tendencies in the Second Century A.D."
Mnemosyne series 4, 18 (1965): 41–56.

Grotemeyer, Hermann. "Excurs über die Echtheir der Schr. adv. Jud. und die Zeit
ihrer Abfassung." *Jahresbericht des Gymnasium Thomaeum zu Kempen* (1896): 16–26.

Grube, G. M. A. "Educational, Rhetorical, and Literary Theory in Cicero." *Phoenix*
16 (1962): 234–57.

Gruen, Erich S. "Cicero and Licinius Calvus." *HSCPh* 71 (1967): 215–33.

Guerra, Anthony J. "Polemical Christianity: Tertullian's Search for Certitude." *The
Second Century* 8 (1991): 109–23.

Hanson, R. P. C. "Notes on Tertullian's Interpretation of Scripture." *JTS* n.s. 12
(1961): 273–79.

Harnack, Adolf. *Die Altercatio Simonis Iudaei et Theophili Christiani nebst Untersuchungen über die antijüdische Polemik in der alten Kirche.* Texte und Untersuchung zur
Geschichte der altchristlichen Literatur 1/3. Leipzig: J. C. Hinrichs, 1883.

———. *Geschichte der altchristlichen Literatur bis Eusebius,* part II: *Die Chronologie,* vol. 2:
Die Chronologie der Literatur von Irenaeus bis Eusebius. Leipzig: J. C. Hinrichs, 1904.

Harris, William V. *Ancient Literacy.* Cambridge, Mass., and London: Harvard University Press, 1989.

Heath, Malcolm. "The Substructure of *Stasis*-Theory from Hermagoras to Hermogenes." *CQ* n.s. 44 (1994): 114–29.

Hendrickson, G. L. "The Peripatetic Mean of Style and the Three Stylistic Characters." *AJPh* 25 (1904): 125–46.

———. "The Origin and Meaning of the Ancient Characters of Style." *AJPh* 26
(1905): 249–90.

———. "Cicero's Correspondence with Brutus and Calvus on Oratorical Style."
AJPh 47 (1926): 234–58.

Higgins, A. J. B. "The Latin Text of Luke in Marcion and Tertullian." *VChr* 2 (1951):
1–42.

Hill, Forbes I. "Aristotle's Rhetorical Theory. With a Synopsis of Aristotle's *Rhetoric.*"
In *A Synoptic History of Classical Rhetoric,* 2nd ed., edited by James J. Murphy and
Richard A. Katula, 51–109. Davis, Calif.: Hermagoras Press, 1995.

Hopkins, Keith. "Christian Numbers and Its Implications." *JECS* 6 (1998): 185–226.

Hoppe, H. *Syntax und Stil des Tertullian.* Leipzig: G. B. Teubner, 1903.

Horbury, William. "Tertullian on the Jews in the Light of *De Spectaculis* XXX.5–6."
JTS n.s. 23 (1972): 455–59.

Horner, Timothy J. *Listening to Trypho: Justin Martyr's Dialogue Reconsidered.* Contri-
butions to Biblical Exegesis and Theology 28. Leuven: Peeters, 2001.

Hubbell, Harry M. "Cicero on Styles of Oratory." *YCS* 19 (1960): 173–86.

Hulen, B. "The Dialogues with the Jews as Sources for the Early Jewish Argument
against Christianity." *JBL* 51 (1932): 58–70.

Innes, Doreen. "Cicero on Tropes." *Rhetorica* 6 (1988): 307–25.

Jacobs, Andrew S. "The Lion and the Lamb: Reconsidering Jewish-Christian Relations in Antiquity." In *The Ways That Never Parted: Jews and Christians in Late Antiquity and the Early Middle Ages,* edited by Adam Becker and Annette Toshiko Reed, 95–118. Texts and Studies in Ancient Judaism 95. Tübingen: Paul Siebeck, 2003.

Johnson, Luke T. "The New Testament's Anti-Jewish Slander and the Conventions of Ancient Polemic." *JBL* 108 (1989): 419–41.

Judant, D. *Judaïsme et christianisme. Dossier patristique.* Paris: Les Editions du Cèdre, 1969.

Katz, Steven T. "Issues in the Separation of Judaism and Christianity after 70 C.E.: A Reconsideration." *JBL* 103 (1984): 43–76.

Kaufman, Peter Iver. "Tertullian on Heresy, History, and the Reappropriation of Revelation." *CH* 60 (1991): 167–79.

Kennedy, George A. "An Estimation of Quintilian." *AJPh* 83 (1962): 130–46.

———. *New Testament Interpretation Through Rhetorical Criticism.* Chapel Hill and London: University of North Carolina Press, 1984.

———. *Aristotle, "On Rhetoric": A Theory of Civic Discourse.* Oxford: Oxford University Press, 1991.

———. *A New History of Classical Rhetoric.* Princeton, N.J.: Princeton University Press, 1994.

Keresztes, Paul. "Tertullian's *Apologeticus:* A Historical and Literary Survey." *Latomus* 25 (1966): 124–33.

Kraabel, A. Thomas. "The Roman Diaspora: Six Questionable Assumptions." *JJS* 33 (1982): 445–64.

Kraemer, Ross S. "On the Meaning of the Term 'Jew' in Greco-Roman Inscriptions." *HTR* 82 (1989): 35–53.

Kraft, Robert A. "The Weighing of the Parts: Pivots and Pitfalls in the Study of Early Judaisms and their Early Christian Offspring." In *The Ways That Never Parted: Jews and Christians in Late Antiquity and the Early Middle Ages,* edited by Adam Becker and Annette Toshiko Reed, 87–94. Texts and Studies in Ancient Judaism 95. Tübingen: Paul Siebeck, 2003.

Krauss, Samuel. "The Jews in the Works of the Church Fathers, part 1." *JQR* 5 (1893): 122–57.

———. "The Jews in the Works of the Church Fathers, part 2." *JQR* 6 (1894): 82–99.

Kroymann, Emil, ed. *Tertulliani Opera,* II, 2. CSEL 70. Vienna: Verlag der Österreichischen, Akademie der Wissenschaften, 1942.

——— ed. "[Q. S. F. Tertulliani]: *Aduersus Iudaeos.*" In *Tertulliani Opera,* part 2: *Opera Montanistica,* edited by Eligius Dekkers et al., 1337–96. CCSL 2. Turnhout: Brepols, 1954.

Labriolle, Pierre de. *Histoire de la Littérature latine chrétienne.* 3rd ed. Collection d'Études Anciennes. Paris: G. Bardy, 1947.

Langmuir, Gavin. "Anti-Judaism as the Necessary Preparation for Anti-Semitism." *Viator* 2 (1971): 383–89.

Lawson-Tancred, Hugh, trans. *Aristotle: The Art of Rhetoric.* Penguin Classics. Harmondsworth: Penguin, 1981.

LeBohec, Yann. "Inscriptions juives et judaïsantes de l'Afrique romaine." *AntAfr* 17 (1981): 165–207.

———. "Juifs et Judaïsants dans l'Afrique romaine: Remarques onomestiques." *AntAfr* 17 (1981): 209–29.

Leeman, A. D. *"Orationis Ratio": The Stylistic Theories and Practice of the Roman Orators, Historians and Philosophers.* 2 vols. Amsterdam: Adolf M. Hakkert, 1963.

Le Saint, William P., trans. *Tertullian: Treatises on Penance.* Ancient Christian Writers 28. New York: Newman Press, 1959.

Lieu, Judith. "History and Theology in Christian Views of Judaism." In *The Jews among Pagans and Christians in the Roman Empire,* rev. ed., edited by Judith Lieu, John North, and Tessa Rajak, 79–96. London: Routledge, 1994.

———. *Image and Reality: The Jews in the World of the Christians in the Second Century.* Edinburgh: T. & T. Clark, 1996.

Lund, John. "A Synagogue at Carthage? Menorah-lamps from the Danish Excavations." *JRA* 8 (1995): 245–62.

McBurney, James H. "The Place of the Enthymeme in Rhetorical Theory." *Speech Monographs* 3 (1936): 49–74.

McDonald, Lee Martin. "Anti-Judaism in the Early Church Fathers." In *Anti-Semitism and Early Christianity: Issues of Polemic and Faith,* edited by Craig A. Evans and Donald A. Hagner, 215–52. Minneapolis: Fortress Press, 1993.

MacLennan, Robert. *Early Christian Texts on Jews and Judaism.* Brown Judaic Studies 194. Atlanta: Scholars Press, 1990.

Marache, René. *La critique littéraire de langue latine et le développement du goût archaïsant au IIe siècle de notre ère.* Rennes: Presses universitaires de Rennes, 1952.

Mohrmann, Christine. "Observations sur la langue et le style de Tertullien." In *Études sur le latin des chrétiens,* vol. 2: *Latin chrétien et médiéval,* 235–46. Rome: Edizioni di Storia e Letteratura, 1961.

Monceaux, Paul. *Histoire littéraire de l'Afrique chrétienne,* vol. 1: *Tertullien et les origines.* Paris: Ernest Leroux, 1901.

Moore, George Foot. "Christian Writers on Judaism." *HTR* 14 (1921): 197–254.

Moreschini, Claudio, trans. *Opere scelte di Quinto Settimio Florente Tertulliano.* Classici delle Religioni, sezione Quarta: La religione cattolica. Turin: Unione Tipografico-Editrice Torinese, 1974.

Murphy, James J. "The Codification of Roman Rhetoric. With a Synopsis of the *Rhetorica ad Herennium.*" In *A Synoptic History of Classical Rhetoric,* 2nd ed., edited by James J. Murphy and Richard A. Katula, 111–27. Davis, Calif.: Hermagoras Press, 1995.

———. "The End of the Ancient World: The Second Sophistic and Saint Augustine." In *A Synoptic History of Classical Rhetoric,* 2nd ed., edited by James J. Murphy and Richard A. Katula, 205–11. Davis, Calif.: Hermagoras Press, 1995.

Murray, Michele. *Playing a Jewish Game: Gentile Christian Judaizing in the First and Second Centuries CE.* Études sur le christianisme et le judaïsme 13. Waterloo, Ontario: Wilfrid Laurier University Press, 2004.

Nadeau, Ray. "Classical Systems of Stases in Greek: Hermagoras to Hermogenes." *GRBS* 2 (1959): 53–71.

Neander, Augustus. *History of the Planting and Training of the Christian Church by the Apostles,* vol. 2: *Antignostikus, or the Spirit of Tertullian.* Translated by J. E. Ryland. London: Henry G. Bohn, 1851.

Neusner, Jacob. *What Is Midrash?* Philadelphia: Fortress Press, 1987.

Noeldechen, Ernst. *Die Abfassungszeit der Schriften Tertullians.* Texte und Untersuchung zur Geschichte der altchristlichen Literatur 5. Leipzig: J. C. Hinrichs, 1888.

———. *Tertullian.* Gotha: Friedrich Undreas Berthes, 1890.

———. *Tertullian's Gegen die Juden auf Einheit, Echtheit, Entstehung.* Texte und Untersuchung zur Geschichte der altchristlichen Literatur 12.2. Leipzig: J. C. Hinrichs, 1894.

Norden, E. *Die antike Kunstprosa vom VI. Jahrhundert v. Chr. bis in die Zeit der Renaissance.* Vol. 2. Leipzig: G. B. Teubner, 1909.

O'Malley, T. P. *Tertullian and the Bible: Language-Imagery-Exegesis.* Latinitas Christianorum Primaeva 21. Nijmegen and Utrecht: Dekker and van de Vegt, 1967.

Ophuijsen, Jan M. van. "Where Have the Topics Gone?" In *Peripatetic Rhetoric after Aristotle,* edited by William W. Fortenbaugh and David C. Mirhady, 131–73. Rutgers University Studies in Classical Humanities 6. New Brunswick, N.J.: Transaction, 1994.

Osborn, Eric. "The Conflict of Opposition in the Theology of Tertullian." *Augustinianum* 35 (1995): 623–39.

———. "Tertullian as Philosopher and Roman." In *Die Weltlichkeit des Glaubens in der Alten Kirche. Festschrift für Ulrich Wickert zum siebzigsten Geburtstag,* 231–47. Beihefte zur Zeitschrift für die neutestamentliche Wissenschaft und die Kunde der älteren Kirche 85. Berlin: Walter de Gruyter, 1997.

———. *Tertullian: First Theologian of the West.* Cambridge: Cambridge University Press, 1997.

———. "The Subtlety of Tertullian." *VChr* 52 (1998): 361–70.

Otranto, G. *Giudei e cristiani a Cartagine tra II e III secolo. L'Adversus Iudaeos.* Bari: Adriatica, 1975.

Perry, B. E. "Literature in the Second Century." *CJ* 50 (1955): 295–98.

Powell, Mark Allen. *What Is Narrative Criticism?* Minneapolis: Fortress Press, 1990.

Price, Simon. "Latin Christian Apologetics: Minucius Felix, Tertullian, and Cyprian." In *Apologetics in the Roman Empire: Pagans, Jews and Christians,* edited by Mark Edwards, Martin Goodman, Simon Price, and Christopher Rowland, 105–29. Oxford: Oxford University Press, 1999.

Quacquarelli, A., ed. *Q. S. F. Tertulliani: "Ad Scapulam." Prolegomeni, testo critico, traduzione e commento.* Opuscula patrum 1. Rome: Desclée, 1957.

———, ed. *Q. S. F. Tertulliani: "Ad martyras." Prolegomeni, testo critico, traduzione e commento.* Opuscula patrum 2. Rome: Desclée, 1963.

Quasten, Johannes. *Patrology,* vol. 2: *The Ante-Nicene Literature after Irenaeus.* Utrecht: Spectrum, 1953.

Quispel, Gilles. *De bronnen van Tertullianus' Adversus Marcionem.* Utrecht: Burgersdijk en Niemans, 1943.

———. "African Christianity before Minucius Felix and Tertullian." In *Actus: Studies in Honour of H. L. W. Nelson,* edited by J. den Boeft and A. H. M. Kessles, 257–335. Utrecht: Instituut voor Klassieke Talen Boeft and Kessels, 1982.

Rajak, Tessa. "Talking at Trypho: Christian Apologetic as Anti-Judaism in Justin's *Dialogue with Trypho the Jew.*" In *Apologetics in the Roman Empire: Pagans, Jews and Christians,* edited by Mark Edwards, Martin Goodman, Simon Price, and Christopher Rowland, 59–80. Oxford: Oxford University Press, 1999.

Rankin, David I. "Was Tertullian a Jurist?" In *Studia Patristica* 31, edited by Elizabeth A. Livingstone, 335–42. Papers presented to the twelfth Oxford Patristics Conference, Oxford 1995. Leuven: Peeters, 1997.

Raven, Susan. *Rome in Africa*. 3rd ed. London and New York: Routledge, 1993.

Rebillard, Éric. "Les *Areae* Carthaginoises (Tertullien, *Ad Scapulam* 3,1): Cimetières, communautaires au enclos funéraires de Chrétiens?" *MEFRA* 108 (1996): 175–89.

Rives, J. B. *Religion and Authority in Roman Carthage from Augustus to Constantine*. Oxford: Clarendon Press, 1995.

Robbins, Vernon K. *The Tapestry of Early Christian Discourse: Rhetoric, Society and Ideology*. London and New York: Routledge, 1996.

Rokeah, David. "Anti-Judaism in Early Christianity." *Immanuel* 16 (1983): 50–64.

Rowe, Galen O. "Style." In *Handbook of Classical Rhetoric in the Hellenistic Period, 330 B.C.–A.D. 400*, edited by Stanley E. Porter, 121–57. Leiden: E. J. Brill, 1997.

Ruether, Rosemary Radford. *Faith and Fratricide: The Theological Roots of Anti-Semitism*. New York: Seabury Press, 1974.

Russell, D. A. "Rhetoric and Criticism." *G&R* 14 (1967): 130–44.

———. "Introduction: Greek and Latin in Antonine Literature." In *Antonine Literature*, edited by D. A. Russell, 1–17. Oxford: Clarendon Press, 1990.

Rutgers, Leonard Victor. *The Jews in Late Ancient Rome: Evidence of Cultural Interaction in the Roman Diaspora*. Religions in the Graeco-Roman World 126. Leiden: E. J. Brill, 1995.

Säflund, Gösta. *De pallio und die stilistische Entwicklung Tertullians*. Skrifter utgivna av Svenska Institutet I Rom, 8, VIII. Lund: C. W. K. Gleerup, 1955.

Sanders, Jack T. *Schismatics, Sectarians, Dissidents, Deviants: The First One Hundred Years of Jewish-Christian Relations*. London: SCM Press, 1993.

Satterthwaite, Philip E. "The Latin Church Fathers." In *Handbook of Classical Rhetoric in the Hellenistic Period, 330 B.C.–A.D. 400*, edited by Stanley E. Porter, 671–94. Leiden: Brill, 1997.

Schäfer, Peter. *Judeophobia: Attitudes toward the Jews in the Ancient World*. Cambridge, Mass., and London: Harvard University Press, 1997.

Scholer, D. M. "Tertullian on Jewish Persecution of Christians." In *Studia Patristica* 17, part 2, edited by Elizabeth A. Livingstone, 821–28. Papers presented to the eighth International Conference on Patristic Studies, Oxford 1979. Oxford: Pergamon, 1982.

Schreckenberg, Heinz. *Die christlichen Adversus-Judaeos-Texte und ihr literarisches und historisches Umfeld (1.–11.Jh.)*. Frankfurt am Main: Peter Lang, 1982.

Schütrumpf, Eckart. "Some Observations on the Introduction to Aristotle's *Rhetoric*." In *Aristotle's "Rhetoric": Philosophical Essays*, edited by David J. Furley and Alexander Nehamas, 99–116. Princeton, N.J.: Princeton University Press, 1994.

———. "Non-Logical Means of Persuasion in Aristotle's *Rhetoric* and Cicero's *De oratore*." In *Peripatetic Rhetoric after Aristotle*, edited by William W. Fortenbaugh and David C. Mirhady, 95–110. Rutgers University Studies in Classical Humanities 6. New Brunswick, N.J.: Transaction, 1994.

Schwartz, Seth. "The Rabbi in Aphrodite's Bath: Palestinian Society and Jewish Identity in the High Roman Empire." In *Being Greek under Rome: Cultural Identity, the Second Sophistic and the Development of Empire*, edited by Simon Goldhill, 335–61. Cambridge: Cambridge University Press, 2001.

Segal, Alan F. *Rebecca's Children: Judaism and Christianity in the Roman World.* Cambridge, Mass., and London: Harvard University Press, 1986.

Semler, Johann Salomo, ed. *Q. S. Fl. Tertullianus, Opera recensuit.* 6 vols. Halle: Hendel, 1770–1776.

Setzer, Claudia. "Jews, Jewish Christians and Judaizers in North Africa." In *Putting Body and Soul Together: Essays in Honor of Robin Scroggs,* edited by Virginia Wiles, Alexandra Brown, and Graydon F. Snyder, 185–200. Valley Forge, Pa.: Trinity Press International, 1997.

Shoemaker, Stephen J. "'Let Us Go and Burn Her Body': The Image of the Jews in the Early Dormition Traditions." *CH* 68 (1999): 775–823.

Shotwell, Willis A. *The Biblical Exegesis of Justin Martyr.* London: S.P.C.K., 1965.

Sider, Robert Dick. *Ancient Rhetoric and the Art of Tertullian.* Oxford: Oxford University Press, 1971.

———. "On Symmetrical Composition in Tertullian." *JTS* n.s. 24 (1973): 405–23.

———. *The Gospel and Its Proclamation.* Message of the Fathers of the Church 10. Wilmington, Del.: Michael Glazier, 1983.

Simon, Marcel. *"Verus Israel": A Study of the Relations between Christians and Jews in the Roman Empire (AD 135–425).* 2nd Eng. ed. Translated by H. McKeating. The Littman Library of Jewish Civilization. London: Vallentine Mitchell, 1996.

Skarsaune, Oskar. *The Proof from Prophecy: A Study in Justin Martyr's Proof-Text Tradition. Text-Type, Provenance, Theological Profile.* Supplement to *Novum Testamentum* 56. Leiden: E. J. Brill, 1987.

Solmsen, Friedrich. "The Aristotelian Tradition in Ancient Rhetoric." *AJPh* 62 (1941): 35–50, 169–90.

Souter, Alexander. *A Study of Ambrosiaster.* Texts and Studies 7. Cambridge: Cambridge University Press, 1905.

Spira, Andreas. "The Impact of Christianity on Ancient Rhetoric." In *Studia Patristica* 18, part 2, edited by Elizabeth A. Livingstone, 137–53. Papers presented to the ninth Oxford Patristics Conference, Oxford 1983. Kalamazoo, Mich.: Cistercian Publications, 1989.

Sprott, S. E. "Cicero's Theory of Prose Style." *PhQ* 34 (1955): 1–17.

Sprute, Jürgen. "Aristotle and the Legitimacy of Rhetoric." In *Aristotle's "Rhetoric": Philosophical Essays,* edited by David J. Furley and Alexander Nehamas, 117–28. Princeton, N.J.: Princeton University Press, 1994.

Stanton, G. N. "Aspects of Early Christian-Jewish Polemic and Apologetic." *NTS* 31 (1985): 377–92.

Stark, Rodney. *The Rise of Christianity: A Sociologist Reconsiders History.* Princeton, N.J.: Princeton University Press, 1996.

Stroumsa, Guy G. "From Anti-Judaism to Antisemitism in Early Christianity?" In *Contra Iudaeos: Ancient and Medieval Polemics between Christians and Jews,* edited by Ora Limor and Guy G. Stroumsa, 1–26. Texts and Studies in Medieval and Early Modern Judaism 10. Tübingen: J. C. B. Mohr (Paul Siebeck), 1996.

Stylianopolous, Theodore. *Justin Martyr and the Mosaic Law.* Dissertation Series 20. Missoula, Mont.: Society of Biblical Literature, 1975.

Swain, Simon. *Hellenism and Empire: Language, Classicism, and Power in the Greek World AD 50–250.* Oxford: Clarendon Press, 1996.

Swift, Louis J. "Forensic Rhetoric in Tertullian's *Apologeticum*." *Latomus* 27 (1968): 864–77.

Taylor, Miriam. *Anti-Judaism and Early Christian Identity: A Critique of the Scholarly Consensus*. Studia Post-Biblica 46. Leiden: E. J. Brill, 1995.

Tränkle, Hermann. *Q. S. F. Tertullian, "Adversus Iudaeos." Mit Einleitung und kritischem Kommentar*. Wiesbaden: Franz Steiner Verlag, 1964.

Ugenti, Valerio. "Norme Prosodiche nelle Clausole Metriche del *De Idololatria* di Tertulliano." *Augustinianum* 35 (1995): 241–58.

Wardy, Robert. "Mighty Is the Truth and It Shall Prevail?" In *Essays on Aristotle's "Rhetoric*," edited by Amélie Oksenberg Rorty, 56–87. Philosophical Traditions 6. Berkeley: University of California Press, 1996.

Waszink, J. H. "The Technique of Clausula in Tertullian's De Anima." *VChr* 4 (1950): 212–45.

———, trans. *Tertullian: The Treatise against Hermogenes*. Ancient Christian Writers 24. New York: Newman Press, 1956.

———. "Tertullian's Principles and Methods of Exegesis." In *Early Christian Literature and the Classical Intellectual Tradition: In Honorem Robert M. Grant,* edited by W. R. Schoedel and R. L. Wilken, 17–31. Paris: Beauchesne, 1979.

Wiles, M. F. "The Old Testament in Controversy with the Jews." *SJT* 8 (1955): 113–26.

Williams, A. Lukyn. *"Adversus Judaeos": A Bird's-Eye View of Christian "Apologiae" until the Renaissance*. Cambridge: Cambridge University Press, 1935.

Wilson, Stephen G. *Related Strangers: Jews and Christians 70–170 C.E*. Minneapolis: Fortress Press, 1995.

Winterbottom, Michael. "Quintilian and Rhetoric." In *Empire and Aftermath: Silver Latin II,* edited by T. A. Dorey, 79–97. London: Routledge and Kegan Paul, 1975.

———. "Schoolroom and Courtroom." In *Rhetoric Revalued: Papers from the International Society for the History of Rhetoric,* edited by Brian Vickers, 59–70. Medieval and Renaissance Texts and Studies 19. Binghamton, N.Y.: Center for Medieval and Renaissance Studies, 1982.

Wisse, Jakob. *Ethos and Pathos from Aristotle to Cicero*. Amsterdam: Adolf M. Hakkert, 1989.

General Index

Aalders, G. J. D., 149n38
Aaron, 69, 110
Abel, 74, 113, 115, 140, 155
Abraham, 74, 92, 108, 113, 115, 155
accomodatus, 144, 145n14
Adam, 112–15, 155, 157
adjunction *(adiunctio)*, 162n118
Aduersus Iudeos: date of composition, 7, 9–13, 15, 149, 177–78. *See also* Index of Citations to Tertullian
adultery, 37, 157
advantage, 104
Africa, 35, 51, 58, 167
Ahaz, 122
Åkerman, Malte, 7, 10, 89, 148
Albucius Silus, C., 32n2
Alexander the Great, 118
allegory, 119, 124, 126, 163n119, 164, 170, 178
Allen, Pauline, viii
alliteration, 151, 154–55, 157, 159
Altaner, B., 13
Amalek, 131n152
ambiguity, 99–101, 105, 108–9, 119, 139
Ambrosiaster, 6n6
amplification *(amplificatio)*, 61, 84–85
analogy, 99–100
Anderson, Graham, 33–34, 36n26, 147
anecdote, 155
animation, 145
anointing, 134, 164n130
anticipation, 145
anti-Judaism, 17–18
antimetabole *(commutatio)*, 154, 159, 162
anti-Semitism, 17–18
antistrophe *(conuersio)*, 159–60, 163
antithesis *(contentio)*, 146, 148, 155, 158, 160, 164
Antonius, M., 100

apodosis, 157
apologetics, 51
apostate of *Aduersus Marcionem*, 7
Apuleius, 31, 36; *Apologeticum*, 35; *Florida*, 35–36; *Metamorphoses*, 35
Argus, 150n44
Aristides: *Orationes*, 42–43
Aristotle, 41, 95, 98, 100, 102
arrows, 126
Artaxerxes, 150n44
Asia Minor, 25n125
assonance, 151
Assyria, 126
asyndeton *(solutum)*, 145, 147–48, 158
Augustus, 121
Aulisa, Immacolata, 6
Aziza, Claude, 13–14, 20, 91–92, 173, 181

Baal, 150n44
Babylon, 126
Babylonians, 162n116
Balfour, I. L. S., 152
Bar Kochba, 22n110
Barnabas, 110, 131, 135nn169–70, 138, 179
Barnes, Timothy D., 14, 20, 29, 39, 40n38, 51n72, 85, 146–47, 177
Barwick, Karl, 98
Bauckham, R., 16n78
Baumgarten, Albert I., 17n83, 21n107
Becker, Adam, 17n78
Becker, C., 11, 142n1
Beersheba, 162n116
Bethlehem, 82, 87, 133–34, 160
Bethsaida, 137
Bingham, D. Jeffrey, 132n157
Blair, Carole, 100
Blanchetière, F., 17
Blumenkranz, B., 17

Bodenmann, Reinhard, 120nn105–6
Bonner, Stanley F., 29n144, 32n1, 37, 60n2, 61
Borleffs, J. W. P., 6
Bouchier, E. S., 35n22
Boyarin, Daniel, 17n78, 54n92, 55, 110n67
Braet, Antoine, 99n4
Bratton, Fred Gladstone, 18n84
Braun, René, 12, 20
Bray, Gerald, 29n145
bread, 132
Britons, 118, 159, 167
Brunschwig, Jacques, 41n41
Bryant, Donald C., 103n36
Buell, Denise Kimber, 106n54
bull: horns, 131; hamstrung, 131, 164n130
Burkitt, F. C., 6, 11
burning bush, 167
Burnyeat, M. F., 102n34

Cain, 115, 140, 155
Caligula, 150n44
Calvus, Licinius, 143n6
Cameron, Averil, 29, 39
Caplan, Harry, 52, 98n3
Carcy, Christopher, 41n41
Carleton Paget, James, viii, 16–17, 20–21, 24–25, 56, 131n153
Carthage, viii, 3, 14–15, 20, 25, 51–52, 56, 141, 158, 170, 173–74, 180–81
Cassius Severus, 32n2
causa, 63; admirabile, 63; anceps, 63n21; dubium, 63n21; honestum, 63n21; humile, 63n21; obscurum, 63n21; turpe, 63n21
Champlin, Edward, 35n23
character, 81, 87, 108n60, 128, 164
Cicero, 43, 45, 60–61, 65, 67, 72, 75, 84, 100, 102, 111, 119, 144, 170; Brutus, 143n6; De inuentione, 63n21, 66, 98–99, 101, 106n52, 108n61, 109n62, 110n69, 112n76, 113n83, 114n85, 115n87, 117n92, 124nn120–21, 127n135, 133n162; De optimo genere oratorum, 143n6; De oratore, 100, 118n97, 143n6, 145–46; De partitione oratoria, 100, 124n121, 145; Orator, 143n6, 171
circumcision, 71, 73–75, 86, 92–93, 111, 113–15, 133, 141, 155, 158–59, 176
Clark, Donald Lemen, 32, 103n36
Clarke, Graeme, viii
Clarke, Martin Lowther, 33n2, 35

Claudius, 121n108
climax (gradatio), 159, 163
Codex Florentinus Magliabechianus, Conv. Sopr. I, VI: 9 (N), 150n44; 10 (F), 150n44
Codex Masburensis, 48n62
Codex Scelestadtensis (P), 150n44
Codex Trecensis (T), 44n55, 48n62, 150n44
Cohen, Shaye J. D., 54, 106, 151n46
Colson, F. H., 142n2
commiseratio, 84
comparison, 99, 111, 118, 133–34, 145
competence, 99, 101, 108n59
composition (compositio), 144n11
concession, 145
conclusio, 60, 84–85
confirmatio, 59, 65n33, 66, 71–73, 75–81, 85–86, 94, 96, 99–101, 104, 116–40, 158–68, 176
confutatio, 59, 72
coniunctis, 144
Conley, Thomas M., 102n34
conquestio, 84
Consigny, Scott, 102n34
constitutio. See stasis
controuersia, 30–32, 36–39, 42–43, 45, 56, 58, 60, 63, 70, 178
Cornificius, 161n114
correction (correctio), 159, 163
Corssen, P., 8–9, 11, 48n64, 130
Countryman, L. W., 128n140
covenant, 54, 74, 76, 111, 116, 159n96, 178–79
coveting, 157
criminals, 62
cross, 80, 82, 92, 131–34, 136, 164
crown, military, 63
Culpepper, R. Alan, 42
Curiatius Maternus, 33n2
curse, 81, 129–30
Cyprian, Testimonia, 6

Damascus, 81, 121, 126, 165, 168
Dan, 150n44, 162n116
Darius, 118, 162n116
David, 127, 133, 135, 139
declamatio, 32, 34, 36–39, 57
defamation, 146
definition, 99–100, 107, 112, 154, 157n85
Dekkers, E., 6n2
de Lange, N. R. M., 17
delectans, 146

desert, 165n130
devil, 62; as serpent: 157n85
digressio, 67, 77, 86–87, 118, 160, 168, 177
disjunction *(disiunctum)*, 159
dispositio, 101
disputatio, 151
distributio, 66–67
diuisio, 59, 66
Dominik, William J., 33n2
Douglas, Alan Edward, 144
Dunn, Geoffrey D., 1, 27n134, 28n139,
    29n145, 54n91, 65n34, 66n35, 73n79, 76n89,
    77n92, 79n97, 83n100, 85n109, 106n54,
    109n65, 110n67, 111n73, 112n78, 113n82,
    114n86, 118n94, 118n96, 119n100, 119n103,
    120nn106–8, 124n123, 127n136, 133n160,
    134n163, 138n182, 139n183, 149n38, 152n59,
    153n61, 160n101, 161n113
Dunn, James D. G., 16n78
dwelling on the point *(commoratio)*, 167

education, Roman, 29
Edwards, Mark, 51n73
Efroymson, David, 8, 17n82, 21, 23, 25–26, 48,
    53, 116n89
Egypt, 126, 165
Egyptians, 162n116
elegantia, 144n10
elimination *(eliminatio)*, 159, 162, 166, 168
Elliott, J. K., 149n38
elocutio, 143, 145n15, 168
emendata, 144
Emmanuel, 81, 121, 123–25, 163
Enoch, 113, 115, 155, 157
enthymeme, 102, 154
enumeratio, 66–67, 84
epanaphora *(repetitio)*, 147, 154n65, 156n76,
    157–60, 162–64
epanelepsis, 159, 163
epigram, 146
Epiphanes, 150n44
epitaphs, 52
equity, 99, 112
Esau, 109
Ethiopia, 162n116
ethnicus, 152
eucharist, 138
Euergetes, 150n44
eulogy, 34–36, 39

Evans, Craig A., 18n84
Evans, Ernest, 1, 8
Evans, R. F., 52, 179
Eve, 112–13, 115, 157
exculpation, 99
exemplum, 146, 151
exordium, 59, 61–65, 68, 86, 106–8, 150–53, 176
expositio, 66, 76

fable, 147
family, 81, 87, 127, 165
Fantham, Elaine, 33n2, 37n33, 103n36, 144n13
figura, 61, 145, 152, 153, 155, 157–60, 163,
    168–69, 171, 180. See also *in sententiarum
    exornationes; in uerborum exornationes*
figurata, 145
flax, 165
flectere, 146n19
Ford, J. Massingberd, 23n117
Fortenbaugh, William W., 144n11
fortune, 101
Fredouille, Jean-Claude, 12–13, 20, 39, 91, 125,
    132, 146, 149, 173
Frend, W. H. C., 20
Froelich, Karlfried, 119n99
Fronto, 31, 36; *Ad M. Caesarem*, 34n12;
    De eloquentia, 34n11; *Laudes fumi et pulueris*,
    35n24

Gaetulians, 9, 118, 150n44, 153, 159
Gager, John G., 13n58, 18n84, 23n115, 44, 51n72
Gamble, Harry Y., 51n74, 52n77
Gammarth, 52
Garver, Eugene, 41n41
Gaston, Lloyd, 20, 23, 26n129, 51n71, 181
Geminus, Fufius, 150n44
Geminus, Rubellius, 150n44
genera, 170–71, 180; *attenuatum*, 143; *dissolutum*,
    144; *exile*, 144; *fluctuans*, 144; *graue*, 143;
    mediocre, 143; *plenum*, 143; *sufflata*, 144;
    tenue, 143
genera dicendi, 149
gens, 106n54, 152–53
Gentiles, 64, 66, 68–71, 82–83, 87, 90, 93, 105–8,
    110, 112, 118, 133, 137, 139, 151n46, 152–53,
    165, 178
Germans, 118, 167
Ghelen, 48n62
goat, 138, 163–64

gold, 126
golden calf, 69, 110
Goldhill, Simon, 33, 36
Goodman, Martin, 51n73
gospel, 50, 73, 168
grace, 64, 68–71, 73, 80, 93, 105, 108, 137
Groningen, B. A. van, 33n2
Grotemeyer, Hermann, 9
Grube, G. M. A., 143n6
Gruen, Erich S., 143n6
Guerra, Anthony J., 64n23, 106n50, 115

habit, 101
Hadrian, 135n170
Hanson, Richard, 118, 124n123
hapax legomena, 150
Harnack, Adolf, 10, 13, 18–21
Harris, William V., 51n74
Hauses, Regina, viii
Heath, Malcolm, 99n4
Hebrew Scriptures, 3, 7, 15, 18, 23, 26, 39, 64,
    105–6, 111–12, 115, 127–29, 131–32, 140, 152–53,
    155, 168, 175–76, 178–79
Hendrickson, G. L., 143n6, 144n8
heresy, 65, 73
heretics, 18, 22n110, 53, 149n41
Hermagoras, 99
Herod, 126n129
hesitation, 145
Hezekiah, 122–23, 126
hidden meaning, 145
Higgins, A. J. B., 149n38
Hill, Forbes I., 98n3
homoeoptoton, 154, 161n113
honor, 104
Hopkins, Keith, 51n74
Hoppe, H., 142n1
Horbury, William, 17, 20
Horner, Timothy J., 25–26, 35n18
Hubbell, Harry M., 143n6
Hulen, B., 19
hyperbaton, 170
hyperbole, 167
hypophora, 167

idolatry and idols, 53, 92, 110, 137, 154, 165
Ignatius of Antioch: Ephesians, 122n110
imitation, 145
impersonation, 145

in sententiarum exornationes, 144–45. See also
    figura
in uerborum exornationes, 144–45. See also figura
incest, 103
indecision (dubitatio), 159, 163
India, 150n44, 162n116
indignatio, 84
Innes, Doreen, 145n18
interlacement (conplexio), 159, 163
interpolation, 87–88, 95, 177
interpretatio, 151, 153
inuentio, 98–101, 140
Irenaeus, 13, 97, 110, 131, 175, 179; Aduersus
    haereses, 122nn110–11, 129, 135; Demonstratio
    Apostolicae Praedicationis, 133
irony, 145, 167
Isaac, 131
isocolon, 158–59, 164, 169
Israel, 69, 165
Iudaeus, 53–54, 107

Jacob, 109, 131, 167
Jacobs, Andrew S., 27n136
Jchozadak, 150n44
Jericho, 115
Jeroboam, 69, 110
Jerome: Commentarii in Danielem, 6n6
Jerusalem, viii, 2, 58, 78–79, 81–83, 86–87,
    90–91, 114, 119–20, 132–40, 155, 180
Jesse, 127, 165
Jesus, viii, 54; baptism, 164n130; birth, 78–81,
    87, 92, 94, 120–23, 125, 133–34, 139, 141, 165;
    coming, 13, 71, 76–83, 86, 90, 119, 164,
    169–70, 176; resurrection, 132, 164; second
    coming, 82, 87, 90, 135, 138, 140–41, 164;
    suffering and death, 78–82, 87, 90, 92, 94,
    119–21, 128–37, 139–41, 161–63, 166
Jews, rejection of, 13, 105, 110, 137, 176, 178–79
John Chrysostom, 26n128
John the Baptizer, 127
Johnson, Luke T., 20, 64n23
Joseph, 131, 164n130, 167
Joshua, 80, 115, 127
Judaea, 81, 83, 162n116
Judaism, viii, 5, 8, 12–13, 15–16, 19–24, 26–28,
    40, 44n51, 52, 54, 56, 92, 106, 116, 151
Judaizers, 105
Judant, D., 13
Juster, J., 17

Justin Martyr, 13, 35n18, 97, 122, 125–27, 129, 138, 141, 175, 179; *1 Apologia*, 122n110, 123–24, 133–35; *Dialogus cum Tryphone*, 9, 12, 25–26, 44, 56, 110, 122, 127, 131–35, 174
Juvenal: *Satirae*, 35, 103n36

Katz, Steven T., 22n110
Kaufman, Peter Iver, 126n131, 127n132
Kennedy, George A., 33n2, 35, 41, 98n3, 100, 102, 103n36, 143n5
Keresztes, Paul, 103n39
killing, 128, 157, 164n130
Kraabel, A. Thomas, 54
Kraemer, Ross S., 54
Kraft, Robert A., 27n136
Krauss, Samuel, 17
Kroymann, Emil, 6, 45n55, 48n61, 88, 128, 150n44, 157n87, 161n115

Labriolle, Pierre de, 7, 13
Langmuir, Gavin, 18n84
law: conflicting, 99–101, 108; Jewish and Christian 13, 24, 92–93, 112, 154–57; lawgiver, 71, 73, 76–77, 94, 117–18, 121, 128, 139–40, 164, 166, 176; legal custom, 99; natural and written, 112–13, 115; old and new, 70–71, 74–76, 78, 80, 86, 93–94, 96, 111, 113, 137, 139, 141, 158, 164, 166, 176; Roman, 37; statute, 99–101
Lawson-Tancred, Hugh, 98n3
LeBohec, Yann, 52n75
Leeman, A. D., 32n1, 37n31, 143n6, 144n7
Le Saint, William P., 147
letter and spirit, 99–100, 105, 111–13
Levi, 131
Levites, 150n44
Lieu, Judith, 25, 52n79, 56
lion, 165n130
loci communes, 101–2, 104, 106, 108, 110, 111, 118, 124, 128, 179. *See also topoi*
logic, 63–64, 76, 80, 102, 106, 116, 147, 154, 177,179
Lot, 113
Lund, John, 180n2
lying, 157

Maccabees, 115, 155
MacLennan, Robert, 17, 29, 48, 91
magi, 81, 126

manner of life, 87, 99, 101, 111, 131
Marache, René, 146
Marcion, 7, 23, 26, 49n67, 50n70, 62, 65, 115, 123–26, 140, 175, 179
Marcionism, 12, 50, 133n161
Mary, 30, 127, 165
Masoretic Text, 120
McBurney, James H., 102n34
McDonald, Lee Martin, 181n3
Mediterranean, 17, 42
Melas, 150n44
Melchizedek, 112–13, 115, 155
Melito of Sardis, 22
messiah, 21, 26, 121–24, 167
metaphor, 145, 148, 151, 157, 164–65, 168, 171
Midrash, 111, 166
modesty, 62
Mohrmann, Christine, 146
Monceaux, Paul, 12, 20
Moore, George Foot, 44n51, 181n3
Moors, 118, 153, 159
Moreschini, Claudio, 14
Moses, 54, 74, 80, 112–15, 127, 131, 157, 167, 178
motive, 99, 104, 110–12
mouens, 146
Murphy, James J., 33n2, 100n11, 145n17
Murray, Michele, 17n83, 21n104, 51n71

Nadeau, Ray, 99
nails, 132
name, 77, 81, 87, 101, 124–25, 127–28, 160n100, 167
narratio, 59, 62–63, 65–67, 176
narrative criticism, 41
natio, 46n58, 106n54, 118, 152–53
Neander, Augustus, 7–9, 11, 27n138, 141
Nebuchadnezzar, 118, 162n116
necessity, 104, 109, 113, 154
Neusner, Jacob, 111n75
New Testament, 64n23, 105–6, 128
Noah, 112–13, 115, 155
Noeldechen, Ernst, 8–11, 178
Norden, E., 142n1, 146
Nun, 127

O'Malley, T. P., 124n123, 149n38, 170n151
oaths, 102
occupation, 81, 87, 128
Ochus (Cyrus), 150n44

officia, 144
Old Greek version of Hebrew Scriptures, 120
Old Latin Bible, 148–49, 169
Old Testament prophecy, 21, 121, 125, 127–29,
132–33
Ophuijsen, Jan M. van, 101n22
Osborn, Eric, 29, 91, 118n98, 137n177, 140n184,
147
Otho, 150n44
Otranto, G., 15
Oxford-Princeton Research Partnership, 16

pagans, 18, 22, 30, 38, 40, 51, 56, 62, 105
pallium, 34
paradox, 146, 148, 167
paralipsis *(occultatio)*, 166
parenthesis, 148, 164–66, 170
Parkes, J., 17
paronomasia, 161n114
Parthians, 9, 12, 162n116
partitio, 30, 59, 62, 65–71, 75–76, 86, 93, 95, 105,
108–11, 117, 139, 153–54, 176–78
Passover, 132, 165–66
Paul, 110, 129–30, 147
Pentateuch, 74
periphrasis *(circumitio)*, 155
peroratio, 59, 83–85, 139–40, 168–69, 177
Perry, B. E., 33
persecution of Christians by Jews, 20, 22
perspicuitas, 144
Pharaoh, 118, 162n116
Pharisees, 132
Philo, 127
Philopator, 150n44
Philostratus, *Vitae Sophistarum*, 33
Plato, 42–43, 146
plea for mercy, 99
Pliny the younger, 37, 39; *Epistulae*, 33n2
polemics, 12, 19, 21–22, 24, 27, 49, 51, 64, 87,
122, 142, 149–50
polyptoton, 159, 161n114, 162
polysyndeton, 159, 163
Powell, Mark Allen, 30, 41–42
praemunitio, 61, 81, 84–85, 87
Price, Simon, 51n73
prison, 165n130
probare, 146n19
probatio, 59
proemium, 59

prophesy. *See* Old Testament
prophet, 71, 73–74, 77, 113
propositio, 62, 64, 66–69, 117
proselyte, 2, 9, 14, 36–37, 40, 44, 50, 54, 57, 62,
69, 73, 106–7, 151–52, 155, 174
proselytizing, 15, 24
protasis, 157
ps.-Augustine: *Quaestionem ueteris et novi
testamenti*, 6n6
ps.-Quintilian, 37
Ptolemy VI, 121n108

Quacauarelli, A., 1, 142n1
quaestio legalis, 101
Quasten, Johannes, 7–8, 13, 146
Quintilian, 39, 61, 66–67, 69–70, 72, 75, 84, 100,
102, 119, 158, 168–70; *Institutio oratoria*, 33n2,
37, 60n1, 63n21, 65n28, 65n33, 69n55, 70n58,
98n1, 101, 103n40, 105, 106n52, 108nn59–61,
109n62, 110n69, 112n79, 114nn84–85, 115n87,
117, 118n95, 118n97, 121, 124nn120–21,
127n135, 143–45, 151n54, 152n55, 153nn62–63,
154n65, 154n68, 154n1/1, 156n75, 159nn97–98,
160n103, 161n114, 163nn123–27, 166n142,
167nn143–44, 167n147
Quispel, Gilles, 7, 11, 13, 52n78, 124n118

rabbis, 111
Rajak, Tessa, 51n73, 56n94
Rankin, David, viii, 29n145
Raven, Susan, 35
reader-response criticism, 41n42, 42n45
Rebekah, 66, 69, 108–10, 153
Rebillard, Éric, 52n75
reduplication *(conduplicatio)*, 154n65, 156,
161n114, 162–63
reed, 165
Reed, Annette Yoshiko, 17n78
refinement of topic *(expolitio)*, 71, 156
refutatio, 59, 69–76, 80, 86, 91–94, 96, 104,
110–17, 121–22, 133, 139, 154–59, 176
reprehensio, 59, 72
res, 143; *decorum*, 144; *dignitas*, 144; *explanatio*,
144; *Latinitas*, 144; *ornatus*, 144–45; *planum*,
144
Rhenanus (R), 45n55, 150n44
Rhetorica ad Herennium, 60n1, 61n6; 63n21,
65n28, 66–67, 72, 84, 98–102, 108n61, 109n62,
110n69, 117n92, 118nn95, 118n97, 124n121,

133n162, 143–45, 151, 152n55, 153nn62–63,
154nn65, 154n68, 154n71, 156n75, 158n90,
158n92, 159nn97–98, 160n103, 161n114,
162n118, 163n123, 163n125–27, 166n142,
167nn143–44, 167n147
rhetorical criticism, 41
rhetorical question, 160n105, 162, 166
ridicule, 146–47
Rives, J. B., 52n77
robbery, 157
Robbins, Vernon K., 41, 45
Rokeah, David, 20, 64n23
Romans, 22, 114, 118, 133, 159, 167
Rome, 22, 52n77
Rousseau, Philip, ix
Rowe, Galen O., 145n17
Rowland, Christopher, 51n73
Ruether, Rosemary Radford, 17n82, 18n84,
20, 23
rumor, 99, 101–3
Russell, D. A., 34n15, 35n22, 103n36
Rutgers, Leonard Victor, 52n77

Sabbath, 71, 73–75, 86, 92–93, 111, 114–15, 155,
158–59, 176
sacrifice, 71, 73–75, 86, 93, 111, 115, 138, 155,
158–59, 176
sacrilege, 104–5
Säflund, Gösta, vii, 10, 12, 14, 20, 48–49, 89,
94, 119, 128n138, 142n1, 147–48, 150nn44–45,
160n104, 164–65, 173, 177
Samaria, 121, 126, 163n119, 165, 168
Sanders, Jack T., 56n94
sarcasm, 126, 140, 165, 170
satire, 146, 170, 180
Satterthwaite, Philip E., 38n34, 146
Schäfer, Peter, 18n84
Scholer, D. M., 20n101
Schreckenberg, Heinz, 14, 20, 44n51, 89–91
Schütrumpf, Eckart, 41n41, 98n3
Schwartz, Seth, 36
Second Sophistic, 31–36, 146, 174
Segal, Alan F., 54n92
Semler, Johann Salomo, 6, 8
Seneca: Controuersiae, 32n2, 37, 60
Septimius Severus, 3, 15
Septuagint, 6, 11, 126n129, 128n138, 148
serpent: bronze, 131; in desert, 165n130; as
devil, 157n85

Setzer, Claudia, 27
Shoemaker, Stephen J., 30
Shotwell, Willis A., 129n142
Sider, Robert, vii, 1–2, 5, 27–29, 58–63, 65,
67–68, 72, 75, 84–85, 91, 95, 97, 102–5, 142, 173
signs, 78, 81, 87, 94, 99, 102–4, 107, 113–14, 119,
121, 125, 128, 133, 163n120, 176
Simeon, 131
simile (imago), 151–52, 157
Simon, Marcel, 13, 17–21, 23, 25, 44–45
simulation, 145
Skaraune, Oskar, 122–24, 127–29, 131, 135–36,
141
slander, 64n23, 146, 170
soldier, 63
Solmsen, Friedrich, 98, 100n11, 100n15, 144n11
Solomon, 118, 139, 162n116
soul, 103
Souter, Alexander, 6n6
Spira, Andreas, 38n34
Spirit, 134n166, 136, 159n95
Sprott, S. E., 143n3
Sprute, Jürgen, 41n41
Stanton, G. N., 17n82
Stark, Rodney, 51n74
stasis, 99–101, 103, 119; coniecturalis, 99, 101;
definitiua, 99–100; finitiuus, 101; generalis,
99–100; iuridicalis, 99–100; legitima, 99–101;
qualitas, 101; translatiua, 99–100
status. See stasis
stealing, 157
Stoicism, 29
Stroumsa, Guy, 16–21, 24–25, 56
Style: Asiatic, 143n6, 146; Attic, 143n6
Stylianopolous, Theodore, 129n142, 130n149
suasoria, 32
subsequent behavior, 99
Suetonius: De rhetoribus, 32n2
supersession, 3, 23, 27, 108, 137, 153, 179
Swain, Simon, 33–34
Swift, Louis J., 103n39
sword, 80, 126, 156n79, 165
syllogism, 101–2, 136–37, 154
synagogue, 129, 134n166, 136, 141
syndeton, 147
synecdoche, 145, 155
synonymy, 156–57, 159–61
Syria, 9, 178

Tacitus, 39; *Dialogues de oratoribus,* 32n2
Taylor, Miriam, 20–25, 28, 44
temple, destruction of, 120–21, 134, 165n130
Tertullian: as Christian sophist, 34; as jurist, 29n145; as legalist, 20; and philosophy, 29; rhetorical aims, 28. *See also Adversus Iudeos; Index of Citations to Tertullian*
testimonia, 10, 122, 135, 141, 179
Theodotion, 6, 11, 120
Theophrastus, 144n11
Thyestean banquets, 103
time, 112, 118–19, 121, 134, 139–40, 179
Titus, viii, 2
topoi, 81, 87, 103, 108, 118, 121–22, 124, 126–29, 133, 137–41, 179. *See also loci communes*
torture, 99, 101–2
Tränkle, Hermann, vii, 11–14, 27n138, 45n53, 49, 79, 93–96, 107n59, 110, 111n72, 124n118, 128, 130, 134–36, 149, 158, 165, 173, 177
transplacement *(traductio),* 159, 161
treason, 37, 104–5
tree, 81, 129, 131n153, 167
trope, 145, 167
trough, 165n130
Trypho, 25, 44
typology, 119n99, 126n131, 131, 138, 170, 178

Ugenti, Valerio, 147n32
understatement, 145

Vespasian, 121
Vipstanus Messala, 32n2, 37
virgin, 121–22, 125
Votienus Montanus, 32n2
Vulgate, 128n138

War, Second World, 17
Wardy, Robert, 41n41
warrior, 121, 126, 161n110, 165
Waszink, J. H., 124n123, 147
Wiles, M. F., 106n51, 126n131
Wilken, Robert, 17
Williams, A. Lukyn, 10, 13, 16–18, 27
Wilson, Stephen G., 17, 26n128
Winterbottom, Michael, 33n2, 37
Wisse, Jakob, 99
witnesses, 99, 101–3, 178
wood, 165n130
woodcutter, 167

Yom Kippur, 18n2

Index of Citations to Tertullian

Ad nationes, 95, 151n47

Ad Scapulam, 1

Aduersus Hermogenem, 45n54, 147

Aduersus Iudeos

    1.1: 40, 63nn20, 22, 106n55, 151, 152n55

    1.1–2: 92

    1.1–3a: 62–64, 86, 106–8, 150–53, 176

    1.2: 54n91, 64n24, 68, 106

    1.2–3: 93, 141

    1.3: 46n58, 47n61, 64, 68, 92, 107n58, 108n60, 111, 150n44, 151n51, 152n56, 152n60, 153n64, 154nn68–69

    1.3b–2.1a: 66, 68–71, 86, 108–10, 153–54, 176

    1.3b–7: 65, 68–69, 110, 176

    1.4: 66, 92, 153

    1.5: 46n58, 66, 92, 109n6, 153, 154n66, 154n72, 170

    1.6: 66, 150n44, 154n67, 154n70

    1.6–2.1a: 110

    1.6–7: 69n56, 92, 110n70

    1.7: 46n57, 47n61, 66, 150n44

    1.8: 68n54, 70, 92–93, 137

    1.9: 92

    2.1: 46n57, 70, 73, 112, 150n44, 156n77

    2.1–3.6: 177

    2.1b–6.1: 71, 73–75, 86, 110–16, 154–58, 176

    2.1b–10a: 73, 86, 111, 154, 176

    2.2: 112, 150n44, 151, 155, 158

    2.2b–6: 112

    2.3: 46n60

    2.4b–5: 113, 157

    2.6: 46n60, 155–56

    2.6–7: 113

    2.7: 45n55, 150n44, 156nn76–77, 157

    2.7–9a: 112

    2.9: 46n60, 47n61, 113, 158

    2.10: 46n60, 47n61, 73–74, 111n74

    2.10b–3.13: 113

    2.10b–3.6: 73, 86, 155, 176

    2.10–11: 74

    2.11: 156n77

    2.11–3.1: 113

    2.12: 74n81

    2.13: 46n60, 157n82

    3.1: 48n62, 73, 150n44

    3.2: 46n59, 114

    3.4: 134, 155

    3.4–6: 114, 133

    3.5: 153, 156n77

    3.6: 46n60, 134

    3.7–13: 74, 86, 93, 114, 176–77

    3.8: 46n58, 46n60, 80, 152n60

    3.9: 46n58, 152n60

    3.10: 46n58, 93, 150n44, 156, 170

    3.11: 46n57, 155

    3.12: 46n58, 155, 156n77

    3.13: 46n58, 47n61, 74, 93

    4.1: 48n61, 70n59, 73

    4.1–5: 74, 114

    4.1–11: 73, 86, 114, 155, 176

    4.2: 46n60, 156n77

    4.3: 46n60

    4.4: 46n60, 80, 151

    4.5: 150n44

    4.6: 46n57, 48n61, 74, 115

    4.7: 48n61, 73

    4.7–11: 115

    4.8: 155

    4.10: 48n61, 92, 156

    4.11: 45n55

    5.1: 46nn57–58, 150n44

    5.1–3a: 74, 115

    5.1–7: 73, 86, 115, 155, 176

    5.3: 46n59, 48n61, 73, 150n44, 156

    5.3b–7: 115

    5.4: 152n60, 156

Aduersus Iudeos (cont.)

5.7: 152n60

6.1: 75n82, 86, 93, 150n44, 158n91, 170

6.2: 46nn59–60, 48n61, 70n60, 71, 75–76, 80, 116, 150n44, 159n96, 161, 164, 170

6.2–7.1: 76, 84, 86, 96, 117

6.2–14.10: 75–84, 86, 93, 116–39, 158–68, 176

6.3: 45n55, 71n62, 76, 80, 116n90, 150n44, 159–60

6.3–4: 166n140

6.4: 71n63, 76

7.1: 46nn57–60, 71n64, 76–80, 86, 94, 117n90, 118, 121, 128, 132, 160, 176

7.1–2: 161

7.1–8.1a: 177

7.2: 46nn59–60, 48n61, 71, 76, 77n92, 79, 86, 93, 117, 152n60, 166

7.2–5: 118

7.2–8.1a: 133, 177

7.3: 161, 166–67

7.3–8.1a: 77, 86, 118, 167

7.4: 9, 118, 150n44, 153, 166, 167n145

7.5: 150n44, 161, 167

7.6: 166

7.6–7: 162

7.6–8.1a: 118

7.6–9: 170

7.7: 150n44

7.7–8: 9, 45n55, 159n99

7.8: 150n44, 153, 166, 167n146

7.9: 153, 160n100

8.1: 48n62, 78, 86, 162

8.1b–14.10: 86, 92, 118

8.1b–18: 119

8.2: 46nn57,60, 78, 81–84, 86, 94, 96, 119, 121, 128, 132, 139, 163, 176

8.3–6: 86, 119

8.3–8: 78

8.3–14: 92

8.3–18: 176

8.5: 120n106

8.6: 162n116

8.7: 46n59, 120n106

8.7–8: 86, 119

8.8: 162n116

8.9: 46n59, 166

8.9–10: 120, 162

8.9–15a: 78, 86

8.10: 46n59, 134, 150n44

8.11: 46n59

8.11–15a: 120

8.12: 164n130, 166

8.13: 48n61, 167

8.14: 150n44, 164n130

8.15: 46n57, 81, 89, 164n130

8.15b–16: 120

8.15b–18: 78, 86, 92

8.16: 150n44

8.17: 48n61, 134, 162

8.17–18: 120

8.18: 88, 150n44

9.1: 46n59, 48n61, 79, 86, 121–26

9.1b–3: 87, 124

9.1–10.19: 177

9.1–16a: 179

9.1–31: 79, 81, 86, 92, 94

9.2: 46n60, 48nn61–62, 49n67, 123–24, 126

9.3: 45n55, 48n62, 49n67, 81, 125, 163

9.4: 49n68, 126

9.4–6: 87, 125–26

9.4–9: 168

9.5: 48n62, 49n67, 150n44, 166

9.5–20: 165

9.6: 45n55, 48n62, 49n69, 126n130, 160, 165, 170

9.7: 48n61, 126

9.7–9: 87, 122, 125

9.8: 46n60, 48n62, 49n69, 81

9.10: 48n62, 49n67, 81

9.10–16: 126, 167–68, 170

9.10–20a: 87

9.11: 165n132

9.12: 9, 162, 165n133, 178

9.14: 48n62, 49n69, 126n128

9.15: 46n57, 160, 161n108

9.16: 46n59, 48n61, 49n68

9.17: 48n62, 148, 165n134, 166

9.17–20a: 126

9.18: 46n59, 80

9.19: 161n109

9.20: 48nn61–62, 49n67, 161n110, 163

9.20b–25: 87, 127

9.21: 46n59, 48n62, 49n67, 80, 127n133, 159n95

9.22: 46n58, 80n99

9.22–23a: 127, 150n44

9.23: 48n62, 127, 159n95, 167, 170

9.23b–24: 127

9.24: 162

9.26: 46n57, 127n136, 128, 149n38, 165n135

9.26–27: 87, 127

9.27: 128

9.28: 87, 128, 148, 165n136

9.29: 45n55, 46n59, 128

9.29–31: 87, 128

9.31: 48n62

10.1: 48n62, 49n69, 129–30

10.1–5: 87

10.1–19a: 79, 80n98, 81, 87, 94, 128

10.3: 129, 160, 162

10.4: 46n57, 48n62, 81, 132, 134–35

10.4–5: 130

10.5: 130n144, 131n150, 132, 160–61

10.6: 81, 159n95, 164n130, 167

10.6–10: 131

10.6–14a: 87, 132

10.7: 131n151, 159n95, 160, 164

10.8: 164

10.8b–10a: 167

10.9: 132, 164n130

10.10: 150n44, 161–62, 165n130, 166

10.11: 45n55, 48n62, 49n67, 81, 132, 135, 166–67

10.11–14: 135

10.11–19: 131

10.12: 48n62, 49n67, 132, 165n130, 166

10.13: 48n62, 49n67, 134, 165n130

10.14: 46n57, 48n62, 49n67, 132, 135, 159n95, 161

10.14b–19a: 87, 132, 170

10.15: 45n55, 132

10.16: 46n57, 132, 164, 166

10.17: 132, 150n44

10.17–12.2: 90, 94

10.17–19: 131n154

10.18: 48n62, 49n69, 132, 165n138

10.19: 48n62, 49n69, 82, 166n139

10.19b–11.9: 79, 81, 83, 87

10.19b–14.10: 83, 132

11.1: 48n62, 177

11.1–9: 83, 90, 177

11.1–14.10: 177

11.2–8: 132

11.9: 48n61, 82, 133

11.10: 46n57, 8, 83

11.10–11a: 81–83, 87, 177

11.10–12: 140

11.10–12.2: 88

11.10–13.7: 81–83, 96

11.11: 46n57, 46n60, 48n61, 83n101, 89, 131n154

11.11b–12: 82, 85, 87

11.11–12.1: 89

11.11b–12.2a: 83–84, 88, 90, 94

11.12: 88

12.1: 48n62, 49n67, 152n60

12.1–2: 87, 90, 177

12.1–14.10: 83

12.2: 46n60, 48n62, 139, 152n60, 165n130, 166n141

12.2–13.7: 83

13.1: 46n57, 46nn59–60, 48n61, 79, 90, 133, 136, 160, 164n128

13.1–3: 121, 133

13.1–7: 82, 87

13.1–23: 90, 94

13.1–29: 177

13.2: 166

13.2–3: 162

13.3: 46n60

13.4: 48n62, 49n69, 82, 133, 134n164, 165n130

13.5: 48n61, 133, 166

13.5b–7: 134

13.6: 150n44

13.6–7: 162

13.7: 83, 159n95, 160, 166

13.8: 46n57, 83, 135–36

13.8–23: 136, 140, 170

13.8–29: 79, 81–83, 87, 179

13.9: 46n59, 136, 160, 164n128, 166

13.10: 82, 90, 134n165, 135, 150n44, 164n128

13.10–11: 135

13.10–23: 135, 167

13.11: 48n62, 161n112, 164n128

13.11–23: 82, 134, 136

13.12: 46n60, 150n44, 164

13.13: 153n60, 166

13.14: 135n169, 162–63, 166

13.14b–16: 134n166

13.15: 48n61, 136, 141, 150n44, 164n128, 165n130

13.16: 48n61, 159n95

13.17: 46n59, 164n128

13.17–20a: 136

13.18: 159

13.19: 46n60, 162, 165n130, 166

Aduersus Iudeos (cont.)
13.20: 48n61, 160, 164n128
13.20b–23: 136
13.21: 150n44
13.22: 164n128, 166
13.23: 136, 166
13.24: 46nn58,60, 48n61, 83, 136
13.24–14.13: 90, 94–95
13.24–25: 137
13.24–29: 90, 136
13.25: 48n61, 137n179, 161n113
13.25–26: 137
13.25–29: 83
13.26: 48n61, 133, 137n176, 137n180, 153n60
13.26–27: 137n178
13.27: 46n59, 48n61
13.28: 48n61, 137n181
13.29: 48n62, 49n67, 138, 153, 166
14.1: 47n60, 48n62, 49n69
14.1–2: 138
14.1–10: 82, 87, 90, 138
14.3: 161, 164
14.7: 164
14.8: 48n62, 150n44
14.9: 45n55, 159n95, 163n122, 164, 165n130, 166
14.10: 48n61, 85
14.11: 47n60, 88n116, 88n119
14.11–12a: 83, 88, 90
14.11–14: 83–85, 87–88, 94, 96, 139, 168–69, 177
14.12: 46n57, 48n62, 49n67, 88, 139, 152n60, 168

14.13: 48n62, 49n67
14.14: 48n62, 168–69
Aduerus Marcionem, vii, 2, 6–14, 18, 26, 45n55, 49–50, 53, 59, 62–63, 65, 68, 87–89, 96, 104–5, 109, 122nn110–11, 123–28, 130–34, 136–39, 141, 146n19, 148–53, 165, 169, 175, 177–80
Aduersus Praxean, 62, 65, 67, 85, 130n145
Aduersus Valentinianos, 62, 65, 146n19, 147
Apologeticum, 12, 62, 65, 67, 85, 103, 105, 178

De anima, 146n19
De baptismo, 73
De carne Christi, 62, 68, 73, 85, 104, 122n110
De corona, 62–63, 65
De fuga in persicutione, 130n145
De idololatria, 45n54, 151n47
De ieiunio, 180n2
De monogamia, 73, 85, 105
De pallio, 34, 147
De patientia, 130n145, 151n47
De praescriptione haereticorum, 62, 65, 68, 105, 151n47
De pudicitia, 62, 65, 67, 105, 109, 110n67
De resurrectione mortuorum, 62, 65, 72, 85, 104–5, 122nn110–11, 135
De testimonio animae, 45n54, 103
De uirginibus uelandis, 146n19, 151n47

Scorpiace, 85

Index of Citations to Scripture

Genesis, 113
  2.2–3: 114
  4.3–11: 115
  4.14: 115
  22.1–14: 136
  25.23: 66, 69, 108, 109n64,
    115, 153n65
  49.5–7: 131

Exodus, 82, 133n159
  4.24–26: 113
  12.2–10: 131
  12.11: 166
  23.20–21: 127
  32: 69
  32.1–4: 110

Leviticus
  16.5–28: 138, 164

Numbers
  21.6–9: 131n153

Deuteronomy
  21.23: 129–30
  27.26: 129
  28.64–66: 133
  31.2–3: 127
  33.17: 131, 164

Joshua
  6.3–5: 115
  6.15–20: 115

1 Kings
  12.25–33: 110
  12.28: 69

14.15: 69
16.31: 69

2 Kings
  6.1–7: 136
  17.7–17: 110

1 Maccabees
  2.38: 115
  2.41: 115

Psalms
  2: 85
  2.7–8: 133, 139, 152n60,
    169, 177
  17(18).44–45: 155
  18(19).5: 118
  21(22).16: 130
  21(22).17: 131, 134–35
  21(22).18: 130, 134–35
  21(22).22: 131
  34(35).12: 130
  44(45).2–3: 126, 165
  44(45).5–6: 126, 148
  49(50).14: 115
  50(51).19: 115
  58(59).12: 137
  66(67).7: 135
  68(69).4: 130
  68(69).22: 130, 134–35
  95(96).7–8: 115, 152n60
  95(96).10: 131, 135

Isaiah, 92, 124–26, 132, 151
  1.4: 153
  1.7–8: 133, 137
  1.11–13: 115

1.13: 114
1.20: 137
2.2–3: 152nn60–61, 156
2.4: 152n60
2.20: 137
3.1: 137
5.6–7: 137
7.13–15: 121–22
7.14: 123–24
7.16: 122
8.3: 122n111
8.4: 121–24, 126, 165
9.5: 131–32
11.1–2: 127, 149n38
13.21: 128n138
14.1: 128n138
16.1–2: 135n170
16.3: 135n170
33.17: 133
35.4–6: 128
40.15: 64, 107–8, 152
42.2–3: 128, 165
42.6–7: 133, 152n60
45.1: 77n92, 117–19, 152n60,
  167
50.11: 137
52.5: 137, 153n60
53.3: 128
53.7: 128, 148
53.7–8: 136
53.8–10: 131
55.4–5: 133n161
57.2: 131
58.1–2: 128
65.2: 134–35
65.13–14: 136
66.23: 114

Jeremiah
2.10–12: 135, 153n60
2.12–13: 135nn169–70, 141, 162
3.8: 135n170
4.3–4: 114
11.19: 131
31.31–32: 114

Ezekiel, 81, 90
8.12–9.6: 132
16.3: 126n128
22.8: 114
36.20: 137
36.23: 137

Daniel, 92, 120–21
6: 78
9: 86, 139, 141
9.1–2a: 119
9.21–27: 78, 119
9.25: 120n106
9.26: 134, 136, 162

Hosea
6.1–3: 136

Joel
2.22: 135

Amos
8.9–10: 131, 135, 150n44

Micah
5.1: 133
5.2: 150n44

Malachi
1.10–11: 115, 152n60

Matthew
1.23: 122
2.6: 133, 150n44
11.10: 127
11.13: 137n176
11.31: 150n44
27.29: 150n44

Mark
1.2: 127
15.17: 150n44

Luke
7.27: 127
15: 109
16.16: 137n176

John
5.18: 128
10.33: 128
19.2: 150n44

Acts
2.5: 118
2.9–10: 118

Romans
9.12: 110

Galatians
3.13: 129

Tertullian's Aduersus Iudaeos: *A Rhetorical Analysis* was designed and typeset in Dante by Kachergis Book Design of Pittsboro, North Carolina. It was printed on 60-pound Natures Natural and bound by Thomson-Shore of Dexter, Michigan.